# CREATING
# EQUITABLE
# CLASSROOMS
# THROUGH
# ACTION RESEARCH

D0469087

# CREATING
# EQUITABLE
# CLASSROOMS
# THROUGH
# ACTION RESEARCH

EDITORS
## CATHY CARO-BRUCE
## RYAN FLESSNER
## MARY KLEHR
## KENNETH ZEICHNER

FOREWORD BY ELIZABETH BURMASTER

A Joint Publication

**CORWIN PRESS**
A SAGE Publications Company
Thousand Oaks, CA 91320

*For information:*

Corwin Press
A Sage Publications Company
2455 Teller Road
Thousand Oaks, California 91320
www.corwinpress.com

Sage Publications Ltd.
1 Oliver's Yard
55 City Road
London EC1Y 1SP
United Kingdom

Sage Publications India Pvt. Ltd.
B 1/I 1 Mohan Cooperative Industrial
    Area
Mathura Road, New Delhi
India 110 044

Sage Publications Asia-Pacific Pte. Ltd.
33 Pekin Street #02-01
Far East Square
Singapore  048763

Printed in the United States of America.

*Library of Congress Cataloging-in-Publication Data*

Creating equitable classrooms through action research/edited by: Cathy Caro-Bruce . . . [et al.].
       p. cm.
Includes bibliographical references and index.
ISBN 978-1-4129-3666-8 (cloth : alk. paper)
ISBN 978-1-4129-3667-5 (pbk. : alk. paper)
   1.   Educational equalization—United States.  2.   Action research in education—United States.   I. Caro-Bruce, Cathy.

LC213.2.C74 2007
379.2′6—dc22

                                                                2006102774

This book is printed on acid-free paper.

07   08   09   10   11   10  9   8   7   6   5   4   3   2   1

| | |
|---|---|
| *Acquisitions Editor:* | Rachel Livsey |
| *Editorial Assistant:* | Phyllis Capello |
| *Production Editor:* | Sarah K. Quesenberry |
| *Copy Editor:* | Bill Bowers |
| *Typesetter:* | C&M Digitals (P) Ltd. |
| *Proofreader:* | Sally Jaskold |
| *Indexer:* | Kay Dusheck |
| *Cover Designer:* | Scott Van Atta |
| *Graphic Designer:* | Karine Hovsepian |

# *Contents*

# *Foreword*

In schools today, raising the achievement levels of all students and closing the achievement gap between students of color and economically disadvantaged students and their peers must be our highest priority. To meet this goal, we know that there is nothing more important than the quality of the teacher in the classroom.

Action research brings the voices and expertise of those closest to the classroom—our teachers—to our educational improvement efforts. Teachers who examine their practices through action research bring relevant, authentic information to our efforts to close the achievement gap and make schools more equitable places for all children. While enrolled at the University of Wisconsin–Madison in Professor Ken Zeichner's graduate course, I conducted my own action research project. I can attest from this firsthand experience the positive impact action research had on my knowledge and skills as an educator, and on my students' performance.

It is incumbent on educational leaders to support and empower teachers' ability to examine their own practices and make changes in their teaching based on research they do in their own classrooms or school settings. Educators will tell you that they often learned far more from their students than they probably ever taught them. During my tenure as principal of West High School in Madison, Wisconsin, I promoted our teachers' efforts to pursue action research, and found their work to be a critical component of our continuous improvement efforts.

*Creating Equitable Classrooms Through Action Research* provides teachers, principals, district administrators, and professional development specialists with compelling insight into the workings of a successful action research program, and 10 excellent teacher action research projects focused on increasing student achievement in diverse school settings. At the heart of education is a belief in the power of quality teaching. I encourage all schools to include the voices of action researchers in their systemwide improvement efforts.

Society is shaped by the care and respect we show for the hearts, souls, and minds of children. Action research provides teachers with a thoughtful, proactive tool for helping children achieve their dreams and add value to our communities. Good teaching is an art form and a science. Action research provides teachers with the tools to enhance their art and improve their science.

—Elizabeth Burmaster
Wisconsin State Superintendent
of Public Instruction

# *Preface*

By almost every measure that exists, there is a crisis of inequality in our public schools that continues to deny many poor children and children of color a high-quality education. A number of gaps in educational outcomes have continued to exist, and in some cases have grown larger, despite all the reform efforts that have taken place in schools. These gaps include inequalities in: achievement as measured by standardized tests in reading and mathematics (Rothstein & Wilder, 2005); in high school graduation rates (Greene & Winters, 2002); in the increased segregation of students according to their race, ethnicity, and social class backgrounds (Orfield & Lee, 2005); in school funding (Carey, 2004); in access to fully prepared and experienced teachers (Peske & Haycock, 2006); in access to advanced mathematics courses that provide the gateway to scientific careers (U.S. Department of Education, 2003); and in access to a broad and rich curriculum that educates students to think critically and develop their aesthetic and civic capabilities (Kozol, 2005).

Although the roots of these gaps lie in inequalities in the broader society in access to jobs that pay a living wage, health care, housing, transportation, and so on (Berliner, 2006; Children's Defense Fund, 2005)—and not in the schools and teacher education institutions, as the popular media have frequently suggested (*The New York Times,* 2006)—it has been clearly shown that teachers and schools can make a difference in narrowing these gaps in a limited way (Education Trust, 2006).

Every school district in the nation is currently attempting to address these various gaps and to provide a more equitable and just education to everyone's children within our public schools. There are vast differences among districts in the approaches taken to narrow educational inequalities, including such things as narrowing the curriculum for students who have done poorly on standardized tests and focusing on better preparing them to take the tests (Dillon, 2006); adopting curriculum programs that are closely aligned with state and local standards, which in turn are aligned to the standardized tests; and providing various kinds of professional development to staff.

This book includes a collection of 10 action research studies conducted by educators in Madison, Wisconsin, about achieving greater equity in educational outcomes for all students. These action researchers include teachers, a social worker, and an administrator and represent elementary, middle, and high schools as well as a variety of subject matter specialties. The Madison Metropolitan School District (MMSD), like every school district throughout the United States, is attempting to address the various gaps that exist in education between students from different ethnic, racial, and social class backgrounds.

One way in which this district has attempted to address inequalities in educational outcomes is by investing in the professional development of its teachers and others who work with students on a daily basis to create new ideas for teaching in ways that more adequately address the learning needs of all their students. Student learning is defined broadly in this book in a way that includes but is not limited to standardized test scores.

Since 1990, the MMSD has supported a classroom action research professional development program that, from its inception, has emphasized the closing of educational achievement gaps. All 10 studies in this book were conducted within the district's Classroom Action Research professional development program.

Unlike dominant models of teacher professional development today in the United States, which continue to treat teachers as passive recipients of expert knowledge from external or internal consultants—despite the recommendations in the literature about the design of effective professional development for teachers (Randi & Zeichner, 2004)—action research as it is practiced in the MMSD and in a number of other places across the country (Zeichner, 2003) treats teachers as capable of playing active roles in their own professional development and of creating new knowledge about effective approaches to instruction.

The purpose of presenting these action research studies to a broader audience is not to suggest that the conditions in the MMSD are exactly like the conditions in other districts and that the learning these 10 teachers have experienced is directly generalizable to teachers across the country. Although we think that there is much in these 10 studies that can be fruitfully adapted to other settings in the service of providing pupils with more culturally responsive and powerful teaching, we present these studies as examples of how a district can design an action research professional development program that enables teachers to make concrete improvements with regard to equity in their classrooms and schools.

Just as the learning of the individual action researchers will need to be adapted to fit other circumstances, so too will the action research professional development program described here need to be adapted to other situations in terms of its specific structures and practices. Chapter 2 discusses the core assumptions that form the basis for the program. We think that these underlying ideas about teacher ownership of their research and about the nature of teacher learning can be realized in a variety of different professional development program situations.

This book should be of interest to those who design professional development for PreK–12 educators, as well as to those who work with students on a daily basis. It should also be of interest to teacher educators, who can use individual studies with novice teachers both in terms of the specific things that can be learned from the studies and from the examples provided by the 10 Madison action researchers of how educators can learn and develop through the careful study of their practices. Finally, this volume should be of interest to school administrators and local school board members, who will see that those at the ground level who work with students every day have a great deal to contribute to the creation of new solutions to the enduring problems of schooling.

Although there is little evidence in these 10 studies of improved student learning as measured by standardized test scores, these action researchers report improvements in pupil learning, attitudes, involvement, and behavior as a consequence of specific actions taken in their research. The evidence for these changes is provided by teacher observations, careful documentation of classroom activities, analyses of student work samples, and teacher-designed assessments. As teachers conducted research, they implemented a variety of new practices with their students that addressed learning and behavior issues.

In addition to offering evidence of the power of action research by teachers to provide concrete improvements in classroom practices that contribute to the narrowing of educational achievement gaps in their own classrooms and schools, this book provides an example of teachers who have created new knowledge that can benefit others about how to narrow educational achievement gaps. Unlike most other collections of teacher research studies, which merely lay out a set of studies for readers to make sense of individually and on their own, in the final chapter of this book we look across the 10 studies and situate them in relation to other research by academics and PreK–12 educators about equity issues. There has been a lot of interest in recent years in treating research done by PreK–12 teachers as knowledge production as well as professional development (Hiebert & Gallimore, 2002). This book examines both of these aspects of the action research studies that are reported.

## AN OVERVIEW OF THE ACTION RESEARCH PROCESS IN THE MMSD

The action research process can take many forms, and there is no single recipe that will work for all teachers or contexts. From its inception, the MMSD Classroom Action Research program has taken a decidedly constructivist stance toward knowledge, and views the classroom inquiry process as cyclical and open-ended. Action research groups in Madison follow the school calendar, formulating inquiry projects that run from September through May. During that time, researchers meet monthly in practitioner-facilitated sessions to discuss progress, share ideas, and receive collegial support. The aim of these regular meetings is to actively think, talk, and learn together in ways that value and build on teacher knowledge and classroom experience.

In general, the action researchers whose studies are included in this collection have worked through a cycle of question development, data generation and analysis, reflective writing, identification of next steps, and sharing what has been learned with others.

Teachers are encouraged to study something that they feel passionate about, and to develop questions that are clearly articulated, focused on their own practices, manageable within the classroom context, will benefit students and others, and will lead to deeper questions. Finding a specific research question can take weeks or even months. Some teachers identify a research focus right away, while others start collecting data on their classrooms before finalizing their questions. A common way we start thinking about a question is through a series of "starting points" questions: I would like to improve . . . ; I am perplexed by . . . ; I'm really curious about . . . ; I want to learn more about . . . ; An idea I would like to try out in my class is . . . ; Something I think would really make a difference is . . . ; or Something I would like to change is . . .

There is no one correct technique for generating data. It starts with what teachers can readily observe or already know, and we encourage teachers to think broadly and creatively about selecting methods that are appropriate to the question and context, as well as manageable for the individual researchers. Researchers work to collect various forms of data that represent multiple perspectives at more than one point in time. Teachers typically analyze their data in standard qualitative ways, such as triangulating information, sorting and coding by themes, looking for patterns in the data, and being alert to the unexpected. Ultimately, data analysis should help classroom practitioners to take productive actions on behalf of their students and to identify the next steps in their inquiry process.

Writing plays a central role in these teachers' work during and at the end of the research process, helping them to articulate their practices and to become thoughtful inquirers about themselves and their students. It also serves as a means for synthesizing learning and communicating with others. Short, end-of-year reports are published in-house, are distributed to all schools in the district, and are posted on the district's Web site. Action researchers are also supported in presenting at local and national educational research conferences and in serving as consultants to other school districts. Finally, over the years a number of teachers have published their studies in academic journals.

## THE STRUCTURE OF THE BOOK

Chapters 1 and 2 set the context for the presentation of the studies. Chapter 1 situates the equity action research reported in the book within the various efforts of the MMSD to narrow educational inequalities across the district. Chapter 2 provides background information on the district Classroom Action Research professional development program within which the 10 studies were conducted. Chapters 3 through 12 report the individual action research studies of the 10 teachers. Each action research study includes an epilogue, in which the researchers reflect about the impact of their studies on their practice over time. The final chapter looks across the 10 studies and situates them in relation to what other PreK–12 and academic researchers have learned about narrowing educational inequalities.

We hope that both the individual studies presented in this book and the example of a school district investing in its teachers to create new solutions to enduring problems of schooling will provide the basis for dialogue and stimulate the creation of other opportunities for teachers to engage in action research in school districts across the country.

## REFERENCES

Berliner, D. (2006). Our impoverished view of educational reform. *Teachers College Record*. Retrieved September 10, 2006, from http://www.tcrecord.org/content.asp?contentid=12106

Carey, K. (2004). *The funding gap: Many states shortchange low income and minority students*. Washington, DC: Education Trust.

Children's Defense Fund. (2005). *The state of America's children*. Washington, DC: Author.

Dillon, S. (2006). Schools cut back subjects to push reading and math. *The New York Times*, March 28. Retrieved August 28, 2006, from http://select.nytimes.com/search/restricted/article?res=F30713FF3F540C758EDDAA0894DE404482

Education Trust. (2006). *Yes we can: Telling truths and dispelling myths about race and education in America*. Washington, DC: Author.

Greene, J. P., & Winters, M. A. (2002). *Public school graduation rates in the U.S.* The Manhattan Institute. Retrieved January 26, 2007, from http://www.manhattan institute.org/html/cr_baeo.htm

Hiebert, J., & Gallimore, R. (2002). A knowledge base for the teaching profession: What would it look like and how would we get one? *Educational Researcher, 31*(5), 3–15.

Kozol, J. (2005). *The shame of American education: The restoration of apartheid schooling in America.* New York: Crown.

National Commission on Teaching and America's Future. (2003). *No dream denied: A pledge to America's children.* Washington, DC: Author.

*The New York Times.* (2006). Why the achievement gap persists [editorial]. December 8, p. A30. Retrieved January 26, 2007, from http://select.nytimes.com/search/restricted/article?res=F1071FFD3C550C7B8CDDAB0994DE404482

Orfield, G., & Lee, C. (2005). *Why segregation matters: Poverty and educational inequality.* Harvard Civil Rights Project. Retrieved June 24, 2006, from http://www.civilrightsproject.harvard.edu/research/deseg/Why_Segreg_Matters.pdf.

Peske, H. G., & Haycock, K. (2006, June). *Teaching inequality: How poor and minority students are shortchanged on teacher quality.* Washington, DC: Education Trust.

Randi, J., & Zeichner, K. (2004). New visions of teacher professional development. In M. Smylie & D. Miretszky (Eds.), *Developing the teacher workforce* (pp. 180–227). Chicago: University of Chicago Press.

Rothstein, R., & Wilder, T. (2005, October). *The many dimensions of educational inequality across races.* Paper presented at the 2005 Symposium on the Social Costs of an Inadequate Education, Teachers College, New York City. Retrieved July 14, 2006, from http://www.tc.columbia.edu/centers/Equitysymposium/ResourceDetailsasp?PresId=13

U.S. Department of Education. (2003). *The condition of education.* Washington, DC: Author.

Zeichner, K. (2003). Teacher research as professional development for P–12 educators in the U.S. *Educational Action Research 11*(2), 301–325.

# *Acknowledgments*

We would like to thank all the administrators and staff in the Madison Metropolitan School District who have supported the action research efforts of teachers and other educators since 1990. We would also like to thank Kalani Eggington and Courtney Koestler, two graduate students at the University of Wisconsin–Madison, who contributed enormously to the conception and organization of this book. Without their efforts this book would not have been possible. We also want to express our appreciation to the Teachers Network Leadership Institute for the partial funding of two of the studies in this collection of studies. Finally, we would also like to thank Margie Dewind for her careful editing of the draft manuscript. All royalties from this book will go back into the Madison Metropolitan School District to support the action research efforts of teachers.

—Cathy Caro-Bruce, Ryan Flessner,
Mary Klehr, Kenneth Zeichner

The contributions of the following reviewers are gratefully acknowledged:

Wanda F. Lofton
Instructional Services
  School Coach
Seattle Public Schools
Seattle, WA

Emily Calhoun
Corwin Press Author
Saint Simons Island, GA

Rose Weiss
Adjunct Professor
Palm Beach Community College
Palm Beach, FL

Linda L. Elman
Director, Research & Evaluation
Central Kitsap School District
Silverdale, WA

Roxana DellaVecchia
Professor and Chair
Department of Instructional
    Leadership and
    Professional Development
Towson University
Towson, MD

Gary L. Anderson
Professor
New York University
New York, NY

Jody Westbrook-Youngblood
Office for Professional Learning
San Antonio Independent School
    District
San Antonio, TX

Janna K. Smith
Assistant Principal
Riviera Day and Preparatory
    Schools
Coral Gables, FL

Diane Yendol-Hoppey
Associate Professor
University of Florida
Gainesville, FL

Terry Morganti-Fisher
Consultant
Morganti-Fisher Associates
Austin, TX

Jeffrey Glanz
Professor
Wagner College
Staten Island, NY

Gloria L. Kumagai
Coordinator
Licensure and Leadership
    Development
Educational Policy and
    Administration
University of Minnesota
Minneapolis, MN

Joseph N. Staub
Resource Specialist Teacher
Thomas Starr King
    Middle School
Los Angeles, CA

# *About the Editors*

**Cathy Caro-Bruce** is an educational consultant to school districts with the Wisconsin Department of Public Instruction, developing the department's Statewide System of Support under the No Child Left Behind (NCLB) law. For 30 years, she was a staff and organization development specialist for the Madison Metropolitan School District, and for 15 years coordinated the Classroom Action Research program as part of the district professional development program. She authored a book, *Action Research: Facilitator's Handbook,* published by the National Staff Development Council (NSDC), to assist educators who want to lead and facilitate action research initiatives. She coauthored a chapter in *Educational Action Research: Becoming Practically Critical* (Noffke & Stevenson, Teachers College Press) about implementing action research in a school district. In *Powerful Designs for Professional Learning* (NSDC), she describes the action research design and how it can be implemented in schools. Cathy also works with school districts around the country helping them implement action research based on principles that drive high-quality professional development initiatives.

**Ryan Flessner** is a PhD student at the University of Wisconsin–Madison pursuing a degree in teacher education with a minor in educational leadership and policy analysis. At the university, Ryan supervises preservice teachers in the Professional Development School program and teaches a math methods course for elementary education majors. Ryan taught fourth and fifth grade in Indianapolis and New York City for seven years and received a master's degree in curriculum and teaching from Teachers College, Columbia University. Ryan's interest in action research stems from his own research projects in the areas of literature and mathematics. He currently resides in Monona, Wisconsin, with his wife Courtney and their son Abel.

**Mary Klehr** is a teacher in the Madison, Wisconsin, Metropolitan School District, currently supervising elementary education fieldwork at the Midvale-Lincoln Professional Development Partnership School. She has been a teacher, research practitioner, facilitator, and consultant since 1996, and recently became coordinator of the MMSD Classroom Action Research program. In addition to being a University of Wisconsin–Madison doctoral student in curriculum and instruction, Mary is a founding member of a local, arts-based classroom inquiry collective, funded in part by the National Council of Teachers of English.

**Kenneth Zeichner** is a Hoefs-Bascom Professor of Teacher Education and Associate Dean in the School of Education at the University of Wisconsin–Madison. He is editor of the international journal *Educational Action Research* and coauthor of "Practitioner Research" in the fourth edition of the *Handbook of Research on Teaching*, published by the American Educational Research Association.

# *About the Contributors*

**Diane Coccari** is a sixth-grade teacher of social studies and language arts at Black Hawk Middle School in Madison, Wisconsin. She holds a PhD in South Asian languages and literature and an MA in South Asian studies from the University of Wisconsin–Madison. She received her teaching certification through the Teach for Diversity Master's Program of the University of Wisconsin, and has long been involved in equity issues in education.

**Kalani Eggington** is pursuing her doctoral degree in teaching and learning at the University of Utah. She received her MS degree in curriculum and instruction at the University of Wisconsin–Madison with a focus on teacher education. Her master's thesis examined sheltered instruction for English language learners through action research. Before her graduate work, she taught science and health at a Utah middle school for seven years. Her main academic interests include investigating effective methods of professional development for preservice and practicing teachers. She strongly believes action research to be an integral component for productive teacher development.

**Denise M. Hanson** teaches Spanish in Madison, Wisconsin, and holds a master's in teacher leadership. She has taught French and Spanish to K–12 students, as well as teaching methods to undergraduates. Her past research includes work on paired testing, second languages for community building, and Latino leadership. An ongoing research interest is the role of Spanish in teaching Latino immigrant students. She currently teaches one of the district's first Spanish classes for native Spanish speakers.

**Jane Hammatt Kavaloski** was the school social worker, and later the coordinator of service learning, at Malcolm Shabazz City High School in Madison, Wisconsin. Her goal at Shabazz was to make education relevant and empowering for marginalized youth. Jane was named the Midwest School Social Worker of the Year in 1983. She retired in 2004 after working for 30 years in public education. A wife, mother, and grandmother, Jane lives in a Quaker-oriented intentional community in rural Wisconsin. In retirement, she balances time with her family, a mentoring program for new teachers, and local peace and justice activities.

**Kate Lyman** teaches a multiage, English as a second language (ESL) cluster of second- and third-grade students at Hawthorne Elementary School in Madison. She has taught prekindergarten through third grade in the Madison district for 30 years, in schools with higher densities of low-income families from diverse racial, cultural, and language backgrounds. Kate received her MS from the University of Wisconsin–Madison in curriculum and instruction, with a focus on multicultural education. She recently completed coursework for certification in teaching English as a second language. Kate has published articles for *Rethinking Schools* on a variety of issues from acquired immunodeficiency syndrome (AIDS) education, testing, and gender issues to teaching about civil rights and child labor. When she's not teaching, Kate likes to spend time outdoors with her family and three dogs. She also works evenings and weekends at the Dane County Humane Society.

**Julie Melton** has been an elementary teacher for 25 years. She is currently the instructional resource teacher and math coach at Lincoln School in Madison. She leads math professional development for a staff of more than 60 teachers and education assistants. As an onsite coach, she enjoys the challenge of finding more effective strategies to teach math to all students. Julie received her master's degree in curriculum and instruction from the University of Wisconsin–Madison. She works with the university's teacher education students and partners with the math department to offer a minority student mentoring program. Julie is a member of the National Council of Teachers of Mathematics and the Wisconsin Mathematics Council.

**Quynh T. Nguyen** currently serves as principal of Patterson Elementary School in the Indian Prairie School District in Naperville, Illinois. She began her educational career in the Madison Metropolitan School District in Madison, Wisconsin. Quynh has spent more than 10 years in the public school system as a counselor and as a principal. Her passion and professional focus are equity and social justice issues within the educational setting. At age five, she came to America as a Vietnamese refugee child. She grew up in the Midwest and now resides in Plainfield, Illinois.

**Shannon Richards** is in her eighth year at John Muir Elementary School in Madison, Wisconsin, currently teaching a second- and third-grade multi-age class. This is her second action research project. Her previous project focused on student understanding of mathematical equality. Shannon's passion for action research lies in the opportunity to reflect on her own practice as a teacher and develop authentic and self-created approaches to improve that practice. Shannon received her master's in teaching and learning in 2002. She lives in Madison with her husband and two sons.

**Erik J. Shager,** a Teacher's Network Leadership Institute MetLife fellow, has taught social studies at the Work and Learn Center in Madison, Wisconsin, since 1995 and is the internal coach for Affiliated Alternatives, an Accelerated Schools PLUS National Demonstration Site. Erik has presented at national education conferences and has participated in summer institutes sponsored by the United States Supreme Court Historical Society and Street Law, the Birmingham Civil Rights Institute, the National Endowment for the Humanities, and the Gilder Lehrman Institute of American History. He would like to thank Hilary, Jens, and Ava for their love and support.

**Van E. Valaskey** retired from 36 years of high school science teaching in 2003 and is currently working at the University of Wisconsin–Madison College of Engineering as a K–12 outreach coordinator. As a science educator and outreach coordinator, Van believes that all students need hands-on experience with working together using the processes of science to solve problems. Van received various honors as a teacher, including the 2003 Outstanding Biology Teacher Award for Wisconsin. His educational philosophy embodies the following quotation from Plutarch (c. 46–127): "A mind is a fire to be kindled, not a vessel to be filled."

**Barbara Williams** teaches fourth grade in Madison, Wisconsin. She holds a PhD in curriculum and instruction from the University of Wisconsin– Madison.

# PART I

---

## *How Action Research Can Promote Equity*

# 1

# *Classroom Action Research With a Focus on Equity*

Cathy Caro-Bruce and Mary Klehr

With so many excellent resources available on action research—covering the range from theoretical frameworks for understanding the process to illustrative stories from classrooms and schools—why a book on *equity and action research*? The answer goes deeper than simply understanding the principles driving action research or the complex questions about equity that face our schools. The answer lies in the interface of what happens when teachers use action research to better understand issues of social and educational equity from inside classrooms and schools, in a way that results in significant learning for teachers and students alike.

This book has as its centerpiece the work of teachers who, in the process of facing hard questions about their own instructional practices and the contexts in which they work, have influenced the thinking and instruction of other teachers, other classrooms, and entire schools. While covering a variety of pedagogical topics, the studies share a common focus on equity, race, and closing gaps in opportunity and academic achievement between groups of students. These stories, which range in scope from a close study of one child and how his elementary teacher adapted instructional practices to ensure school success to a study of how a high school science department changed inclusive practices in an effort to eliminate tracking, illustrate the kinds of changes teachers can make in their own thinking and pedagogy on behalf of their students.

This book also gives readers the opportunity to learn how one public school district has sustained its action research program since 1990, starting with a group of eight teachers and including several hundred participants over the years since. The commitment by the Madison Metropolitan School District (MMSD) to this professional development opportunity is a validation of the benefit of self-reflective, inquiry-based research to classrooms and schools. When educators select meaningful questions to explore and then generate data about their own work to help them improve what they do, they act as autonomous, responsible agents who actively direct their own pedagogical development. The classroom action research process has provided a structure through which to pursue questions of immediate importance to teachers and their students, and the MMSD has found that authentic and immediate change can occur when teachers are able to delve deeply into their own values, experiences, and practices in this way.

The MMSD, like a number of other school districts that are highly successful in the areas of academic performance and teacher quality, has struggled to improve the academic achievement of students of color and students living in poverty. Confronting issues of equity and race has been a district focus for many years, and action research is one of many professional development strategies that the MMSD has supported over time as a method for making progress in understanding and improving achievement for all children.

In this chapter, you will learn about the district's focus on equity issues and how action research fits with other efforts to make schools places where all children can be successful. Chapter 2 describes how action research fits into broader professional development efforts and outlines the MMSD's action research story: how the program is organized, the principles that guide the work, the method of facilitation, and the nitty-gritty details that have helped to make this experience so successful. The 10 studies that make up the heart of this book illustrate the range of action research questions that teachers have pursued, how they conducted their research, and what they learned, while the final chapter analyzes the studies through the lens of academic literature on equity pedagogy, to identify key findings and their pedagogical implications for teachers, classrooms, and districts.

## EQUITY ACTION RESEARCH

Madison, Wisconsin—not an unlikely place to start up action research as a professional development practice in the 1980s, but unusual in that the first group would focus on equity issues. Madison, the state capital and home of the University of Wisconsin–Madison, has a strong history of community support for and involvement in education. The MMSD serves approximately

25,000 students in 31 elementary schools, 11 middle schools, four large comprehensive high schools, and an alternative high school. For the most part, our schools have much to celebrate. Among statistics of note are that nearly half our teachers have at least one master's degree, and an unusually high number have doctorates. Our high school graduation rate is higher than the national average, and Scholastic Aptitude Test (SAT) scores for Madison students are 20 percent higher than the U.S. average. Each year Madison has more than 50 National Merit Scholar semifinalists, five times as many as the average for other districts of its size.

In the 1980s, MMSD staff throughout the district were starting to notice the effects of subtle but increasingly significant changes in the demographics of the student population. The minority population had risen to 22 percent, and the poverty rate hovered around 19 percent. Teachers who had felt successful working within the norms of a generally homogeneous student population were alternately excited, bewildered, and challenged by the growing diversity of their students, the broader range of learning styles, and different forms of parental support. Schools began to recognize the importance of understanding the contributions and needs of this changing population so that all students could be successful.

During the mid-1980s, a staff development specialist organized two different yearlong action research groups that focused on bringing teachers together to inquire and reflect on their evolving instructional practices. Participants were enthusiastic and felt that it was a powerful experience on an individual level. However, the experience had little noticeable impact at schoolwide or district levels. When the staff development specialist left the MMSD, these initiatives were not continued.

By the late 1980s, when the MMSD was looking at different strategies to support schools with higher numbers of minority and low-income students, another member of the staff development team, who had observed the early success and enthusiasm of the action research groups, formed a partnership with the MMSD coordinator of research and evaluation. With patience and persistence, these two individuals spent three years trying to find funding and support for action research in the MMSD. They presented their proposal to various groups—principals, administrative cabinets, and MMSD leadership groups—and were met with mild interest. The groups made several suggestions for how to fund release time for teachers to do this work, which the organizers believed was essential to attract teachers and sustain the initiative. One of the most challenging issues that repeatedly surfaced at that time was the lack of acceptance or understanding on the part of these leadership groups of the need to help teachers become more reflective about their teaching practices.

It became apparent that efforts by individual schools to meet the needs of an increasingly diverse student body were not having the desired impact, and that district resources needed to be organized more effectively to support specific schools. The MMSD directed funds to the schools with high poverty populations and also set up professional development activities to support teachers in these schools. In the late 1980s, understanding and improving minority student achievement emerged as an MMSD priority. One of the key initiatives was a project called "Cultural Differences and Classroom Strategies." For two years, teachers in high-need elementary schools participated in this effort to help them increase their repertoire of teaching strategies to meet the many needs of students from different ethnic groups and socioeconomic backgrounds. During the third year of the project, the expectation was that teachers would be able to implement some of the strategies that they had been learning and try to figure out what made a difference in the success of their students. Action research had the potential to provide the structure for teachers who had participated in the Cultural Differences and Classroom Strategies initiative to explore their topics more deeply.

In the spring of 1990, the two coordinators of the action research program sent a letter to all elementary teachers in the MMSD, inviting them to participate in an action research group called "Meeting the Needs of Diverse Learners." Funding tied to the district initiative to understand cultural differences had been found, and when eight people signed on, the organizers were ecstatic. Although they were on their way to bringing action research to the MMSD, at the time they had little idea what that meant. From month to month, they learned more about how to maintain the momentum of designing experiences that would promote ongoing reflection and how to consciously bring the action research process to the participants. They also began to see how quickly teachers embraced this kind of professional development activity and began to plan for sustaining action research in the district on a long-term basis.

This experience taught the program coordinators a lot about what it takes to implement a new way of providing staff development, and how to move toward institutionalizing it across the district by making it available to all staff and schools. In the second year, the project grew to two groups, with 12 teachers in one and 12 principals in the other. Since this beginning, the program has annually supported 30 to 75 participants in various themed groups, led by experienced action researchers who facilitate their colleagues during the yearlong action research process.

## FAST-FORWARD TO THE PRESENT DAY

The changes in MMSD demographics that were subtle in the 1980s have since become dramatic. For example, the number of low-income students as a proportion of all students enrolled in the MMSD has increased to 38 percent (doubling since 1988), while the proportion of students of color has doubled as well, to 44 percent of the student population. The number of English language learners (ELLs) enrolled in the district has risen by roughly 300 percent during that time span, and the percentage of Latino students in third grade receiving English as a second language and/or bilingual support has increased from 16 percent to 70 percent. The calls to improve how services are delivered throughout the district—and explore how to meet the varied needs of an increasingly diverse population—have now become top priorities.

Opportunities to join action research groups focusing on equity, race, and the achievement gap have been offered annually to all MMSD teachers, support staff (psychologists, social workers, nurses, and school counselors), and administrators. Groups have worked on themes including "Meeting the Needs of All Learners"; "Race, Class, Gender, Culture, Language and Learning"; "English Language Learners"; and "Closing the Achievement Gap."

## OTHER EQUITY INITIATIVES

Action research is only one part of a much larger initiative around equity that has had a significant impact on teacher effectiveness and student achievement across the district. Other key activities include:

- **Districtwide data collection and analysis.** Through the continual improvement of the district data systems, teachers and other staff can now easily access data about individuals and groups of students. Initially, the MMSD Research and Evaluation Department responded individually to the hundreds of yearly requests for data. A critical recent professional development effort has been to build the knowledge and skills of all staff to directly access data about students so that they can engage in thoughtful dialogue within their schools. Action researchers, who are comfortable with data collection, data analysis, and the inquiry process, help the district model positive attitudes to other staff about the importance and usefulness of data.

- **Leadership development.** During its annual summer Principals Institute in 2000, the MMSD brought in a national consultant on race and equity, who helped principals and administrators engage in self-reflection about race and identity and how each individual's personal assumptions affect our schools and students. With strong leadership from the MMSD assistant superintendents, principals have continued to build competence in leading their schools and addressing issues of race and equity at their monthly professional development meetings. The MMSD also put together a district equity team and has offered ongoing professional development to the MMSD superintendent's cabinet.

• **Districtwide professional development.** For many years, the MMSD has offered courses for teachers that are focused on strategies to help all students succeed. Once the principals experienced the equity-based summer training, the district management team decided to implement a systemwide professional development program for all staff. Under the direction of the superintendent's special assistant for parent and community relations, the MMSD offered workshops and supported both district- and school-based professional development. Each school and MMSD department has its own equity team, which designs continuing staff development opportunities, including ongoing reflective conversations, book groups, and workshops, and addresses equity issues in their schools or departments.

• **Minority Student Achievement Network.** The MMSD is a member of the Minority Student Achievement Network, a national coalition of multiracial, relatively successful school districts that have come together to study the disparity in achievement between White students and students of color through intensive research and professional development. The network was established to discover, develop, and implement the means to ensure high academic achievement of minority students. MMSD representatives attend regular conferences and are part of the research arm of the network, which has also promoted leadership among students from the MMSD's high schools.

All these key district activities focusing on equity and race have resulted in several important outcomes:

• Staff clearly understand the MMSD's mission and vision regarding the ability of all students to achieve at the highest level.
• Staff use a common language to communicate about expectations and anticipated outcomes.
• Increasingly, thoughtful and honest conversations occur about equity and race and their impact on student achievement.
• Schools examine systems, structures, and instructional practices that are barriers to student achievement.
• Leaders at all levels of the MMSD are committed to equity and race work.
• There is a climate and expectation of accountability, ensuring that schools achieve their school improvement goals.

While action research is just one cog in the wheel of the many efforts in which the MMSD is engaged to make schools equitable, the focus on teachers' capacity to understand how to make a difference in the lives of students, and the in-depth, reflective dialogue that pushes teachers to understand equity and race issues in thoughtful ways give action research a unique place in the larger district work.

## WHAT HAPPENS IN AN EQUITY-FOCUSED ACTION RESEARCH GROUP?

Themes of race and achievement thread themselves through the questions and conversations of action research groups that focus on educational equity, as action researchers strive to build both competence and confidence in this complex and challenging area facing the schools. While teachers in an action research group generally follow an inquiry process of developing questions, collecting and analyzing data, and writing about findings, the group's facilitators and members take responsibility for educating each other about equity and race in order to build common knowledge and talk more honestly about the issues they are facing.

Action research groups also incorporate various activities to build a foundation and knowledge base among practitioners for talking with others about equity beliefs and practices. Some of the specific activities that groups have done include:

- Constructing a working definition of *equity.*

*Action researchers do not work from a textbook definition of equity. Instead, in the constructivist spirit of the action research process, researchers build a definition that is based on specific knowledge, context, and experience. The term "working definition" is used to reflect how the understanding of equity shifts and evolves throughout the action research experience.*

- Writing about *equity* as it is observed in classrooms and schools.

*In order to examine, critique, and change practices, group members spend time thinking and writing about equity issues in their own classrooms—assumptions, observations, concerns—and then they highlight two or three compelling ideas that stand out as important to develop further. A list of potential action research questions for further study is created from what has been written.*

- Reading and discussing articles about *equity.*

*Group members deepen their understanding of issues of equity, race, and closing the achievement gap through discussions of articles and the impact of the readings on them as teachers and administrators. Articles that challenge and verify their assumptions about equity issues, extend their knowledge, and help them become more interculturally competent are emphasized.*

- Writing a story about *equity* in the teacher's classroom or school.

*Sharing written narratives about interactions with students or colleagues provides a rich opportunity to describe and discuss a range of authentic experiences.*

- Creating cause-and-effect/root cause (fishbone) diagrams.

*Teachers use a cause-and-effect diagramming exercise to identify important questions and potential root causes of unequal achievement of students (see Chapter 11). This exercise also uncovers potential data sources and pedagogical strategies.*

- Reading other action research studies focusing on *equity.*

*Teachers read what other action researchers have studied, as another source of data for their own research, but also to deepen their own understanding of the issues that they are studying. They are especially curious to find out what their district colleagues have learned and what actions they have taken.*

- Interviewing school staff about diverse experiences with and concerns about issues of *equity.*

*An important source of data for action researchers is the perspectives and experiences of colleagues. Teachers are often pleasantly surprised by the willingness of their peers and administrators to help them with their research.*

- Having each group member share his or her racial autobiography.

*One of the most powerful activities in which groups engage is taking the time to listen to each group member's racial autobiography. This process helps everyone understand how personal experience influences who we are and what we believe, as well as learn about different life experiences and perspectives people bring to teaching and learning.*

- Describing what it means to work for *equity* in one's school.

*Action researchers typically come to the groups with a strong commitment to issues of equity and social justice. Time is spent in the group talking about specific leadership actions that members can take to affect classrooms and schools, and often how to find the courage to take action in some challenging environments.*

As a result of questioning assumptions and articulating ideas in the safe environment of a research group, action researchers appear to be more inclined to take risks in discussions and practices that are necessary for engaging in equitable practices, eliminating the achievement gap, and acting on behalf of colleagues, students, and families in their school communities.

\* \* \* \*

The 10 studies that make up the core of this book lay out an array of areas that teachers were drawn to study through classroom action research. Each account is set in the context of a particular classroom in a particular community, and taken together they tell the story of how teachers bring different filters and experiences to the important discussions about how equity and race affect children in schools. As you read through the studies, keep in mind that although the district has come a long way in making the schools more humane and equitable for children and families, there is still a long way to go as individuals and as an educational community. While some of the results may have direct implications for other districts, this particular story can serve as a road map for doing the critical work that is essential to the future of the students. Enjoy the journey!

* * * *

# 2

## Implementing a School District Action Research Program

Cathy Caro-Bruce and Mary Klehr

K nowing how action research fits into the larger discussion of effective professional development, as well as the specifics of what a district program looks like, is essential to understanding how to implement a quality action research program. Having this foundation is helpful to teachers, principals, staff developers, curriculum coordinators, and other educators who have the interest and ability to coordinate groups of people who want to examine and improve their practices.

### ACTION RESEARCH IN THE LARGER CONTEXT OF DISTRICT PROFESSIONAL DEVELOPMENT

> *By validating teachers as knowers as well as doers, teacher research can turn traditional professional development on its head, offering the possibility of major long-term changes that are generated by teachers themselves, based on their own investigations of practice.*
>
> —Check, 1997, p. 6

Action research, a form of inquiry that involves teachers in developing their own research questions and investigating their own classroom practices, is an activity that reflects the current consensus about quality professional development activities. Since the Madison Metropolitan School District (MMSD) classroom action research program began in 1990, numerous organizations, including the U.S. Department of Education, the National Staff Development Council, and various content area associations (including the National Council of Teachers of English) have articulated standards or "design principles" for describing good professional development activities. These standards, which are linked to research on teacher learning, emphasize the importance of providing teachers with intensive, participant-driven opportunities to engage with colleagues in inquiry and reflection over time about issues that matter to them in the course of their daily work. This vision of professional development—while recognizing the need for teachers to learn new skills and content that address school reform initiatives—emphasizes the need for opportunities that respect and build on the knowledge and expertise that teachers already have and that nurture and support teachers' intellectual leadership capacity.

What distinguishes action research from other forms of educational research? Action research is a distinct genre by virtue of who the researchers are (teachers); what they do (inquire into their own practice in systematic ways); and where the research takes place (inside classrooms and schools.) It is markedly distinct from other forms of educational research, in that teaching and researching are actively intertwined. The results of this process, which mirror current developments in qualitative and social science research, is often more personally reflective, context-specific, and open-ended than are the findings typically found in controlled experimental design or strictly quantitative studies.

Opinions differ regarding the validity and usefulness of teachers researching their own practices. Skeptics wonder if teacher research contributes anything of significance to broad-based educational knowledge beyond "small stories" and technical skills (Hodgkinson, 1957; Huberman, 1996). Supporters of action research question whether educational research that is grounded in scientific theory with the aim of broad generalizability is capable of addressing the contextualized realities of actual classrooms. Even when the intention of more traditional research is to influence classroom practice, teachers are typically not the primary audience.

The purpose of researching one's own practice from inside the classroom is different from the purpose of educational researchers, who examine the behaviors and practices of other people. Action research, which by design is immediate and relevant to teachers' lives and work, allows practitioners to make productive changes in classroom practice based on analysis of authentic and contextually specific data. Because it is created by and for teachers and intentionally tailored to respond to specific classroom contexts, classroom action research is therefore *necessarily* and *appropriately* different from the kind of research done by those who are more removed from schools.

## STRUCTURE AND ORGANIZATION OF ONE SCHOOL DISTRICT'S ACTION RESEARCH PROGRAM

While it has become increasingly common for teachers across the country to engage in some form of action research, there is no common recipe for doing so. Districts and staff development organizations across the country take a wide variety of approaches to conceptualizing, organizing, and supporting teachers through the process. Variations are reflected in: (1) the purposes and motivations of those who engage in the research; (2) the structure and context of research groups; (3) ideas about research process and methodology; (4) facilitation process; (5) writing and dissemination; and perhaps most important, (6) the underlying philosophical assumptions about knowledge, teacher learning, and school change. We will now discuss in turn how each of these plays out for the action researchers included this study.

## PURPOSE, MOTIVATION, AND THEMES

Teachers are motivated to conduct research in their own classrooms for a variety of reasons. Noffke (1997) and Fisher (1996) have outlined several different, sometimes overlapping motives, which are mirrored in the studies that appear at the heart of this book:

(a) Individual progress—to better understand and improve one's instructional practices and classroom environment;
(b) Student progress—to know more about and improve student learning;
(c) Knowledge production—to produce and share knowledge useful to other educators;
(d) Social change—to contribute to greater equity and democracy in schooling and society; and
(e) Personal meaning—a search for connections and meaning in one's work.

When teachers are not given the power to determine the research focus or the methodology of their inquiries, they may react negatively to what they perceive as attempts to control and manipulate them under the guise of empowerment (Zeichner, 1999). Nonetheless, one of the goals of the Madison District's action research program is to build a body of knowledge around topics that will help the schools and district accomplish a range of goals and priorities. One strategy to address possible tensions between district improvement priorities and teachers' own definitions of their individual development needs is organizing research groups on topics that are MMSD priorities and allowing teachers to develop their own research foci within these broad areas. Themes of importance to the district on which recent action research groups have focused include: "English Language Learners," "Closing the Achievement Gap," "Special Education," "Equity," "Technology," "Six Trait Writing," "Health and Wellness," "Culture and Climate," and "Reading Comprehension." This system of identifying broad areas for research and then giving teachers the autonomy to develop their research projects within these priority areas taps into the power of teacher inquiry to promote both individual and district goals.

## STRUCTURE AND CONTEXT OF RESEARCH GROUPS

While most of the teachers pursue individual questions, they also work on their questions in a group setting when they meet on a monthly basis to support and challenge each other. The experience of working in a group in which all members are engaged in self-study helps teachers develop new attitudes and skills to work collaboratively. When teachers feel safe and supported in these groups, communication among members becomes more authentic and informative than the usual daily talk in staff rooms. In the group context, individuals are pushed to be clear about their thinking in a public way, to be vulnerable with colleagues when they are struggling, and to be thoughtful listeners as they support other group members in their studies. These sustained discussions with other teachers over long periods of time seem to be uncommon in teachers' previous experiences and important for helping them learn to analyze their practices in depth.

The action research groups are typically made up of six to ten participants from throughout the district, which promotes cross-school sharing among participants about different practices and ideas. Each year, some school-based groups focus on a topic of particular importance to that school. Most groups meet monthly in the morning, with three additional afternoons built in during the year to work individually on their projects. Other groups meet once a month for three or four hours after school. Participants do not receive a stipend for participating in action research, but express strongly their appreciation for being able to have release time to meet during the school day. The program coordinator searches creatively for sources of funding to cover the costs of substitutes, including securing support from district departments that are interested in participating in this kind of professional development. Over the years, funds to support groups have come from the budgets of departments, such as Special Education, English Language Learners, Staff Development, and Teaching and Learning, as well as specific grant initiatives such as Comprehensive School Reform and Safe Schools.

At the beginning of the action research experience, each group member signs an agreement to attend all sessions and to write a paper describing the work that has been accomplished. Over the years, it has become clear how important it is to have participants attend all the meetings, especially when the meetings occur only once a month. If people miss meetings, they often lose momentum with their projects and, just as important, have a hard time feeling a part of the group, which is essential to the quality of the experience. Participants in action research groups can earn university credit at the University of Wisconsin–Madison (at a prearranged reduced fee), can receive district professional advancement credit for hours worked beyond the contract day, or can use this experience as part of the state licensure requirements for individual professional development plans.

## RESEARCH PROCESS AND METHODOLOGY

> *[Teacher] research is a process in which participants examine their own educational practice, systematically and carefully, using the techniques of research.*
>
> —Watts, 1985, p. 2

Teachers have traditionally been seen primarily as subjects or consumers of research done by others. In contrast, the MMSD's action research program is based on the assumption that teachers are capable of determining research methods to articulate what they know about classroom practice, to question and change what goes on in schools, and to contribute to general educational knowledge. One of the central practices tied to this philosophical view is that teachers are expected to choose research questions of interest to them, to select their own data methods, and to do their own analysis.[1]

While MMSD action researchers conduct their studies in a careful, systematic manner following many of the common steps of research—question development, data generation, analysis, and reporting—the approach strives to be more aligned to the way teachers, not academicians, inquire into practice. For example, questions evolve and change over time, with some teachers working with multiple questions simultaneously. Analysis and action occur throughout the process, often in a cyclical, iterative pattern. Teachers judge the validity of their work on its systematic process, its trustworthiness to other practitioners, and its catalytic (leading to action) and democratic (taking other perspectives into consideration) qualities.

Action researchers ground their work in classroom context and practice and look to many sources for finding the right action research question, including: data about their students; observations of their classrooms; areas in which they want to improve their teaching practices; challenges presented by individual students; school or classroom systems and structures that they believe are not serving students well; promoting greater equity in their classrooms or schools; observations and discussions with other staff; or schoolwide goals. Researchers often have to start down the pathway of collecting initial data about their question before determining if the question is appropriate and if it's one in which they can be invested for the entire school year. Initial data can reveal that the researchers already know what they think are good instructional practices, and that pursuing a question on that topic is not a good use of time.

Finding the right question is critical. Some action researchers come to the group with a question in mind and are willing to be influenced by other group members as they continue to refine the question. Other action researchers are not clear on the specific question when they arrive and access the group, with its systematic listening and questioning process, to clarify their action research questions. Action researchers learn the importance of their questions *being clear* (conveying the focus and not filled with jargon-laden phrases); *being doable* (something that can be accomplished within the context in which they work); *being open-ended* (written in such a way that it leads to a range of ideas, insights, and new questions); *providing tension* (giving the researcher an opportunity to grow as a result of the study); and *being* one to which the researcher *feels commitment* (this is hard work—it's essential that the question is of great importance to the teacher).

While many teachers are interested in learning what others have written about their areas of study, they do not always find it useful to review academic or teacher research literature. Therefore, individual researchers are encouraged to decide for themselves whether to incorporate external research into their studies. In some of the studies included in this book, literature reviews are part of the action research, but in others, there are no references to external research.

## FACILITATION

Groups are cofacilitated by two experienced action researchers who can be teachers, central office staff, or support staff (psychologists, social workers, or nurses). Those who are new to the role of facilitation are paired with veterans in order to build a core group of skilled facilitators. Facilitators also gain support by attending regular afterschool meetings that focus on three things: problem-solving around issues that arise at monthly meetings; learning more about specific aspects of the action research process; and sharing successful group facilitation strategies.

Facilitators are encouraged to exercise their professional judgment and leadership abilities as they facilitate their action research groups. Unfortunately, funding is not available to pay stipends to facilitators for their work with groups. They do receive other resources, including a handbook of suggested processes and handouts, articles, and a support structure for their work. Throughout the years, facilitators consistently describe the joy and sense of reward they feel in planning a quality experience for their colleagues and learning more about the challenges and issues that go with working with adults.

### What Happens at Monthly Action Research Group Meetings?

It is both hard and simple to define what happens in an action research group. Without a step-by-step manual, facilitators new to action research often become concerned about how to take people through the stages of developing an action research question, collecting and analyzing data, and doing a final write-up of the study. Facilitators know that the heart of the meetings is in how they create the opportunity for everyone to engage in thoughtful and meaningful conversations. By having everyone follow a set of behavioral norms, group members are willing to speak openly about their work and are appreciative of the time to talk with each other, an activity that seems desperately lacking in the lives of educators. Action researchers frequently compare the "deep discussions" that they engage in as teacher researchers with the shallowness of many of their other professional development experiences. This combination, of providing safety and security on the one hand, and intellectual challenge on the other, is similar to what Lord (1994) refers to as "productive disequilibrium," one aspect of the concept of "critical colleagueship," which he considers to be important to good professional development.

So, what does a typical action research group meeting look like? At the beginning of each meeting, facilitators structure time for a check-in activity that connects teachers to their action research focus and allows group members to get to know each other better. Typical check-ins might include: "What three words would your colleagues use to describe you?" "Describe one of your most influential teachers." "What is one positive thing that has occurred so far as a result of your action research study?"

A portion of the meeting is also spent learning more about or practicing some aspect of the research process. This might include exploring different ways to refine questions, learning about conducting effective interviews, or having group participants design a data collection plan that uses triangulation of data. Later in the year, the facilitators introduce peer editing strategies and have group members work together to offer suggestions on drafts of each other's papers.

Structuring time for action research participants to write at each meeting has become an essential part of the process. Usually, it's a 10- to 15-minute time block, during which participants often focus on their questions and prepare for the ensuing discussion as they share their progress with the group. Facilitators offer a writing prompt, such as asking group members to respond to a quotation, write about other questions they have about their action research question, or describe what they have learned so far. Participants soon learn how their monthly reflections are another source of data for them as they look at their question over an entire school year.

The most important part of the meeting, and the aspect that takes the most time, is having individuals talk about a salient aspect of their research work—what their plan is, what data they have collected, what challenges they are facing, how they are revising their question based on what they have learned, or what they have learned from analyzing their data. Each group member decides what to discuss during this time. This is the aspect of action research meetings with which most districts struggle: the tension between expecting people to respond to a formulaic protocol and trusting the group members to focus on what they know they need. As group members develop confidence in the power and usefulness of action research, they become very focused on what they want to accomplish to ensure that the meetings are addressing their issues.

So, what is the role of the group members while each person is sharing his or her work? It is to be thoughtful listeners—to think about questions or paraphrased statements to offer the presenter that will help him or her go more deeply with the question. It is not to offer solutions to the presenter or to solve the problem for the person who has the question—even if group members think that they have *the very best idea that will solve the problem!* Individuals who are talking about their action research question will often physically withdraw from the conversation as other people take over the problem solving and the entire presentation. Facilitators play a critical role here by monitoring who is talking and ensuring that group members who might be dominating the discussion—or just enthusiastically trying to be helpful—are not taking over the discussion. Encouraging teachers to play a more listening and thoughtful questioning role is probably the hardest behavior to change in an action research group. Teachers are generally very helpful and don't like seeing anyone struggle when they have an issue or problem about which they might know something.

One of the ways that a district can more effectively implement an action research program is to take the time to talk about what it hopes to accomplish and what might be some guiding principles for its work. When the MMSD began its program, it was not clear how it would evolve. What *was* clear was that the organizers had some strong philosophical beliefs about teachers and their capacity to improve and make changes on behalf of their students. Programs do not need to look alike, but it is essential to know the guiding principles of a program that a district is developing. This description of a district action research professional development program is one example—in one district. You could not, nor would you want to, replicate the elements from the Madison Metropolitan School District in your own district. What this description *can* provide you, however, is a place to launch your own discussions about what you hope to accomplish and some ideas for getting there.

## WRITING AND DISSEMINATION

> *It is teachers who, in the end, will change the world of the school by understanding it.*
>
> —Lawrence Stenhouse, 1975
> (quoted in Rudduck, 1988, p. 30)

In the early years, action researchers wrote about their work because it seemed as if writing about the experience was a good thing to do, but not essential. It has become clear over time how essential writing is to the learning that occurs during the year and the impact it has on the researcher's overall learning. Some action researchers have said: "I didn't realize what I had really learned until I had to write about it." "The writing pushed me to choose words carefully and to think in purposeful ways about what I had experienced." Each action researcher writes a report that the school district publishes. Categorized abstracts of all the studies are available on the district's Web page,[2] and some of the abstracts are linked to .pdf versions of the full reports. Although the quality of the writing varies, as do individuals' experiences with writing papers, it is important to communicate and disseminate what has been learned. Publishing the work also contributes to teachers' sense of professionalism and their belief that what they have done can have an impact on students, staff, and their schools.

Over the years, the collective knowledge that has been produced has been disseminated in a variety of other ways as well. For seven years, a collaborative partnership of district, university, and state department representatives organized an annual action research conference that brought together a couple of hundred people, who sat with each other in small groups, discussed the current studies, and learned from colleagues. Another strategy to share the work was a program on the MMSD cable television network featuring action researchers who described their work and what they had learned. Many action researchers have also spoken at conferences and written papers for journals. In the past few years, action researchers have shared their work with the MMSD Education Services Department about potential policy implications, including how the district might think differently about how services are delivered to special education and English language learner (ELL) students, as well as the kind of professional development needed by staff. These are always very powerful meetings.

In addition to the extensions of the individual action research studies described above, other leadership opportunities for action researchers have included facilitating research groups and serving as consultants to other districts.

## PHILOSOPHICAL ASSUMPTIONS

In 1998, a study of the MMSD action research program was conducted through a grant awarded to the Madison Metropolitan School District and the UW–Madison from the Spencer and MacArthur Foundations in order to clearly identify key principles from the action researchers that enable the transformation of teacher thinking and practices that lead to student success. The following five key areas illustrate the guiding principles that ground all elements of the MMSD program.

(1) **Voluntary participation.** The program is voluntary. Because teachers are able to choose their own research questions, data collection and analysis strategies, and how they write up their findings, they can become personally invested in the process.

(2) **Creating a culture of inquiry that respects the voices of teachers and the knowledge they bring to the research experience.** Provision of release time, opportunities to present and publish work, and the way in which meetings are conducted support teachers' struggles while providing intellectual challenge and collegiality.

(3) **Investment in teachers' intellectual capital.** Teacher researchers in this program can take control of most aspects of the research process, building on a strong belief that teachers have the capacity to find answers to questions that they are pursuing.

(4) **Collaboration over time in a safe and supportive group environment.** The experience of working in a group in which all members are engaged in self-study aims to help teachers develop new skills and ways to work collaboratively.

(5) **Intellectual challenges and stimulation**. Contrary to the popular images of teachers as wanting quick fixes or being incapable of serious intellectual activity, MMSD action researchers say that they value the difficulty and challenges provided by group discussions of their inquiries.

## DISTRICT-UNIVERSITY COLLABORATION AROUND ACTION RESEARCH

As researchers whose work is personally meaningful and of consequence to others, teachers and academic researchers share many of the same questions, concerns, and purposes. Unfortunately, little attention has been given to how research conducted by K–12 teachers can inform educational policy and the process of educational change at a level beyond individual teachers' own classrooms and schools. Understanding that teacher action researchers are unique and important sources of pedagogical knowledge—and that their intellectual and leadership capacity remains largely unrecognized and untapped by the academic community—reflects a potential for new working relationships between teacher researchers and academics.

The MMSD program reflects an unusual collaboration between university faculty members, school district staff developers, and teachers. In the dominant model of school-university collaborations, a university conception of research shapes the structure, nature, and impact of the collaboration. In contrast, the Madison Metropolitan School District–University of Wisconsin–Madison collaboration has taken a unique form that is aligned with the philosophy of the action research program. The collaboration has not meant that the university has taken control of the program or serves as its gatekeeper. Rather, the university recognizes that teachers develop valuable pedagogical skills and knowledge while teaching, and the university tries to promote a constructivist understanding of teachers as learners. Thus, the university takes a collegial rather than an "expert" stance. In practical terms, the MMSD owns the program, by taking responsibility for structuring, funding, and facilitating the research groups. The university supports the program by providing university credit, periodic study grants, funding for teacher researchers to attend and present at conferences, assistance with journal articles, and other resources. It also makes an effort to incorporate teacher research work into its course syllabi so that both undergraduate and graduate students can learn from the studies of classroom teachers.

The University of Wisconsin–Madison and the MMSD collaborate in various ways to support action research conducted by preservice teachers at the university and to introduce to student teachers the idea that teachers can control their own professional development and can produce educational knowledge to benefit others. These practices include: (1) placing student teachers in classrooms with cooperating teachers who are doing action research, who question current practices, and who are openly reflective about their own practice; (2) hiring teachers to teach an action research class to School of Education undergraduates; and (3) inviting teacher researchers to discuss their research in undergraduate and graduate university classes.

The broader consequences of this collaboration include a sustained effort to integrate teacher-produced knowledge from action research groups (such as algebraic thinking, outdoor learning labs, ELL students) into the curriculum of the UW–Madison elementary teacher education program; an increase in self-study research conducted by UW–Madison teacher educators (both faculty and graduate students); and collaboratively conducted research projects that bring the skills, resources, and perspectives from the school district and the university together.

## TEN EQUITY ACTION RESEARCH STUDIES

What follows is a representative group of action research studies, all focusing on the themes of equity, race, and closing achievement gaps. The authors include teachers from elementary, middle, and high schools who address questions that show their commitment to improving the lives of students and schools. These chapters are the final reports after a yearlong study by each of the action researchers. Some of the studies are recent, some from several years ago. Each includes a follow-up epilogue, where the action researchers describe the impact of their studies on their own instructional practices, their schools, and the lives of their students. Immerse yourself in the thinking and actions of these practitioners, whose stories have stimulated and challenged them, and opened them up to new, more thoughtful practice.

## NOTES

1. There are many articles, chapters, and books to help people understand more about action research. At the end of the chapter we list literature that has influenced how we understand and conduct action research in our district.

2. Madison Metropolitan School District Classroom Action Research Web site: http://www.madison.k12.wi.us/sod/car/carhomepage.html.

## REFERENCES

Check, J. (1997). Teacher research as powerful professional development. *Harvard Education Letter, 13*(3), 6–8.

Fisher, J. (1996). Open to ideas: Developing a framework for your research. In G. Burnaford, J. Fisher, & D. Hobson (Eds.), *Teachers doing research: Practical possibilities.* Mahwah, NJ: Lawrence Erlbaum.

Hodgkinson, H. L. (1957). Action research: A critique. *Journal of Educational Sociology, 31,* 137–148.

Huberman, M. (1996). Moving mainstream: Taking a closer look at teacher research. *Language Arts, 73,* 124–140.

Lord, B. (1994). Teachers' professional development: Critical colleagueship and the role of professional communities. In N. Cobb (Ed.), *The future of education: Perspectives on national standards in America* (pp. 175–204). New York: College Entrance Examination Board.

Noffke, S. (1997). Professional, personal, and political dimensions of action research. *Review of Research in Education, 22,* 305–343.

Rudduck, J. (1988). Changing the world of the classroom by understanding it: A review of some aspects of the work of Lawrence Stenhouse. *Journal of Curriculum and Supervision, 4*(1), 30–42.

Watts, H. (1985). When teachers are researchers, teaching improves. *Journal of Staff Development, 6*(2), 118–127.

Zeichner, K. (1999). *Teacher research as a professional development activity for P–12 educators.* Washington, DC: U.S. Department of Education.

## CLASSROOM ACTION RESEARCH RESOURCES

There are many articles, chapters, and books to help people understand more about action research. Listed below is some of the literature that we refer to most often:

### Books About Classroom Action Research

Anderson, G. L., Herr, K., & Nihlen, A. S. (2007). *Studying your own school: An educator's guide to practitioner action research.* Thousand Oaks, CA: Corwin Press.

Caro-Bruce, C. (2000). *Action research facilitators' handbook.* Oxford, OH: National Staff Development Council.

Cochran-Smith, M., & Lytle, S. L. (1993). *Inside/outside: Teacher research and knowledge.* New York: Teachers College Press.

Hopkins, D. (2002). *A teacher's guide to classroom research.* Philadelphia: Open University Press.

Hubbard, R. S., & Power, B. M. (1999). *Living the questions: A guide for teacher-researchers.* York, ME: Stenhouse Publishers.

Hubbard, R. S., & Power, B. M. (2003). *The art of classroom inquiry: A handbook for teacher-researchers.* Portsmouth, NH: Heinemann.

Kemmis, S., & McTaggart, R. (Eds.). (1988) *The action research planner* (3rd ed.). Victoria, Australia: Deakin University.

Maclean, M. S., & Mohr, M. M. (1999). *Teacher-researchers at work.* Berkeley: University of California National Writing Project.

Marion, R., & Zeichner, K. (2001). *Practitioner resource guide for action research.* Oxford, OH: National Staff Development Council.

Mills, G. (2003). *Action research: A guide for the teacher researcher.* Upper Saddle River, NJ: Pearson Education, Inc.

Stenhouse, L. (1975). *An introduction to curriculum research and development.* London: Heinemann.

## Articles About Classroom Action Research

Calhoun, E. (1993). Action research: Three approaches. *Educational Leadership, 52*(2), 62–65.

Calhoun, E. (2002). Action research for school improvement. *Educational Leadership*, March, 18–24.

Caro-Bruce, C., & McCreadie, J. (1995). What happens when a school district supports action research? In S. Noffke & R. Stevenson (Eds.), *Educational action research.* (pp. 154–164). New York: Teachers College Press.

Cochran-Smith, M., & Lytle, S. (1999). The teacher research movement: A decade later. *Educational Researcher, 28*(7), 15–25.

Duffy, G. (1998). Teaching and the balancing of round stones. *Phi Delta Kappan,* June, 777–780.

Hughes, V. (1992). In defense of action research. *Research Forum,* Fall, 6–11.

Joyce, B., & Calhoun, E. (1995). School renewal: An inquiry, not a formula. *Educational Leadership, 52*(7), 51–55.

McKay, J. A. (1992). Professional development through action research. *Journal of Staff Development, 13*(1), 18–21.

Miller, D. M., & Pine, G. J. (1990). Advancing professional inquiry for educational improvement through action research. *Journal of Staff Development, 11*(3), 56–61.

Senese, J. (2002). Energize with action research. *Journal of Staff Development,* Summer, 39–41.

Watts, H. (1985). When teachers are researchers, teaching improves. *Journal of Staff Development, 6*(2), 118–127.

Zeichner, K., Klehr, M., & Caro-Bruce, C. (2000). Pulling their own levers. *Journal of Staff Development, 21*(4), 36–39.

Zeichner, K., & Noffke, S. E. (2001). Practitioner research. In V. Richardson (Ed.), *Handbook of research on teaching* (4th ed., pp. 298–310). Washington, DC: American Educational Research Association.

# PART II

---

*Action Research Studies*

# 3

# Been There, Done That

## Student Inquiry About High School Dropouts

### Erik J. Shager

## EDITORS' INTRODUCTION

A striking example of a teacher engaging students in the action research process, Shager's work highlights the power of a relevant curriculum. Working within an alternative high school setting, Shager draws on his students' experiences and expertise to explore the issue of high school dropouts. Through their research, Shager and his students collect a variety of data (student and teacher journals, survey results, discussion notes, and other classroom artifacts), analyze their findings, and present their research to an assortment of audiences. By encouraging students to capitalize on their own life experiences, Shager's study provides a unique example of how teachers can empower their students to take action.

* * * *

According to the United States Census Bureau, a high school dropout's projected work-life earnings will be $200,000 less than those of a high school graduate. This discrepancy increases as the high school graduate attains more education; a graduate with "some college" will see an additional $300,000 in work-life earnings (Day & Newburger, 2002). Obviously, students who drop out of high school are at a disadvantage in work-life earning potential. As a teacher in a small vocational high school, working with students who have at some time been considered at risk of not graduating, I often remind them of this payoff to finishing high school.

When we began our initial discussions as members of an action research group that focused on equity issues in our classrooms and schools, the idea of doing a study around the topic of high school dropouts seemed like a good idea. Based on what was happening in Madison—and, as I found out, throughout the country—there were questions about why students drop out of school. I was curious about what would happen if my students examined the issue of high school dropouts. I hoped that my students would progress from talking about the issue to conducting their own research, and I envisioned them identifying causes, proposing possible solutions, and taking action. Therefore, my action research question became: **What happens when my students inquire about the issue of high school dropouts in their local community?**

## MY SETTING

For the past nine years I have taught at the Work and Learn Center High School (WLC), a diploma completion program in the Madison Metropolitan School District. Each student who attends WLC was at one time at risk of not graduating from high school. The majority of students who enter the program have earned fewer than five credits after two years of high school and therefore are significantly short on credits. Through a four-semester sequence of academic coursework and community-based vocational placements, WLC students can earn diplomas from their home high schools. For many students, enrollment at WLC is their last chance to graduate. The students involved in this study were scheduled to graduate at the end of the school year.

When this project began, there were 14 students in my class—six males (one African American, one Asian American, and four White) and eight females (four African Americans, one Native American, and three White).

Like many alternative schools, WLC has a low student-to-teacher ratio. The 13 students who participated in this project were the only students I worked with during the semester. We were together for three consecutive class periods each day. This structure provides me with a wonderful opportunity to teach in an interdisciplinary manner. The subjects I cover—language arts, social issues, computer skills, and psychology—rarely have clearly defined boundaries

# WHY FOCUS ON HIGH SCHOOL DROPOUTS?

*"Been there, done that."*

—WLC student response to the question:
"Why should we research the issue of high school dropouts?"

The topic of high school dropouts is typically of high interest to the students who attend WLC. Because they have not experienced much success in the traditional setting and may themselves have even dropped out at some point, they have firsthand knowledge of what might cause a student to leave high school before graduation. They know what it is like to attend high school in Madison, and they know students who have dropped out. Most important, they were at one time—and in some cases still are—at risk of not graduating from high school ("been there, done that"), and now find themselves less than five months away from their own graduation night. In addition, many are students of color—students disproportionately represented in the city's dropout statistics. For these reasons, I was excited to examine what would happen when my students dug deeper into this issue facing their community.

Every semester I have my students at WLC read an article from the *Wisconsin State Journal* titled "Nearly 1 in 5 Madison Students Don't Graduate" (Erickson, 2000). Students are taken aback by the number of students who do not complete high school in Madison, and they are surprised by the dropout rates for students of color in the district: 46 percent of African Americans, 28 percent of Hispanic students, and 54 percent of Native American students do not earn a diploma after four years of high school. Each semester this article prompts a deep discussion within the class about why certain students—especially students of color—leave high school without a diploma. During whole-class discussions, students generate a list of reasons that they think might account for why students stop attending high school before graduation: Students get pregnant. Students are lazy. Students lack focus. Despite the high level of student interest in this topic, until now we had rarely devoted more than two class periods in a semester to the discussion.

I thought it would be interesting to examine what would happen if students were provided with more opportunities to peel back the layers of this issue and create their own data-based knowledge relating to the topic. I also wanted to make certain that the students would be willing to work on this project, that the project could lead to a deeper understanding of the issue, and most important, that participation in the project had the potential to result in action by the students.

## IDENTIFYING A FRAMEWORK

As someone who has experience teaching an issues-centered curriculum, I realize that issue selection is of utmost importance to student engagement. If students do not like an issue or do not feel that it is relevant to their lives, it can be a challenge to get them excited about the topic. In his article "Criteria for Issues-Centered Content Selection," Byron G. Massialas (1996) points out how important it is to select the right issue for students in an issues-centered classroom. He writes, "Little or no learning takes place unless the individual is involved personally in the topic of the presentation or discussion" (Massialas, 1996, p. 44).

Specifically, Massialas identifies five criteria he deems vital to issue selection: relevance, reflection, action, practicality, and understanding. Using these criteria as guides, I have generated a series of questions in order to identify good issues for classroom inquiry (see Table 1). I use this series of questions as a litmus test to help me to identify what issues might work best within my classroom.

When I positioned the issue of high school dropouts within this framework, it appeared to be a good issue to explore. Based on my previous experience with the topic, I knew it was definitely relevant to the students and would provide an opportunity for reflection. I also knew that the students would have an opportunity to understand and to build their knowledge using a variety of the social sciences; I had seen this occur in previous classes. I was confident we would be able to develop a project that would be practical and have support from others in our building. Equally important, this issue provided the *potential* for student action—a step the students in my previous classes had never reached.

I had high expectations for this project and hoped that students would find the intrinsic drive to take action while they were in the process of investigation. However, I did not want to force my students to take action. I envisioned them becoming what Westheimer and Kahne refer to as "justice-oriented citizens"—students who "[c]ritically assess social, political, and economic structures and explore collective strategies for change that challenge injustice and, when possible, address root causes of problems" (Westheimer & Kahne, 2002, p. 3).

## DATA COLLECTION

Various forms of data collection were used in this project. I wrote in my teaching journal as the students completed the various components of the project, documenting their interactions and insights. I also kept notes of

**Table 1**    Selecting an Issue for Student Inquiry

1. Relevance
   - How does the curriculum relate to the students and the social context in which they find themselves?
   - Does it affect students inside and outside of the classroom?
   - Does it contain "burning issues" involving students that stem from larger societal issues?
   - Can traditional subject content be used as background data?

2. Reflection
   - Does it trigger thinking in the students?
   - Does it engage the students?
   - Are all sides heard? Are students asked to form a position based on explicit evidence?
   - Is it open-ended?
   - Is there a classroom climate that provides for an exchange of views?

3. Action
   - Will the critical and systematic analysis produce action?
   - Will the action transfer out of the classroom?

4. Practicality
   - Can the project be implemented?
   - Is there support for this type of project in the school community?

5. Understanding
   - Will it promote understanding in students?
   - Does it promote or hinder reflection on perennial or persistent problems of humankind?
   - Does the issue connect with relevant sources?

SOURCE: Adapted from Massialas (1996).

class and group discussions. I observed the students as they developed a survey, administered it to students in our building, tabulated it, and analyzed the results. Student journal entries about the topic of high school dropouts and the students' thoughts on the progress of the project provided a wealth of information; many of the quotations used to begin sections in this paper were taken from those entries. In addition, the results of student small-group work shed light into students' thought processes.

The students and I also worked together to consolidate our findings, with the students explaining their thoughts, which I recorded on the computer. In addition, a student from UW–Madison pursuing his teacher certification was present in our class four hours per week, often while we were working on this project. His observations provided another perspective on what was occurring. Informal conversations with students and their parents also provided some insight.

## PROJECT DESCRIPTION

We began the project with a single question: Why do students drop out of high school? The students spent 15 minutes writing about this question in their journals, and the rest of the class period (30 minutes) discussing what they had written. As the discussion facilitator, I tried not to steer the conversation in any specific direction.

The theories that my class came up with at this initial stage about why students drop out were similar to those mentioned by my previous classes. A lack of support at home, or simply a lack of will to succeed, were cited as possibilities. Some teenagers, they wrote, were "lazy," while others were "crazy." Other students in my class mentioned the need for teenagers to work and earn an income for themselves and their families.

Many of my students also mentioned teen pregnancy as a reason for dropping out. One of the four teenage parents in our class related her struggle to be both a good parent and a good student. Many students, she explained, simply cannot handle both responsibilities. Some students in class who did not have children asked how she was able to juggle both. She replied that she just tells herself that she has to finish high school— that she has been in school too long (she is one year behind the class with which she began high school as a freshman) to not finish now. She also said that she felt a responsibility to show her daughters how important it is to finish school. "How will I be able to tell them how important school is if I don't graduate?" she asked. She did say, however, that she often gets upset when she is at school because she does not see her children as often as she would like; her busy work and school schedules leave little time for her to have quality contact with them. "Sometimes I get so sad, because I miss my kids so much," she said with tears in her eyes. Later in the semester, this student told me that she was offered a job change that would include a promotion and, most important, some desperately needed additional income but would also eliminate some of the "awake" time she spends with her children. At the time of this writing, she was still trying to decide whether to make the job change.

Our next step was to read about the local dropout situation. During one class period, I had the students read the article mentioned earlier in this paper: "Nearly 1 in 5 Madison Students Don't Graduate" (Erickson, 2000). As they read, I asked them to identify things they found important in the article. Most of the students pointed to the fact that almost 20 percent of students who start high school in Madison do not finish. The high number of dropouts surprised them. Only a few mentioned the disproportionate number of students of color who drop out of school, and the students seemed uninterested in discussing why African American, Native American, and Latino/Hispanic students drop out at such high rates. "I don't know" and "How would I know?" were common responses to the question of why this phenomenon was occurring. At this stage, my students seemed to be more interested in the total number of dropouts than in the breakdown by racial groups.

We also read articles that pointed to specific reasons why students might leave school early. One column, written by the father of a high school student in Madison, mentioned that African American male students feel pressure not to do well in school out of fear of being looked down upon by their peers. "To gain friendship, to be considered 'hip,' even to be defined as a black man, my son must hide his brain," the author/father wrote (King, 2003, p. B1). I asked my students if they agreed with the premise of the article. Had they seen this type of behavior? Some students said that they had seen it, while others emphatically denied that it occurs. The conversation quickly turned to anecdotal evidence of students they knew or had known who fit this profile. Most students agreed that there was some evidence of this occurring, but they did not quite agree that students felt pressured to hide their "school smarts." Rather, the class believed that skipping school provided more opportunity for fun than did attending school. They also said that they had grown out of that phase of their lives and were ready to focus on completing their education.

Following the initial brainstorming on the topic and discussion of the newspaper articles, students worked together in teams, deconstructing their hypotheses. The students formed research teams based on the themes they had identified as reasons why students might drop out of high school. The three themes that evolved were: student as the reason, family/community as the reason, and school as the reason. Each team used a cause-and-effect map to peel away the layers of their identified problem, repeatedly asking why a certain problem exists. What follows is one example from the "school" team:

*One reason:* Students drop out of school because they *don't want to go to class.*

> *Question 1:* Why don't they want to go to class?
>
> *Answer 1:* Because classes are boring.
>
> *Question 2:* Why are classes boring?

*Answer 2:* Because they're not interesting to a lot of students.

*Question 3:* Why aren't they interesting?

*Answer 3:* Because all students do is sit around and listen to teachers talk all the time.

*Question 4:* Why don't some students like listening to teachers lecture?

*Answer 4:* Some students learn better through hands-on activities.

In the end, each team had a list of reasons why students might drop out of high school. Although this activity tended to take a long time and at times seemed repetitive, it did force the students to narrow their focus. They knew, based on their earlier discussions, that the reasons why students might drop out seemed limitless. Getting to the heart of each thematic area helped students decide which questions to ask in the surveys they planned to give to other WLC students.

## THE DEVELOPMENT OF THE SURVEY

> *"The best thing I like about the project is that we are letting them know what the outcome of it is, because I hate doing surveys and not knowing what becomes of them."*

> *"I'm actually pretty geeked up about it! I just wanna hand it out and explain what the survey is about. I like going to classrooms and explaining stuff. Makes me feel special and important!"*

> *"I don't think we should do a multiple choice, and do a q/a so people will put down the truth."*

One of the most challenging aspects of the project was to develop a survey to distribute to the students in our building. After discussing the various ways students could acquire more information about their topic, they decided that a survey would give them the best information. The students were very concerned about the format of the survey they were creating; they said that when they had been asked to complete surveys in the past, they did not take them very seriously. Some even admitted to "just filling in dots" instead of providing honest responses. They decided that they needed to take steps to ensure that their survey would not meet with similar negative reactions.

The students said that it was important that people taking the survey should know its purpose, that it was created by students, and that the tabulated results would be made available to all the students who completed the survey. They felt that sharing this information up front would garner the most genuine and accurate responses.

The students also felt it was important to keep the survey concise enough to keep respondents interested, yet thought-provoking enough to elicit the honest, informative responses they wanted. Some students thought that only open-ended questions would allow for these types of responses and wanted to steer clear of multiple-choice questions. Others wanted to limit the survey to statements that could be answered using a scaled list of predetermined responses. I encouraged the students to think about the effort it was going to take to compute and analyze the data they would collect. The students struck a compromise and decided that the survey should include both open-ended questions and statements that required the person to select at what level they agree or disagree with specific reasons why students might drop out.

The entire class helped develop the survey. Using the ideas they had generated earlier in the project and independent Internet research they had done, students met in their thematic groups—student, school, family/community—to come up with a series of statements stemming from the prompt: *Students drop out of school in Madison because . . .* Students viewed various online surveys in order to select the scale of responses that fit best with what they wanted to determine: How students feel about the issue of high school dropouts in Madison. The students selected a scale with responses ranging from "strongly agree" to "strongly disagree." The students also decided to include a "neither" or "neutral" option. Originally, the students wanted to limit the number of these statements to 10, fearing that the survey takers would "zone out" if they were required to do more. When the groups combined their work, they realized that they had a total of more than 30 statements. Due to overlaps in the statements, however, they were able to settle on 16 statements to include in the survey (Appendix A).

The class created the open-ended questions during a whole-group activity. Each student submitted one question that he or she thought should be included in the survey. As each student shared his or her question, I entered the question into a PowerPoint slide, which I projected onto a screen at the front of the room. Once again, the students saw overlap in their questions and combined several of them. Eventually, the students selected three to be included in the survey and agreed on the wording of each question. The three questions focused on issues they felt were vitally important to their research: why students drop out; what students' motivation is for finishing school; and what changes the survey takers would make in order to keep more students in school. At this point in the project, the students also decided to ask the respondents to provide their age, gender, grade, and race/ethnicity on the surveys (Appendix B). The surveys were color-coded in order to determine which school or program the respondent attended. Students also decided to have the survey takers answer the open-ended questions first, fearing that the statements on the survey might influence responses.

In the end, three students volunteered to administer the survey to the classes at WLC and WLC–Park and to the other alternative programs in our building—the School Age Parent Program (SAPAR), Alternative Education Resource Options (AERO), and the Cluster Program. When the students were not able to administer a survey in person, they attached a note that stated what the survey was for and why they would appreciate honest responses.

The students chose to administer the survey to these students because they felt that they had the knowledge and school experience that could provide them with the best information. Many students who attend either of the WLC sites or SAPAR are very close to graduation and could explain how they achieved that goal despite the obstacles they encountered along the way. The younger WLC and SAPAR students and the students in the middle school programs—AERO and Cluster—could give some insight about the thinking of younger students regarding school.

## ADMINISTERING THE SURVEY

*"The next steps for the survey would be to make sure we try to get it to everyone and get everyone's responses."*

Once they had prepared a draft of the survey, the students developed a plan to administer it to the students in our building and at the other WLC site. Luckily, the survey administrators were able to meet with the entire student bodies of SAPAR, AERO, and Cluster. The survey was administered on a class-by-class basis to WLC students, because at no time during the school day are all WLC students together in the building.

The students enjoyed this part of the project. The three survey administrators explained why our class was gathering this information and how important it was for respondents to give honest responses. They also stressed their willingness to share the results of the survey. Although, just as predicted, some students expressed resistance to filling out the survey, the survey administrators were satisfied that they had convinced the survey takers to complete the survey as honestly as possible. I was able to observe my students administering the survey on two occasions and was impressed with how they handled the pressure of being in front of a large group of students.

## TABULATING THE SURVEY DATA

*"I personally liked writing the information down into the computer. I like to type. So not only was it something that I'm good at, but it was somewhat easy and had a good flow to it. It's hard to find something that you're good at and like to do in school. So that was really cool for me."*

One of the biggest challenges in this project was deciding how to tabulate responses from the 118 completed surveys. After toying with the idea that students could break into teams to tally the results by hand, we decided to locate a computer program that could help us with this process. I had some familiarity with the database program Filemaker Pro and suggested that we ask Larry, our building's Filemaker expert, if he would be willing to give us a quick tutorial. He agreed, and we began the process of tabulation.

In order to record all the responses, we had to create a new survey form within Filemaker. This form contained all the information from the original survey. It also included a field to record a survey number (in case we wanted to check the hard copy of a survey) and a field in which we could record the program affiliation of the student who completed the survey. (It was at this point in the project that we realized we could have saved a lot of work by creating the survey directly in Filemaker—a thought I will keep in mind for the next time my class works on a research project.)

Although we now had a means to tabulate the survey, we still had to physically enter the data into the computer. Larry once again helped us, this time by setting up the computer at my desk to be the "host" computer to collect all the data. We then set up four stations at which students took turns entering the data. Because we had formatted the demographic questions and the 16 scaled-response statements using a drop-down menu of choices, students were able to enter that data relatively quickly. Transcribing the responses to the open-ended questions tended to take more time and, due to the handwriting of the survey takers, some patience. Some students liked this part of the process more than others did and ended up entering more of the surveys.

Another benefit of this part of the project was that it gave the students an opportunity to work directly with the data to assess the quality of the survey they had developed. Although some surveys contained what the students felt were immature responses—"These kids need to grow up!" one student observed—or no responses at all, the majority of the surveys met with the class's approval. The students were particularly interested and surprised by the depth and length of the responses to the open-ended questions. On some occasions, students would stop their typing to read a response to the rest of the class and identify how the response connected with the hypotheses they had created.

The class was able to tabulate the answers to the scaled-response statements by using a feature in Filemaker. I then helped the students export their data into a spreadsheet program in order to create a table of raw data (Appendix C) and a table that displayed the percentage of students who chose each response (Appendix D).

Working with the qualitative responses was more labor-intensive. In fact, the tabulation of the responses actually morphed into an early form of data analysis as students began to see patterns emerging in the responses. Due to some problems that we were having printing out the responses to each of the open-ended questions, students had to use the original completed surveys. Working in three groups, the students sorted through the completed surveys, identifying themes that emerged in the responses to each of the questions. The class then consolidated the findings from each group and created a list of new themes identified for each question. For example, some of the themes identified in response to the questions "If you could change anything that would help keep students in school, what would it be? Why?" were:

- Better classroom activities
- Less time in the school building
- More community-based learning
- Different ways of teaching
- More encouragement of students
- Be more understanding of students
- Get to know students better
- More one-on-one help for students

Using the themes they had identified in this process, the students then returned to the computers and began doing keyword searches using the "find" option in Filemaker. Each group was responsible for searching for thematic keywords for one of the questions and recording the number of hits they got on each search. The themes that received the highest number of hits were selected for further analysis. The group mentioned above, for example, found that the following searches yielded the most hits:

- "Teach" (mentioned in 21 surveys)
- "Help" (mentioned in 18 surveys)
- "Fun" (mentioned in 17 surveys)
- "Work" (mentioned in 15 surveys)
- "Learn" (mentioned in 14 surveys)

The groups then printed all the survey hits and collated them for further analysis.

## SURVEY RESULTS

The analysis of the survey data was also completed in both small-group and whole-class settings. One group of students analyzed the results of the scaled-response statements, and the other three groups analyzed the results of the three open-ended questions. Each group's goal was to synthesize its findings and submit them to be included in a report authored by the entire class.

The group that worked with the scaled response statements combined the results of the "strongly agree" and "agree" selections for each statement in order to determine which statements had the highest level of support. They also combined the "strongly disagree" and "disagree" selections for each statement to determine which statements had the highest level of disagreement. In addition, the group used a graphing program on the computer to create charts showing some of these results. They then presented their findings to the entire class for inclusion in a final report. Their findings included the following:

- Many students don't find school interesting (82.1 percent).
- Many students find it easy to skip (73.6 percent).
- Many students feel that it's hard to catch up after falling behind (72.4 percent).
- Many students feel that students are afraid to ask for help after falling behind (68.6 percent) and are not getting the help they need (70.3 percent).

The remaining three groups were responsible for analyzing the results of the responses to the open-ended questions. Each group was responsible for one of the questions. They analyzed the responses from each of the thematic groupings that had been identified during the tabulation process, wrote short summaries of what they found, and shared these results with the entire class.

The final step in the analysis process was the production of a list of findings and recommendations (Appendix E). Two students also volunteered to write a story for *The Link*, the student newspaper that "links" the various alternative programs in our building; they also e-mailed the story to a member of the MMSD Board of Education, who is the father of one of the students in class. At the time of this writing, students were scheduling visits to classrooms to share the results of the survey and discuss their recommendations; a presentation to district-level administration was also under consideration.

## STUDENT ENGAGEMENT IN THE PROJECT

> *"I guess what surprised me the most was how hard it was to put all of the information together to get a response. I was also surprised that most of the students took the survey, especially the younger students."*

> *"I'm not really sure what we're supposed to be doing right now."*

> *"I have learned that not everyone is as cooperative as you think they would be. It's not as easy as you think it would be. You have to persuade people into wanting to do the survey and answer questions that they have. I also found out that a lot of people are really determined to grad-uate and make something of themselves. I didn't think people would share this information to others so openly, either."*

Toward the end of my research project, when I was busy sifting through the mountains of data I had collected, I attended an educational retreat with four other members from our building. The purpose of the retreat was to reflect and to develop goals for next year. I saw this as an opportunity to step away and take a break from my research. On our first day, however, I was brought back to my research as I listened to our keynote speaker, a professor from the University of Wisconsin–Milwaukee, describe his idea of a "developmental contextual learning environment" in classrooms. Simply put, in a "developmental contextual learning environment" the classroom operates in such a way that it pulls the potential out of each student. I think that this project had that effect on many of the students. The size of our class, the interest and experience with the topic, the instructional time devoted to the topic, and the cooperative nature of the individuals in the class all helped this type of a classroom setting to evolve. There was at least one aspect of this project that provided an opportunity for students' potentials to emerge—each student found his or her niche.

As every teacher knows, it is almost impossible to design a lesson or unit that gets *every* student in the class excited about learning. Although it may sound as though this project captured the interest of every student, not every student attacked this research with the same degree of vigor and energy as others. While they all seemed to feel vested in the project and completed the required work, some students seemed to believe in it more than others. For example, some students were disappointed on days when we did not devote any class time to the project. Some appeared to enjoy certain aspects of the project and were willing to do extra work if needed. For example, some students preferred entering the data into the computer, while others preferred creating graphs or charts of the data. Three students volunteered to administer the survey, while other students agreed to write up our findings. One student spent additional time analyzing the data, trying to identify certain demographic trends in the respondents. Overall, students seemed to view this project as worthwhile.

## STUDENTS AS EXPERTS

*"I know because I have been there and done that."*

*"Because of my past experiences and changes I have been through."*

*"Because it might have happened to one of us before, or it might have happened to someone we know."*

*"Some of the girls down the hall need to know what's up!"*

—Student responses to the question:
"What qualifies you to do this type of research?"

In addition to the level of student engagement in the project, I also noticed that the students increasingly viewed themselves as experts on this subject—and they were. When I asked them what qualified them to do research like this, students were eager to share the experiences that had led some of them to drop out of school and left others hanging on the edge. They were also excited to highlight the changes they had made in their lives in order to graduate. They brought a lot of knowledge to the project in the form of anecdotal information and personal experience; as they gathered more evidence, they built upon that knowledge.

They also felt that they had a lot to share about the subject with the other students in our building. Even before they had gathered their data, a group of students asked if they could go speak to the younger students in our building. Based on some of the behavior they had witnessed, they assumed that these students needed the guidance of successful older students like themselves in order to avoid the same path that they had taken: the path of the high school dropout. They viewed it as a responsibility to talk with "the girls down the hall."

As my students set out to administer the surveys, I noticed a level of conscientiousness; they were the all-knowing ones, visiting those who needed their guidance. And even though their task was simply to administer the survey, it did become a teaching moment. In sharing why they were doing the research, they had an opportunity to talk about their own experiences as struggling high school students. After she had administered the survey to a group of students in the AERO program, the student who was the mother of two young children shared how her pregnancies had affected her high school career. Although she was graduating one year behind her class, she was proud of what she had accomplished. She also pointed out that school would have been a lot easier had she not gotten pregnant.

The knowledge my students were creating also became visible to people outside our classroom. It sparked the interest of the survey takers. As groups were presented with the survey, they asked my students why they were doing this project. "Do you *have* to do this?" they asked. Third-semester WLC students, who will be in my class in the fall, asked me if they were going to be able to do a similar project. It also sparked interest among both building and district staff. Some students' parents also expressed interest in the project, asking to see the results.

## DESIRE TO TAKE ACTION

> *"I liked when we went to talk to the AERO and WLC children about our research project. I felt like I can inspire some students to continue to stay in school. Even though some might drop out, at least in the long run, I can say I tried to help them, or I tried to prevent it."*

> *"They asked a lot of questions about my life and how it is as a parent of two. Hopefully by me talking to them, some of the females will get the message and wait until they're ready to have kids."*

As I mentioned earlier, students were anxious to devise solutions to the problem of high school dropouts. From the first day of the project, students were suggesting ways to solve the problem of dropouts in Madison. They were anxious to speak to the younger students in the building about what it takes to become a high school graduate, and they wanted to address the school board. I tried to rein in that enthusiasm and have them focus on the research. By the end of the project, students were asking if they could go out and share our results; two students wrote an article for the school newspaper. Other students asked if we could expand our research in order to gather even more information; they noted that the data would be strengthened by the inclusion of student responses from Madison's four traditional high schools—the high schools my students had previously attended. Due to time constraints, we were not able to survey students at these other schools. This could become a project for future classes, however.

Another example of this desire to take action occurred while our staff was hosting a meeting of teachers from Milwaukee and northern Illinois as part of the Accelerated School Project. As one of the meeting's coordinators, I had arranged for a panel of WLC graduates to speak to the group about their experience at WLC and their accomplishments since they had graduated. I arranged the meeting so that my current students could also attend; I felt that they could benefit from listening to the graduates. I encouraged my current students to share their experiences with the group of teachers as well.

Two of my current students, however, thought that they did not receive the same opportunity to tell their stories as did the graduates; they thought that they had just as much, if not more, to share as did the graduates on the panel. I asked them if they wanted me to arrange a time when they could address the group by themselves, even if it would require that they do so after the rest of the class had been dismissed. They agreed and proceeded to lead the group in a wonderful discussion of what they had accomplished as students at WLC and the class's progress on our dropout project. These same two students took the lead in writing an article for our school newspaper and helped to compose a sheet of talking points to use while addressing groups about the project's results.

Although the students did not become the "justice-oriented citizens" (students who take action to address the root causes of the problem) I had hoped for at the beginning of this project, they did take more action on this issue than had any of my previous classes. My experience with this project has laid the groundwork for future projects. I am excited to research new ways to bring about more collective action from my classes.

## INCREASED UNDERSTANDING OF THE ISSUE

> *"What surprised me the most is that all the students know that they don't want to be dropouts, and they know what can happen if they were to become a dropout."*

> *"The thing that has surprised me the most is that a lot of kids say that the biggest reason that they drop out of school is their family life, but the biggest thing that inspires them to stay in school is younger brothers and sisters. That to me was just kind of surprising because it contradicts what they just said before, but it makes sense overall."*

> *"Why do they think it's easy to skip, but they don't think high schools are too big? That's why it's so easy to skip!"*

*"The reasons students are using to drop out are things that can be pre-vented and worked around, but they don't want to bear the stress that it's going to take."*

Student understanding of the issue of high school dropouts in Madison increased during this project. As shown in the statements above, their writ-ten responses at the end of the project were more multifaceted than those at the outset, highlighting the complex nature of the problem of high school dropouts. The students used all the resources at their disposal—newspaper articles, Web sites, class discussions, small-group work, survey results, and each other—to craft for themselves a more complete under-standing of the issue.

At the beginning of the project, many of my students felt that students who were at risk of dropping out simply did not care whether or not they graduated. This assumption was partially contradicted by the survey results. A large number of responses, particularly from older survey tak-ers, indicated a strong desire to finish school and the importance of having a high school diploma. However, the survey results of younger respon-dents supported some of my students' hypotheses. For example, one pop-ular idea among the students in class was that middle school–age students and those just beginning high school do not value the importance of grad-uating from school. This lack of belief in the importance of a high school diploma was seen more often in the responses from younger students.

My students' deeper level of understanding is also seen in the recom-mendations they made at the end of the project (Appendix E). The blame they attached to both the individual students and the school at the begin-ning of the project evolved and was replaced with a list of proactive steps that could be taken in schools—steps that should make a lot of sense to anyone who spends time in a high school. After I asked my students to create a list of recommendations based on what they saw in the data, I observed that they viewed the problem as a progression of activities and interactions that led to students dropping out—it was not simply one fac-tor. For example, students do not feel comfortable in a large school, so they do not go to class. Because they are not in class, they fall behind. Since they already do not feel comfortable in class, they will not seek additional help from teachers in order to catch up. Eventually, they end up getting so far behind that they stop attending school.

It is interesting to note the great emphasis that my students placed on the relationship between students and the adults in school. One reason for the significance of this factor may be the positive experiences they have had as students in the smaller setting of WLC. When I asked these current students why they are graduating when many of the classmates with whom they began high school are not, they pointed to the changes they made once they began attending WLC. They pointed out that because of the intimacy of the program, teachers got to know each student better and were able to provide one-on-one attention. They also credited the other support staff in the building and some of the adults with whom they interacted at their school-sponsored job placements for their recent successes.

The value the students placed on a strong student-teacher relationship mirrors results from some of the research on preventing students from dropping out of high school. Croninger and Lee (2001) found that a teacher's guidance can provide a form of "social capital" that can reduce the probability of dropping out by nearly half. Most important, they found that "[s]tudents who come from socially disadvantaged backgrounds and who have had academic difficulties in the past find guidance and assistance from teachers especially helpful" (Croninger & Lee, 2001, p. 548).

There is also research that supports the students' suggestion to utilize adult mentors as role models for students. Zirkel (2002) found that positive relationships with adult role models who were matched to students by race and gender had a positive impact on student achievement. In Zirkel's longitudinal study of 80 adolescents, she found that "[s]tudents who reported having at least one race and gender-matched role model at the beginning of the study performed better academically up to 24 months later, reported more achievement-oriented goals, enjoyed achievement-relevant activities to a greater degree, thought more about their futures, and looked up to adults rather than peers more often than students without a race- and gender-matched role model" (Zirkel, 2002, p. 357).

## WHAT DID I LEARN?

As a result of my participation in this project, I learned a lot about my teaching and the students I teach. I learned about how students who enter my classroom came to be considered at risk of not graduating from high school. I was able to participate with my students as they took an in-depth look at a social issue that was very close to them, and I witnessed how powerful this level of authenticity was to the students. I also learned how to organize a research project that will result in student action outside the classroom. Although there are some things I wish I had done differently—such as using more community resources—I was pleased with what occurred during this project. I look forward to working on similar projects with future students.

Like my students, I also increased my understanding about the issue of high school dropouts. Many of the survey results helped inform me about what current students were thinking about their educational opportunities. It was fun to help my students as they sifted through the same types of qualitative data that I was collecting for my own research. In helping my students construct their survey and the summary of their findings, I educated myself about the types of students who will be entering my classroom. I also learned more about the various strategies being used throughout the country to address the problem of high school dropouts; my students' interest in dropouts prompted me to do my own research on the topic. I was encouraged to find that some of the same strategies recommended by my students had also been identified by other researchers.

One thing that surprised me, however, was that the issue of race as a factor did not show up much in the work my students did or in the results from the student surveys. In fact, the issue of race did not show up in any of the survey responses or in any student journal entries. Based on what I knew about the achievement gap in Madison and about the disproportionate number of students of color who were dropping out, I expected race to show up somewhere in their findings. The only time race was even mentioned was in a graduation speech by a Hmong student in my class. In the speech, he reflected on the experiences he had in high school before he came to WLC. WLC, he felt, was the best school he had ever attended; he wished he could stay at WLC for another two years. He contrasted his experience at WLC with his previous school, where a teacher often marked him absent even though he was present. The teacher had confused him with another Hmong student in his class who had not been attending. My student reasoned, "If my teacher doesn't know who I am, why should I be here?" So, he stopped going to school. Student research specifically on the topic of race is a possibility for a future project. Different data-gathering techniques, such as ethnography, might help to focus on this particular issue.

Finally, I learned how challenging it is to do a project like this. It is hard to know when to lead and when to let students proceed at their own speed. It is impossible to know exactly what students will find in an inquiry project such as this. At the same time, the unknown answers make this type of project all the more exciting to both teacher and student.

## EPILOGUE

"Been there, done that" chronicles my effort to engage my students in a high-level, meaningful research project. As a member of an action research team focusing on equity, I appreciated the opportunity to reflect on what it means to promote equity in education. Teaching in a small alternative high school for students who are at risk of not graduating provided me with a unique perspective on issues of equity in education. After all, my students were not receiving the same education they would get at a traditional high school.

In many ways, this study is structurally similar to other action research projects I have completed in the past: I posed a question regarding my classroom practice; I gathered data to help me answer that question; I discussed my progress with other action researchers; and I presented my findings in the form of a written reflection. The major difference was that while I was gathering data regarding my question, my students were doing the same concerning a question of their own: Why do students drop out of high school in our specific community? As a result of these simultaneous examinations, a product developed that was more rich and far-reaching than what resulted from my previous classroom action research studies.

This richness is a testament to the capabilities of and effort put forth by the students in an alternative high school setting. They come to our school with plenty of ideas, thoughts, and knowledge; a research project like this helped them build on those ideas, thoughts, and knowledge. I discovered that this group of students was very capable of doing this kind of work, but also that it is not easy to facilitate. For example, facilitating this project required collaborative effort both inside and outside the classroom. In class, the students worked in teams to complete the tasks necessary for good social science research. Outside the classroom, other students and staff in our building provided my students with opportunities to gather information and share their findings. Student inquiry of a social problem is high-level work, analogous to the work done by teacher researchers and social scientists. I had hoped that it was possible for students to engage in similar investigations of social issues, and this project validated that belief.

The impact of this project was more far-reaching than that of previous action research I had completed. Whereas previous projects helped me become more aware of my teaching, the effects of this project traveled beyond the limits of our classroom walls and our academic calendar year. While the project provided numerous opportunities for my students to learn new skills and build on the strengths they already possessed, it also gave them an audience for the knowledge they had created. The reasons they heard from others about why students drop out mirrored their own experiences. They took on the role of expert in this project—they had experienced the life of a high school dropout and felt the need to learn more and, most important, to try to do something about this social problem.

My role as teacher also expanded as a result of this project. I ventured beyond the classroom door to help with the logistics of student data gathering. I also assisted in the dissemination of the students' findings. As I interacted with other educators—at local and national conferences, in

Listserv conversations, at MMSD meetings—I was able to talk about both the process students went through and the products they created. I still find myself quoting my students' findings in the many conversations I have with educators about how we can make schooling—especially at the high school level—better for all students. Since the completion of the project, school board members, professional researchers, and educators from both inside and outside our district have commented on the methodology of the project and the importance of the students' findings.

More than a year after I finished this study, I ran into Jessica Doyle, the wife of Wisconsin Governor Jim Doyle. She had agreed to speak at a celebration recognizing WLC's selection as a national demonstration site for Accelerated Schools PLUS. While I was in the beginning stages of this action research project, Ms. Doyle met with me and other members of my action research team; as a former teacher, she took interest in all the action research projects. At the end of the school year, I sent her a copy of my students' findings. Before I could thank her for coming to our celebration, she greeted me by asking, "So what project are your students working on this year? I still share your students' research every time I can."

This project and the students' findings are powerful pieces of evidence that support the push for small high schools presently occurring in this country. The recommendations the students identified—building better relationships with adults, smaller school and class sizes, improving communication between teachers and students—are found in educational research in support of small high schools. In fact, three years before we conducted our project, the school district's Research and Evaluation Department had conducted a study regarding students not completing high school. I sent my students' completed work to that study's lead researcher, explaining the process the students had gone through to generate their findings. His response in an e-mail confirmed what I already knew: "What a great project! The findings are very similar."

Now more than ever, I understand that education is not a one-size-fits-all proposition. My students' work on the project demonstrated that given the opportunity, these students are capable of doing high-level, authentic, meaningful work despite their checkered school histories and lack of academic credits. Their written findings are now part of my curriculum "canon." The knowledge they created is now a resource for other students, and their work has served as an impetus for students to conduct their own research projects on similar topics. To me, equity in education requires us to provide all students with the equal opportunity to use their strengths, talents, and abilities to construct knowledge of the world around them. This project is one example of what can happen when students are given the opportunity to tackle a social problem in their community.

# APPENDIX A: SURVEY
# STATEMENTS DEVELOPED BY STUDENTS

| *Students in Madison drop out of school because:* | | | | | |
|---|---|---|---|---|---|
| | *Strongly Agree* | *Agree* | *Neutral* | *Disagree* | *Strongly Disagree* |
| 1. They lack the discipline needed to succeed in school. | SA | A | N | D | SD |
| 2. They are not getting the help they need. | SA | A | N | D | SD |
| 3. It's too easy to skip school and/or not attend classes. | SA | A | N | D | SD |
| 4. They don't value the importance of graduating from high school. | SA | A | N | D | SD |
| 5. They don't find classes interesting. | SA | A | N | D | SD |
| 6. They don't feel that they belong in school. | SA | A | N | D | SD |
| 7. It's not "cool" to be a good student or get good grades. | SA | A | N | D | SD |
| 8. Health issues get in the way of school (pregnancy). | SA | A | N | D | SD |
| 9. Their parents are not involved enough in their children's lives. | SA | A | N | D | SD |
| 10. There is a lack of communication between school and home. | SA | A | N | D | SD |
| 11. Schoolwork is not challenging enough. | SA | A | N | D | SD |

*(Continued)*

(Continued)

|  | Strongly Agree | Agree | Neutral | Disagree | Strongly Disagree |
|---|---|---|---|---|---|
| 12. There is a lack of hands-on/relevant activities in classes. | SA | A | N | D | SD |
| 13. The high schools are too big; it's easy to get lost in the crowd. | SA | A | N | D | SD |
| 14. Counselors are too busy; aren't available at all times. | SA | A | N | D | SD |
| 15. They are afraid to seek out help after they have fallen behind. | SA | A | N | D | SD |
| 16. It's too hard to catch up after falling behind in class work. | SA | A | N | D | SD |

SOURCE: E. Shager (2004).

## APPENDIX B: OPEN-ENDED SURVEY QUESTIONS AND DEMOGRAPHIC INFORMATION

| Age:                           Race/Ethnicity: |
|---|
| Gender: |
| Grade: |
| What do you think is the biggest reason students drop out of school in Madison? Why? |

| What motivates you to stay in school and *not* become a dropout? Why? |
| --- |
| If you could change anything that would help keep students in school, what would it be? Why? |

SOURCE: E. Shager (2004).

## APPENDIX C: SURVEY RESULTS/RAW NUMBERS

| *Students in Madison drop out of school because:* | | | | | | |
| --- | --- | --- | --- | --- | --- | --- |
| | *Strongly Agree* | *Agree* | *Neutral* | *Disagree* | *Strongly Disagree* | *Total* |
| 1. They lack the discipline needed to succeed in school. | 15 | 43 | 33 | 21 | 6 | 118 |
| 2. They are not getting the help they need. | 30 | 53 | 16 | 17 | 2 | 118 |
| 3. It's too easy to skip school and/or not attend classes. | 47 | 40 | 18 | 9 | 4 | 118 |
| 4. They don't value the importance of graduating from high school. | 19 | 54 | 29 | 7 | 7 | 116 |

*(Continued)*

(Continued)

| | Strongly Agree | Agree | Neutral | Disagree | Strongly Disagree | Total |
|---|---|---|---|---|---|---|
| 5. They don't find classes interesting. | 44 | 53 | 15 | 4 | 2 | 118 |
| 6. They don't feel like they belong in school. | 28 | 40 | 31 | 17 | 2 | 118 |
| 7. It's not "cool" to be a good student/get good grades. | 5 | 13 | 33 | 47 | 20 | 118 |
| 8. Health issues get in the way of school (pregnancy). | 17 | 45 | 26 | 26 | 4 | 118 |
| 9. Their parents are not involved enough in their child's life. | 25 | 42 | 29 | 20 | 2 | 118 |
| 10. There is a lack of communication between school and home. | 17 | 40 | 37 | 20 | 4 | 118 |
| 11. Schoolwork is not challenging enough. | 8 | 12 | 26 | 53 | 19 | 118 |
| 12. There is a lack of hands-on/ relevant activities in classes. | 24 | 32 | 37 | 19 | 5 | 117 |
| 13. The high schools are too big; it's easy to get lost in the crowd. | 11 | 19 | 22 | 45 | 20 | 117 |
| 14. Counselors are too busy; aren't available at all times. | 17 | 32 | 33 | 29 | 6 | 117 |

| | Strongly Agree | Agree | Neutral | Disagree | Strongly Disagree | Total |
|---|---|---|---|---|---|---|
| 15. They are afraid to seek out help after they have fallen behind. | 34 | 46 | 21 | 12 | 3 | 116 |
| 16. It's too hard to catch up after falling behind in class work. | 42 | 42 | 16 | 13 | 3 | 116 |

SOURCE: E. Shager (2004).

## APPENDIX D: SURVEY RESULTS/PERCENTAGES

| Students in Madison drop out of school because: | | | | | |
|---|---|---|---|---|---|
| | Strongly Agree | Agree | Neutral | Disagree | Strongly Disagree |
| 1. They lack the discipline needed to succeed in school. | 12.7% | 36.4% | 28.0% | 17.8% | 5.0% |
| 2. They are not getting the help they need. | 25.4% | 44.9% | 13.6% | 14.4% | 1.7% |
| 3. It's too easy to skip school and/or not attend classes. | 39.8% | 33.8% | 15.2% | 7.6% | 3.3% |
| 4. They don't value the importance of graduating from high school. | 16.3% | 46.5% | 25.0% | 6.0% | 6.0% |
| 5. They don't find classes interesting. | 37.2% | 44.9% | 12.7% | 3.4% | 1.7% |
| 6. They don't feel like they belong in school. | 23.7% | 33.8% | 26.2% | 14.4% | 1.6% |
| 7. It's not "cool" to be a good student/get good grades. | 4.2% | 11.0% | 27.9% | 39.8% | 16.9% |

*(Continued)*

(Continued)

|  | Strongly Agree | Agree | Neutral | Disagree | Strongly Disagree |
|---|---|---|---|---|---|
| 8. Health issues get in the way of school (pregnancy). | 14.4% | 38.1% | 22.0% | 22.0% | 3.3% |
| 9. Their parents are not involved enough in their child's life. | 21.1% | 35.6% | 24.6% | 16.9% | 1.7% |
| 10. There is a lack of communication between school and home. | 14.4% | 33.8% | 31.3% | 16.9% | 3.3% |
| 11. Schoolwork is not challenging enough. | 6.7% | 10.1% | 22.0% | 44.9% | 16.1% |
| 12. There is a lack of hands-on/relevant activities in classes. | 20.5% | 27.1% | 31.6% | 16.2% | 4.2% |
| 13. The high schools are too big; it's easy to get lost in the crowd. | 9.4% | 16.2% | 18.8% | 38.4% | 17.0% |
| 14. Counselors are too busy; aren't available at all times. | 14.5% | 27.4% | 28.2% | 24.8% | 5.1% |
| 15. They are afraid to seek out help after they have fallen behind. | 29.3% | 39.3% | 18.1% | 10.3% | 2.5% |
| 16. It's too hard to catch up after falling behind in class work. | 36.2% | 36.2% | 13.7% | 11.2% | 2.5% |

SOURCE: E. Shager (2004).

## APPENDIX E: STUDENT LIST OF FINDINGS AND RECOMMENDATIONS

What do we know now after looking at the survey data? (statements)

- Many students don't find school interesting (82.1 percent).
- Many students find it easy to skip (73.6 percent).

- Many students feel that it's hard to catch up after falling behind (72.4 percent).
- Many students feel that students are afraid to ask for help after falling behind (68.6 percent) and are not getting the help they need (70.3 percent).

What do we know now after looking at the survey data? (open-ended questions)

Things that motivate students to stay in school:

- One reason that motivates students to stay in school is that they want to be successful and have a good job after earning a diploma.
- One reason that motivates students to stay in school is that they realize that having an education will help them in the future.
- One reason that motivates students to stay in school is to be able to further their education in the future (college).
- One reason that motivates students who have children to stay in school is to show their children that they did it—be a good role model.
- One reason that motivates students to stay in school is to set an example for other family members. "I'll be the first one to earn a high school diploma."

Things that students would like to see changed:

- Students feel that there is too much homework and not enough variety of assignments—more fun and hands-on activities.
- Students feel that teachers need to make activities more interesting and fun.
- More one-on-one help would help keep students in school.
- Teachers need to understand student needs—develop good working relationships with students.
- Students need more opportunities to get help when they've fallen behind.

Reasons why students drop out:

- Some students are scared to seek help when they fall behind—make students feel better about school/class/teachers.
- Family issues (pregnancy) have a big impact on whether or not students graduate. It's easy for students to fall into the "wrong" crowd and start doing drugs.

What are some recommendations that we have?

What should be done to help all students graduate from high school?

- Have better adult partnerships in school (mentors, counselors, advisors, older students in the school).
- Utilize older students to teach younger students or peer-to-peer teaching.
- Smaller classes/smaller schools
- Better student/teacher ratio—more one-on-one time with teachers
- Improve communication with students—get to know students better.

---

SOURCE: E. Shager (2004).

## REFERENCES

Croninger, R., & Lee, V. (2001). Social capital and dropping out: Benefits to at-risk students of teachers' support and guidance. *Teachers College Quarterly, 103*(4), 548–581.

Day, J. C., & Newburger, E. C. (2002). The big payoff: Educational attainment and synthetic estimates of work-life earnings. (Current Population Reports, Special Studies, P23–210). Washington, DC: United States Department of Commerce, Economics and Statistics Administration, Census Bureau. [Online]. Retrieved September 18, 2006, from http://www.census.gov/prod/2002pubs/p23–210.pdf.

Erickson, D. (2000). Nearly 1 in 5 Madison students don't graduate. *Wisconsin State Journal*, March 11, A1.

King, R. (2003). Problem: Teens shun academic achievement. *Wisconsin State Journal*, December 7, B1.

Massialas, B. (1996). Criteria for issues-centered content selection. In R. W. Evans & D. W. Saxe (Eds.), *Handbook on teaching social issues*. Washington, DC: National Council of Social Studies.

Westheimer, J., & Kahne, J. (2002). *What kind of citizen? The politics of educating for democracy*. Paper presented at the American Political Science Association annual meeting, Boston.

Zirkel, S. (2002). Is there a place for me? Role models and academic identity among white students and students of color. *Teachers College Quarterly, 104*(2), 357–376.

# 4

# *What Strategies Can I Incorporate So That the English Language Learners in My Classroom Will Better Understand Oral Directions?*

Shannon Richards

## EDITORS' INTRODUCTION

Concerned that her English language learners (ELLs) are having difficulty understanding her oral directions, Richards sets out to uncover ways in which she can communicate more effectively with her second- and third-grade students. By reading relevant literature, observing classroom interactions, and interviewing her students—ELL students and native speakers alike—Richards finds that all children can benefit from small changes in classroom practices. Richards's study is unique in that it provides readers with an example of student empowerment, showcases teacher self-examination, and provides practical applications for others who work with English language learners.

\* \* \* \*

## MY STORY

I teach second- and third-grade students in a multiage class at John Muir Elementary School. Muir School is part of the Madison Metropolitan School District in Madison, Wisconsin. Each school in the MMSD is site-based managed, meaning that the staff at each school is responsible for developing its own goals and curriculum to correlate with state and national standards.

The enrollment at John Muir is 470 students from early childhood to fifth grade. Students come to Muir from various neighborhoods. Two of the nearby neighborhoods are inhabited mostly by White, middle- to upper-class residents; the third neighborhood contains mostly subsidized housing for low-income families, most of whom are minorities. The population of John Muir is diverse, and several countries and ethnicities are represented. Of the 470 students, 59 percent are Caucasian, 19 percent are African American, 13 percent are Asian, 9 percent are Hispanic, and 1 percent are Native American.

John Muir's school improvement plan includes high academic goals for all students. The plan outlines that every student will perform at grade level in reading and math by the end of each school year. Regular classroom teachers, special education teachers, and support staff work closely with each other to strive to meet these goals.

Because John Muir is a site-based school, it does not have adopted textbooks or curricula for reading, science, or math. Teachers are responsible for generating their own curricula and materials that correlate with state and national standards for their grade levels.

This year my class consisted of 14 second graders and 10 third graders; 14 were boys and 10 were girls. Eleven of my students were Caucasian, four were Asian, three were Hispanic, two were African American, one was African, one was European, and two were biracial. About half of my class received free or reduced-price breakfast and lunch at school. For 10 students, English was a second language. Toward the end of the school year, nine of those students were still receiving English as a second language (ESL) services. I had two students from Korea, two from Mexico, one from India, one from Venezuela, one from Togo, Africa, one from Germany, and one whose father speaks only Spanish. Of this group of ESL students, seven had started school at John Muir in kindergarten or first grade. The other two students, both in second grade, came to Madison during the first week of school, and spoke little or no English. Because John Muir uses an inclusion model, all English language learners stayed in my classroom all day and received support each morning. During math, a bilingual resource specialist (BRS) came into my room, and for the literacy block (spelling, reading, and writing), I was joined by an ESL teacher.

Thanks to a state-funded Student Achievement Guarantee in Education (SAGE) grant, eight of my students worked in another classroom each morning in order to maintain a 16:1 student-teacher ratio.

Because of my class's multiage format, I am able to loop with my second graders every year and welcome them back to my room each fall as third graders. This has helped to create a unique and invaluable sense of community and build a framework that cannot otherwise be duplicated. I truly loved my class this year. They were a very open, honest, and sincere group, always willing to help me or each other without having to be asked to do so. They had amazing, unique ideas and frequently complimented one another on those ideas. My relationship with my students this year was special in that we had a great deal of love, respect, and trust for one another and therefore felt very comfortable having frank and productive conversations as a group or individually. I can only hope to have a group like this again in my teaching career.

## MY QUESTION

When I was given the opportunity to join a classroom action research project, my ears perked up. Because my previous experience with action research had been so positive and eye-opening, I knew I couldn't go wrong in doing another project. I became especially interested when I saw that one of the topics was English language learners. With eight ELL students in my classroom, how could I not accept the chance to learn more about them and my methods of teaching them? I signed up right away and started thinking about forming a question that would help both the ELL students and me.

One thing that I noticed in my classroom early last fall was that the ELL students asked a lot of questions during class. Of course, I expected many questions from these new learners and did everything I could to answer their questions and help them succeed. However, the *timing* of these questions was of particular interest to me. Whenever I finished giving directions for an assignment, task, or project, I offered the students the chance to ask questions for clarification. On a few occasions, maybe one or two hands would go up, but not necessarily the hands of the ELL students. After a few weeks, I began noticing a pattern in my ELL students' questions about my directions. Nearly every time I finished giving directions and then asked, "Do you have any questions?" the room was relatively quiet. However, no sooner did I send the students off to work independently than up to the front of the room came a swarm of students who seemed to have little understanding of the task at hand. It was at this point in the lesson (the point at which I thought everyone knew what to do) that

I heard students saying, "What are we doing?" "I don't get it," and "What should we do first?" Initially, I was very patient with these students and helped them get through the activities, which usually had multistep directions. However, as the first quarter went on, I noticed that this was happening at the same point in *every* lesson, *every* day, week after week, and that each time almost the same students were questioning the routine and asking the same questions. Of the eight ELL students, the same three or four always seemed to need repeated instructions before they could start working. However, two boys were at opposite ends of the spectrum. While neither truly understood what my expectations were, one of them listened to directions yet rarely asked for clarification, and the other never heard the directions in the first place because he simply wasn't listening!

I had to do something. Why was I not reaching the ELL students? I was talking more slowly than usual, giving visual examples of what to do, asking for help from the class, and offering the whole group the chance to ask questions before getting started. Yet, in the end, I had four or five students rushing up to me as if they had not heard me in the first place! What was going on? I knew I had to act fast or we were all bound to suffer. It was from these experiences and reflective turmoil that my research question was born: **What strategies can I incorporate so that the English language learners in my classroom will better understand oral directions?**

## WHY IS THIS HAPPENING?

I set about trying to find answers to my questions. What was leading to this lack of understanding in the ELL students? I figured the best ways to find out were to watch, read, and ask. To learn more, I observed my students during class time and kept a journal of what I saw. In addition, I read the book *Learning to Learn in a Second Language* by Pauline Gibbons (1991). Finally, I developed an interview to conduct with my ELL students that would, I hoped, help me get to the bottom of the issue.

Observing my students during class time turned out to be more of a challenge than I initially thought it would be. Because I had 24 students and limited teaching time and was not as organized as I could have been, I tended to put on the back burner the tasks of making observations and writing in my journal. I did, however, get enough chances to watch my students that I was able to make some valuable conclusions about their behaviors. I also wrote and reflected frequently about my teaching methods and how they affected my students.

In several of my early journal entries, I mentioned that my teaching style might be one of the strongest factors in the ELL students' confusion or lack of understanding. By nature, I am a fast talker, and even native English speakers often misunderstand me. Furthermore, as a teacher with a constructivist teaching philosophy, I want to spend the least amount of time possible on teacher-led instruction in order to maximize my students' experiential learning time. Therefore I tend to rush my explanations and deliberately leave small details out so that my students can explore and learn on their own. My first journal entry, written in October, read as follows:

> Because of my teaching style, I may be missing some of my ELL kids because they don't understand the direction/expectations. I need to make some changes so that they all feel comfortable and "with" the group. I also don't want them to be afraid to ask for help or clarification . . . what can I do so that they "get it" and I am saved from frustration? More directions? Written directions? On overhead? Modeling? Have students repeat directions?

As can be seen in this early journal entry, I knew specifically what the problem was and actually made my own suggestions for making a change in order to solve that problem.

Aside from my speedy delivery of instructions and expectations, I was still confusing the ELL students on a daily basis. Regularly, upon giving directions and/or modeling an activity, I asked my students if they had any questions. As I mentioned earlier, I usually got no more than two or three questions, and they were not necessarily all from the ELL students. However, no sooner had I sent the students off to work independently than I would be approached by two or three ELL students who had little or no idea of what they were supposed to do! Their questions made this obvious. One journal entry that I wrote following a math lesson expressed my frustration:

> Once I thought every student understood the expectations, I gave two separate opportunities to ask questions. At that point, nobody chose to take advantage and ask a question. So I gave one last reminder and set the kids to work. At the moment they set to work, three ELLs approached me and claimed that they did not know what to do! Arrgghh! Why? Why is this happening? Why don't they get it? Why didn't they ask? What did I do wrong?

I began putting pressure on myself. I take great pride in the progress I am able to make with students, and I felt that this issue was a major roadblock in the progress I planned to make with the ELL students. I started monitoring myself during class to try to see what was lacking in my communication with the students. Later in the semester I had a difficult lesson with my students, particularly the ELL students, and wrote this entry in my journal that night:

> Today I made some mistakes in my teaching that directly affected my ELLs and reaffirmed my need and desire for change . . . I only gave the directions orally, and had *several* questions from the ELLs. It was as though a three-step direction was too much or too overwhelming. Was it too much to remember or were the directions too hard? In retrospect, it would have been so easy to write the directions on the board, ask for the steps repeated back to me, or both! This could have helped me reach my ELLs and possibly even more students.

When the ELL students asked for clarification, the most common statements I heard were, "What do we do?" followed closely by "I don't get it," and "What are we supposed to do?" The comments were not limited to these three, but these were definitely the ones I heard most frequently and that frustrated me the most, because they came immediately after I gave full directions. Almost always, the ELL students approached me with their questions rather than raising their hands, and some even waited until there were no other students around before talking with me. Because of the continual necessity for an extra question-and-answer period, as well as the apparent discomfort the ELL students were feeling, I decided to develop a short interview to conduct with each of them in order to find out more.

Interviewing my students proved to be very helpful to me in this situation. Sitting one-on-one with each of the ELL students and asking them questions specific to the issue helped me discover how much I was contributing to the problem without even knowing it. One of the great benefits of these interviews was seeing how comfortable and candid the students were with me. Watching them formulate honest and open answers made me feel good and reinforced my belief that I was doing a nice job with these students.

The interview I created consisted of seven open-ended questions (see Appendix: Student Interview), which asked students about their level of understanding, confusion, and comfort in the classroom. I chose to interview eight of the nine ELL students, because at the time the student who had just arrived from Germany was not comfortable enough with English to have a conversation with me. At home, these students spoke Korean, Spanish, Ewe (from Africa), and Gujrati (from India).

I noticed certain strong themes while analyzing the responses to my interview questions. Of the eight students I interviewed, seven claimed to be confused sometimes when I gave directions in front of the class. The other student, a second-grade girl who received speech and language services, claimed to always understand my directions, yet she seemed to be one of the students who usually needed additional assistance understanding and getting started. I decided to omit this student's interview, as it did not seem to correlate with my other findings regarding her progress. Another student, a second-grade boy who had difficulty paying attention in class, claimed to be confused when I gave directions but, unlike the other students, blamed it on his constant talking and lack of attention during class. I appreciated his honesty, but decided to omit his interview as well and work on that problem with him at another time. A third student went through the entire interview, answered most of the questions accurately, and then after the interview divulged to me, "I don't know what 'confused' means." That was my first important lesson right there! I did keep this student's interview because she gave some helpful answers to my questions.

Of the six students who claimed to be confused during my oral directions, I heard the following responses when I followed up with the question, "Why?"

"I don't get it when sometimes you say something and I don't understand because some words I didn't know before."

"Fancy words."

"I miss directions. I didn't understand you because of how fast you're talking."

"I don't understand English."

"I don't know every one of the words in America."

The students used the words "angry," "confused," "desperate," "sad," and "crazy" to describe how they felt when they were perplexed in the classroom. This broke my heart, but it also surprised me because I hadn't realized before that the problem was this serious.

As reinforcement for both the students and myself, I asked them what strategies I already used that helped them better understand directions. This was useful because it gave me information about strategies I should use more frequently as well as those that were not as helpful as I thought. Helpful strategies mentioned were writing things down, telling what the "fancy" words mean (I interpreted this as focusing more on vocabulary), repeating directions, having students ask a friend for help, showing what to do, and telling how to do things "out loud so everybody can hear it."

The interview question that was the most helpful to me was, "What could I do to help you understand?" Going into the interview, I was not sure I would get strong responses to this question. I was wrong! Almost every student had two or three suggestions ready for me without hesitation. Suggestions included:

"Not talk so fast—slow down."

"Don't read so fast—repeat words."

"Tell about big words. Explain parts again."

"Tell directions two times."

"Slow down."

"Tell me what it means."

These responses were interesting because the same responses were made to the previous question about helpful strategies I already used. I concluded that I was dabbling in helpful strategies but not making them a consistent part of my teaching repertoire.

The final two questions for each student were about their comfort level in asking me for help alone and in front of the other students. All but one of the students said that they were comfortable in both situations; the one student who wasn't said that he feared that other children would stare or laugh at him if he asked questions. With this child, I discussed the safe environment in our classroom and encouraged him to feel better about speaking up. The most thoughtful and heartwarming response was from the second-grade student from Africa. To my question, "Do you feel comfortable asking me for help in front of the other kids? Why?" she responded, "Yes, because it's good to. Because if other kids don't understand they could hear me and they could understand when you answer." What a model response from a student who could not speak English two years before!

Once I noticed the strength of these themes and patterns in my conversations with the students, I decided that it might also be helpful to interview a small sample of the native English speakers to see what they thought. I interviewed two second-grade boys, a third-grade boy, and a third-grade girl. The third-grade students had also been in my class for second grade. I gave these four students the exact same prompts and questions that I did the ELL students. I was sure that their responses to the first question about understanding my directions would be, "I understand you," and that the interviews would take about 7 seconds each. I was wrong. *All four* of these native-English-speaking students said that they sometimes got confused when I was talking! Wait a minute here! If I was confusing the English speakers, then what on earth was I doing to the ELL students? I felt terrible.

I began to feel a little better as the interviews progressed. One student admitted that he was not listening to me, and another tried to blame his confusion on chatty classmates. A third student's response was a bit more helpful in that he claimed to not understand specific math terms. For example, "When you say minus or you say a number I don't get it. I don't get what 'divided' means or 1 equals 1. I don't get it." This reiterated the idea that I should teach vocabulary before a lesson and consistently monitor for comprehension of terms. The fourth student, the third-grade boy, said that he didn't "really understand what you're supposed to do and I get them mixed up, like what to do first, next . . ." I assumed that this might have been because I was speaking too quickly when explaining steps or directions to the group. I did find it helpful when I asked each of these students for suggestions on what was helpful so far and what may be helpful in the future. To these questions, I got the following responses:

What do I do to help you understand?

"Show me how to do it."

"Write it on the board."

"Do stuff on the board because then I can see."

"Explain it to me."

What else could I do?

"Come over and explain it to me."

"Make it easier so that I could understand. Repeat it one or two times."

I found it very helpful to chat with these students and gain different perspectives and feedback on how I was doing. It seemed to me that they had some of the same needs as the ELL students. This excited me, because now I realized that making changes to my teaching methods was really going to benefit everyone.

The conclusion I drew from the interviews confirmed what I already believed. The two main reasons the ELL students were having difficulty understanding were the new English words I was using and the speed at which I was speaking. These results did not surprise me, but why had I not done anything about it yet? I guess I had adopted the theory that immersion and experience would have the same valuable effect as each other, but I was quickly corrected as I had these conversations with the students. Indeed, the students were quickly learning a great deal as they experienced daily life in the classroom. However, the "dive right in" theory didn't prove to be as effective as I had previously thought, because it was not giving the students the academic and curriculum-related vocabulary they needed to succeed.

In *Learning to Learn in a Second Language,* Gibbons (1991) generalizes common characteristics of ELL students in a new or unfamiliar learning environment. Although her study was based on students in Australia, I was amazed at the similarities between the students whom she studied and the students I was working with. I really enjoyed reading Gibbons's work and found it very useful in helping me better understand the ELL population in my classroom.

In Australian schools, roughly 25 percent of the student population speaks English as a second language (Gibbons, 1991). With nine ELL students in my class of 24, I was *exceeding* that average! Was I going to get some sort of award or special training for accepting such a challenge? Not formally, but the benefits and experience that these students gave me were reward enough. The unfortunate part for them, however, is that I did not know much about their past experiences or their learning styles. In order to best meet the needs of this mostly shy and terrified yet eager group of exceptional ELL students, I needed to learn about and become more sensitive to where they were coming from . . . and in the meantime meet the needs of 16 other second and third graders. It was time to act, and act fast.

My group of students was diverse not in terms only of ethnicity but also of culture, family background, and experiences. The nine ELL students represented six countries and five continents. Some of them were from wealthy, educated families; others were from poor, single-parent, refugee families. Most of these children had attended school in their native countries, but the experiences were much different from John Muir, either because of conditions of extreme poverty or extreme wealth. In addition to previous school experiences, it is also important to consider students' oral and writing skills, not only in English but also in their native languages. If students are struggling in their own language, it is likely that they will continue to struggle while learning a second or third language.

Gibbons (1991) suggests that ELL students fit into one of three general categories:

1. Students new to the country from a non-English-speaking background;

2. Students born in the country but who enter school with little or no English; and

3. Students who have received all or a portion of their education in the country, but whose family speaks one or more languages other than English at home.

While two of my students fit into category #1, because they moved to the United States just a few days before starting in my classroom, the remaining seven fit into category #3. Each of these students had moved to the United States at a younger age and then either started school as kindergarteners or joined school at his or her age-appropriate grade level. Every one of the ELL students spoke a language other than English at home. I found that this set them up for challenges in having to assimilate, almost immediately, into an English-speaking classroom.

Another interesting point made in *Learning to Learn in a Second Language* is that there is a difference between conversational, functional English and what Pauline Gibbons calls "playground language." When people (such as myself) assume that children learning English will learn best if they are surrounded by peers who speak English and can provide them the necessary tools to "pick up" the English language, we are right, but within limits. Indeed, young children are quick to pick up English when they are placed in situations in which English is spoken; however, they are obtaining "playground language," quickly acquired language that allows children to survive in social situations with peers. These situations may include interactive play at recess or in physical education class, conversations at lunch or in the halls, or any other situations that require basic conversations with peers. This type of interaction typically occurs between children face to face, and is often dependent on eye contact, gesturing, and body language (Gibbons, 1991).

Playground language differs greatly from the academic language required for survival in the classroom. Language such as mathematics vocabulary, science terms, oral and written directions, and cognitive vocabulary such as "estimate," "infer," "predict," "assume," "hypothesize," "generalize," "rationalize, and a host of other words and terms may pose major challenges to ELL students. This language can take much longer to learn and eventually master than playground language, as it is often more abstract and offers fewer visual cues to assist with comprehension. According to Gibbons, it may take as many as five years before ELL students comprehend these ideas as well as their peers do (Gibbons, 1991). It is very important for teachers to take these ideas of language "type" and language acquisition into account when setting goals and expectations for students.

Some of the strategies Gibbons identifies as commonly used by ELL students who are having difficulties were interesting to me and related directly to the strategies I thought I was seeing in my classroom. These students gain the ability to hide the challenges they are facing and create a façade that helps them to appear as able, competent English speakers. They may use selective listening to block out oral directions and questions, or request additional speaking from the teacher (Gibbons, 1991).

In instances when students do feel comfortable enough to participate in activities or discussions, they will typically display a variety of characteristics that communicate their difficulty with learning a new language. Some of the identified characteristics follow (Gibbons, 1991):

*Listening:* The student has trouble following multistep directions, has difficulty concentrating, demonstrates an inability to predict what is next, has difficulty with key words that may change the meaning of the text, and has continued difficulty distinguishing certain sounds.

*Speaking:* The student shows strengths in both oral language and playground language, may sound especially loud or impolite in certain situations, says the same "comfortable" things frequently, and has trouble with sentence structure, grammar, and sequencing.

*Reading:* The student may read slowly, have difficulty identifying main ideas, comprehending, and retelling, have trouble reading for meaning, making predictions, and drawing conclusions, and may neglect to self-correct while reading aloud.

*Writing:* The student has low written language skills, writes in a "chatty," conversational manner without paragraphs or sequencing, uses simple sentences with limited vocabulary, has poor grammar and spelling, and writes short pieces that tend to be a repeat of previous pieces.

Pauline Gibbons's work in Australia truly intrigued me because her findings so closely paralleled the conclusions I had made about my students. She also identified some characteristics that I had not previously taken into consideration that pertained to the ELL students in my classroom. For example, the third-grade boy from Venezuela always wrote in a very casual, "chatty" manner, and I had assumed that he was picking this up from his high school–age brother. Little did I know that this was such a common habit of ELL students. In addition, it was actually quite comforting and reassuring to see that the students I was working with were progressing at a speed that was expected and were accomplishing no less than the "average" student learning English as a second language.

My research activities of observing, journaling, interviewing, and reading helped me to see that I had a truly exceptional group of ELL students in my classroom. In the end, the most important thing I learned was that I had a lot more to learn about them! Each one of the ELL students brought into my world experiences with culture and education, and exposure to different English language skills. This was truly an enlightening and educational experience, and I could not wait to put my new findings to work.

## MAKING CHANGES FOR EVERYONE

Because of my own learning style as well as the curious, eager, and responsive learning styles of my students, I decided that the best way to find out how I could maximize understanding in my classroom would be to use trial and error. Almost immediately after I identified my question of incorporating strategies to improve oral directions for my ELL students, I began thinking of specific things I could try. I took suggestions from the students whom I interviewed and also invented a few of my own strategies. I tried each strategy for a few days at a time, then watched and waited. The results were astounding, and I have since decided that I should have done this project years ago!

The first and most important changes I made were to slow down my rate of speech even more and to make sure that I was enunciating well when I spoke. Throughout my teen years, one of my mother's most famous quips was, "Shannon, you need to speak slowly and clearly." Naturally, years later, my mother is still right! I am by nature a very fast talker, and my words tend to run together, sometimes to the point of being incomprehensible. Because I had such a large number of ELL students, I knew right away in the fall that I would need to make changes in the way I talked in order to reach all of my students. I did; however, I did not change enough. Later, after identifying my problem, I made even bigger changes and began slowing down, making all sounds clearly, and speaking very deliberately to all my students. These steps were accompanied by more contact with the students as well as increased attentive listening from the whole group, because it seemed as though I was speaking more dramatically. Eventually I found myself using more inflection, expression, and tone and volume changes.

I noticed improvements after making this small adaptation to my teaching style. Students made more eye contact with me, followed along with their eyes and ears, and seemed to better grasp the things I was saying. This was true not only of the ELL students but of other students as well. I also noticed that my communication with the families of ELL students became more positive and effective because, by slowing down, I showed that I had time for them and genuinely wanted them to understand the things I was saying. I found that all students were asking fewer questions when I was finished talking, and in the event that a student did have a question, it was because of a difficult direction or another distraction in the classroom. Sometimes when I didn't have much time, I forgot my new strategy and returned to my old ways of hurried, muddled talking. I could always tell I was making this mistake due to the number of hands in the air and students out of their seats asking for help. I needed several self-reminders in addition to a few student reminders ("Mrs. Richards, could you please talk a little slower?") in order to move toward making this simple change a permanent strategy in my teaching repertoire. It was amazing how such a small change made such a colossal difference to the success of my students. Now they were able to hear and understand my directions the *first* time through and to feel intelligent and empowered when they could get right to work independently like the rest of their classmates.

Another strategy I used was repeating directions. The concept seemed easy, but I quickly found the practice to be tricky. This was because I needed to identify the fine line between helping the students (with repeated exposure) and insulting their intelligence (with unnecessary repetition). I certainly wanted to help them without insulting them, so I knew that I would need to adopt a method of providing the repetition they needed without sounding like a broken record. I decided to use a tone of voice and an attitude that empowered the students and made them feel smart, capable, and in control of their own learning. So I varied my strategies a bit. Sometimes I would say the directions as I demonstrated the task and then repeat them a few minutes later as if reviewing them, not only for the students but also for myself. At other times, I would write the directions on the board while or shortly after I gave them orally, so that students who needed additional exposure or a reminder could refer to them as much as they needed. Sometimes I would write full sentences for each step; at other times I wrote just one word for each step so that students could practice recalling the steps with one clue. Another method of repetition that I tried was asking the students themselves to repeat directions back to me. After explaining the lesson or activity in multiple steps, I would ask a student (either an ELL or a native English speaker) to help me out by telling me what to do first, next, and so on. Sometimes I would ask, "Who can tell me what to do first?" and take volunteers. Occasionally I would choose a student who I knew needed the review or was paying attention during directions. At other times, when the direction was obvious, like putting a name on an assignment, I would ask the whole group what they were going to do first and let them all tell me in unison.

I found all these methods very effective in helping the students understand directions through repetition. Through observations, I noticed that the ELL students began to better understand my oral directions the first or second time, asked fewer questions, and got started on their work more quickly compared to earlier in the school year. In addition, I am sure that these strategies helped some of my native English speakers, because I also noticed several of them asking fewer questions and getting to work faster. It was encouraging to see the whole group benefiting from this experiment. All learners were having their needs met in my classroom through my use of these small extra teaching techniques that took literally seconds to employ.

Modeling is another strategy that I learned I should do more often, particularly with such a high concentration of ELL students in my classroom. Modeling strategies for doing assignments was something that I frequently cast aside, because my eager and capable group seemed not to need it. I failed to see the true value of modeling until I decided to incorporate it into my daily routine. Whenever possible, I stood before my class while giving directions and did exactly what I wanted them to do so that they could see it happening as they heard the directions. This was beneficial not only to my students but also to me. The students were able to see me doing the same work I expected them to do. Sometimes, because the activity was new to me as well as to them, I made mistakes, and then I asked the students questions to help clarify my mistakes. This allowed me to alter my plans as I worked so that the plans were more appropriate for the students. The more I modeled and let the students see me in action, the more we were able to teach and learn from each other, and the more we understood each other. The visual learners were getting what they needed, as were the tactile, oral, and aural learners, because I was covering the assignment from all angles. When I really wanted to ensure complete understanding, I gave directions orally, modeled the assignment, and then wrote the directions on the board. This is what I eventually found myself doing most often. Even though it meant a little extra patience from and listening for the students who got it the first time, I heard very few complaints. I know my efforts helped each and every one of my students at one time or another.

One thing I had to watch out for was what I call "overmodeling." I didn't want students to get to see me do a complete task. I feared that overmodeling would lead to too much direct imitation and limit the authentic work my students were capable of. I found that it was best to model the first couple of steps, leaving the remaining components of the assignment up to each individual student. That way, I was helping everyone get started without hindering their creativity.

Other strategies that I incorporated included teaching vocabulary words in lessons in all subjects, assigning peer helpers who could aid with understanding, and waiting to pass out materials until all students understood the directions. I used these strategies only a few times, but from what I saw they were also effective in assisting the ELL students as well as the other students in my classroom.

I think that I became more patient and more accepting of the fact that I needed to take time to ensure understanding by repeating myself and answering questions. I also set higher standards for behavior during class time when I was giving directions. This way, even the students who blamed their lack of understanding on other students (or on themselves!), were able to gain a better understanding of the expectations.

Finally, I continued providing the students with plenty of opportunities to ask questions to clarify or better comprehend what was going on in the classroom. Although the students (ELL students in particular) did not always take advantage of the chance to ask questions in front of the group, overall the total number of questions decreased significantly, thus meeting my goal for this action research project. From now on, I plan to make all these new teaching strategies a permanent part of my teaching repertoire, because I am confident that they are fail-safe and critical to the success of all of my students.

## THE GREATEST GIFT TO MYSELF

When all was said and done and I was wrapping up another school year, I realized that everyone had benefited from this project. I feel that I definitely attained my goal of improving and adding to my teaching strategies to help the ELL students in the class better understand my directions. Overall, I noticed these students watching me more closely during my teaching time, making more eye contact, participating more in discussions, and asking significantly fewer questions about what they needed to do. This led to better relationships between the ELL students and myself and an overall stronger feeling of trust, cooperative learning, and community.

Going into this project, I wasn't planning to involve my native-English-speaking students that much in the classroom action research process. I figured that they weren't struggling much with my teaching tactics, and that on those occasions when they didn't hear or understand me, it was for a reason other than a lack of language experience or my speaking too fast. Little did I know that some of these students were feeling the same way as the ELL students! I was quite surprised when the responses from the small group of native-English-speaking students showed many similarities to those from the ELL students. They too felt that I was talking quickly and perhaps not explaining or modeling key concepts enough for them to succeed independently. This was a real eye-opener for me, because teaching independent work habits is one of the foundations of my teaching philosophy. I'm so glad that I decided to involve my other students in this study because, along with so many other aspects of this project, doing so forced me to take a look at my teaching practices and to make changes needed to help all of my students reach their maximum potential all day, every day.

Finally, I was the person who may possibly have been the most directly affected by this yearlong project. I made changes to my teaching practice in the interest of my students. Because they are my number one priority day in and day out, it was very important that I stayed focused and strived to be the best teacher I could for them. In doing so, I think I really did help myself become the best teacher I could be. I got to know my students so much better and on a more personal level than in other years because I made such an investment in them when I committed to this project. I developed close, trusting relationships with the ELL students and their families but also grew closer to the rest of my students because I grew to understand them better as well. I learned about the things that I do well in my classroom each day and the things that I may want to change in order to have a positive, one-to-one interaction with each of my students every day for 180 days. I received more feedback this year from students and families than I can remember receiving in the past, and although some of it could be considered "constructive criticism," most of it was positive feedback and encouragement to continue what I was doing with these students in room 29 at John Muir Elementary School in Madison, Wisconsin. This was truly one of the greatest learning opportunities that I have undergone, and I know that the lessons I took away from it will last the rest of my life.

## EPILOGUE

To me, the term *equity* was always something that I thought I could easily practice: the inclusion of all students and their families, equal treatment for all, and a general sense of fairness in everything I did. I had adopted a somewhat "textbook" definition of equity and was willing to give lip service to the concept to anyone who would listen. I assumed that because I had bought into what I thought was the correct definition of equity, everyone with whom I shared it would think I was wonderful and doing the best possible job as a teacher. After completing the classroom action research project, "What Strategies Can I Incorporate So That the English Language Learners in My Classroom Will Better Understand Oral Directions?" my personal definition of equity changed dramatically. Now, to me, *equity* is a place, a state of being, a feeling. To feel and experience equity is to feel safe and comfortable in your own skin, no matter who you are, where you are, or who you are with. To create equity means to create safety and comfort for people from different countries, neighborhoods, and experiences as well as for people with different colors.

We need to keep in mind that diversity is represented by so much more than simply skin color. It is represented by where we live, how we are treated, and how we treat others. To me, diversity runs through the soul. That is one of the most important lessons I took with me out of this classroom action research experience. Because of this lesson, I knew immediately that I needed to make some changes in my behavior, both professionally and personally.

Once I truly opened my eyes and took a look at the students, families, and colleagues I was working with each day, I realized how widespread diversity is in our society. In my classroom, I discovered that I was simply part of a microcosm of the wider world. Not every teacher in every school can say this; many schools across America do not represent the real world. I was fortunate enough to have a true "melting pot" in my classroom that year. Not only did I have students from six different countries learning English as a second language, but my English-speaking students were from a variety of backgrounds, experiences, and socioeconomic levels. This created a wonderful learning experience for my students and me and also for anyone coming into Room 29 to teach or learn throughout the year. I don't think that I would have looked at my class and its population as closely or with as much appreciation if it had not been for this project.

I also have the project to thank for opening my eyes outside the classroom and allowing me to recognize the vast diversity that exists right here in Madison, Wisconsin. I have become more aware of people around me as well as more sensitive to where they may be coming from. I feel that I view people with more respect and patience. After all, isn't that what we all deserve?

It was interesting and enlightening to me when I discovered that the majority of my ELL students were having difficulty understanding me in the classroom. It wasn't especially surprising. I knew that the non-English-speaking children would have a hard time with just about everything at first. However, it was particularly eye-opening to learn that most of them were having trouble for the same main reason: I was talking too fast. As I stated in my study, I felt bad about this and immediately promised myself to make some changes. Originally, I only intended to interview my ELL students and work with their responses. However, once I saw the pattern in those responses, I decided to add a few English-speaking students to my survey group, perhaps to serve as a control group. Again, I was completely taken aback by the fact that these students, too, were missing directions in the classroom because I was saying them too fast! Without the impetus of the classroom action research project, I never would have known that talking at my usual rate was a problem (and such a solvable one at that) preventing many of my students from working to their full potential. Because of the practical, reflective nature of classroom action research, I was able to identify, internalize, and improve something in my teaching that was keeping me from being the best I could be. It is for this reason that I feel that all teachers should be required to complete a classroom action research project at some point in their careers!

Teaching tolerance and acceptance has been a core piece of my curriculum each year. I expect every student in my classroom to be accepting and tolerant of and helpful toward other people, no matter what. I realize each year that I have some students who are not, sometimes because they choose not to be and other times because they have not been taught how to be. I take pride in the fact that, by the end of every school year, I can see my students acting with more kindness and patience toward and acceptance of each other. Now that I have completed this project that had so much to do with equity and diversity, I feel that I myself am a stronger person who is more tolerant, accepting, and patient. I know that I have transferred these characteristics to my students more since the project and will continue to do so in the future.

From this point onward, I hope to spread my newfound knowledge to students, families, and colleagues with whom I work each day. I think it would be beneficial to share my work with others and show how much I have learned and grown by looking at myself not only as a professional, but also as a person and a member of society. The best way to make these changes was to look within myself and my practice, something everyone can and should do not just once but every single day.

## APPENDIX: STUDENT INTERVIEW

Preface: I want you to answer all my questions as honestly as you can. There are no right or wrong answers.

1. When I give directions to the class (when I am talking in front of everyone), do you always understand what I am saying or do you sometimes get confused? Why?

2. How do you feel when you get confused?

3. What kinds of things do I do for you that help you understand?

4. What else do you think I could do to help you understand? What would help you?

5. Do you feel comfortable asking me for help? Why?

6. Do you feel comfortable asking me for help in front of the other kids? Why?

## REFERENCE

Gibbons, P. (1991). *Learning to learn in a second language.* Portsmouth, NH: Heinemann.

# 5

## *Understanding High School Black Male Students' Achievement and School Experience*

### Quynh T. Nguyen

### EDITORS' INTRODUCTION

Nguyen's study employs an interesting mixed-methods approach to teacher research. By mining the district database for information about the success rates of high school–age Black males, Nguyen uncovers intriguing quantitative patterns in the area of minority student achievement that demand her attention. Utilizing a qualitative interview protocol with a sample of young Black men whose standardized test scores indicate a potential for academic success, Nguyen examines the differences in educational experiences that cause some of these students to be labeled "high achievers" while others struggle in school. Through her research, Nguyen is able to delineate ways in which schools and individual teachers can become more deliberate in their attempts to connect with their Black male students.

\* \* \* \*

# INTRODUCTION

My interest in minority student achievement stems from my own experience of growing up as a Vietnamese American student in the American public education system. My experience involved effectively existing within two very different cultures. At home, I was expected to behave under one set of expectations while at school I was expected to function under a completely different set of rules. My complex home and school experience led me to conduct this action research project.

I am currently considering the principalship for a career path through my administrative intern position in the Madison Metropolitan School District (MMSD). I have spent the last 3 years as a middle school counselor in the MMSD. My work both as a counselor and as an administrative intern has led me to the difficult conclusion that minority (especially Hispanic and Black) students are underachieving compared to their majority classmates. More specifically, Black students are the lowest-achieving subgroup in the MMSD. Data show that Black students as a subgroup have the lowest percentage of students scoring proficient or higher on the Wisconsin Reading Comprehension Test (WRCT), complete algebra at the lowest rate, and have the poorest attendance rate. It should be noted that Black students' performance in reading and math has slightly increased over the last three years; however, the overall data continue to have alarming implications.

My action research project is connected with my pursuit of a leadership position in the field of education. My desire to enter into a leadership role stems from my obligation and responsibility to provide all students with equal education opportunity. The Madison Metropolitan School District currently has three priorities:

1. All students will complete third grade able to read at grade level or higher;

2. All students will complete algebra by the end of ninth grade and geometry by the end of tenth grade; and

3. All students will attend at a 94 percent attendance rate.

My hope is that my action research project will provide some valuable insights into Black male students' school experience that will, in turn, allow me to provide some suggestions to teachers for improving Black male students' achievement.

My action research question is: **What are the factors that support Black male students' achievement in MMSD?**

## RESEARCH METHODS

### Methods

The methods I used to conduct my action research study were reviewing the current data and interviewing high school students. I took a number of steps in order to review the existing data on Black male students. First, I requested general data, including grade point average (GPA), Wisconsin Knowledge and Concepts Exam (WKCE) scores, special education status, and free and reduced-price lunch status for all Black high school students in MMSD from the Research and Evaluation Department. I discovered from the data that Black female students were succeeding at a higher ratio than Black male students, based on the above criteria. I then narrowed my research to studying Black male students. Second, I looked specifically at Black male students' data including: enrollment, free and reduced-price lunch status, special education status, and WKCE test scores. I looked for trends, as well as anomalies, within these different data categories. The trends I discovered provided a foundation and starting point for my research.

The second part of my action research project involved interviewing Black male high school students. My initial intention was to interview regular education, high-poverty, high-performing Black male students about factors that supported their academic success. After reviewing the data and speaking with several administrators, however, I realized that a substantial number of Black males showed proficiency on the WKCE but were underachieving according to their GPAs. As a result I decided that it would be valuable to interview both high-achieving and underachieving Black male students, all of whom were proficient on the state standardized tests. My target group became regular education, high-poverty, proficient Black male students, including five high achievers and six underachievers. (See the tables in the Interview Data and Analysis section.) I then requested and received permission from parents and guardians to interview 11 Black male high school students from the three primary high schools. My interviews were conducted on school grounds and lasted between 45 minutes and an hour apiece. I individually interviewed tenth-, eleventh-, and twelfth-grade students about their school experiences. (See the Appendix for a sample interview questionnaire.) The students' stories were extremely rich in depth and powerful in insight.

### Limitations

I believe the findings of my study are quite relevant and powerful. However, as with all studies, there are limitations to my research. The three limitations of my study are:

1. Narrow study—the data I have are specifically on Black male high school students. This is not a comparison study; it is a single study of Black male students in one school district.

2. One-time study—my study looks at one group of students at one point in time and is not longitudinal.

3. Small sample of interviewees—although the data portion represents all high school, Black male students, the total number of interviewees is relatively small. Interviewees represent three of the four high schools in MMSD.

These limitations present possibilities for expanding my study in the future. I do believe, however, that the data and interview results I have are useful to educators.

## DATA

### MMSD Data

The first part of my research consisted of reviewing the current data on all Black male high school students in MMSD. I looked at a variety of data, including general enrollment, lunch status, special education enrollment, tenth-grade Wisconsin Student Assessment System (WSAS) data, and GPA data.

First, I reviewed the general enrollment data. The following table breaks down the current high school Black male enrollment in MMSD by grade level:

Trend Data Enrollment

| Grade Level | Number of Students |
| --- | --- |
| 9 | 210 |
| 10 | 188 |
| 11 | 119 |
| 12 | 94 |
| Total | 611 |

The data indicate that MMSD currently has 611 Black male students at the high school level. In addition, the data tell us that the largest number of Black males are enrolled at the ninth grade and that the number of Black males enrolled decreases with each grade level. Furthermore, the number of Black male students enrolled in Grade 12 is less than half the number of Black male students enrolled in Grade 9. The data also indicate that the largest difference in enrollment is between tenth-grade enrollment and eleventh-grade enrollment. The questions that this data set brings up are: (1) Where are our Black male students "disappearing to"? (2) Is there significance in the large difference in enrollment between the tenth and eleventh grades? The possible hypotheses include students move out of our district, drop out, and/or enter the job market. The concern with the latter two possible explanations is the lack of education of students dropping out and entering the workforce.

I then compiled the data on students' lunch status in order to have a better understanding of the high school Black male population. The following table is a summary of students' lunch status:

Trend Data Lunch Status—Indicator of Poverty Level

| Grade | Number Free | Percentage Free | Number Reduce | Percentage Reduce | Number Regular | Percentage Regular | Total |
|-------|-------------|-----------------|---------------|-------------------|----------------|--------------------|-------|
| 9 | 116 | 55.24 | 21 | 10.00 | 73 | 34.76 | 210 |
| 10 | 99 | 52.66 | 15 | 7.98 | 74 | 39.36 | 188 |
| 11 | 38 | 31.93 | 13 | 10.92 | 68 | 57.14 | 119 |
| 12 | 30 | 31.91 | 7 | 7.45 | 57 | 60.64 | 94 |
| Total | 283 | 46.32 | 56 | 9.17 | 272 | 44.52 | 611 |

The data indicate that a little more than half (55.49 percent) of all Black male high school students receive free or reduced-price lunches. The data also indicate that the percentage of Black male students receiving free lunches decreases in the upper grade levels, while the percentage of regular lunch students increases. One conclusion that can be drawn from our general enrollment and lunch data is that poor Black male students in MMSD are the students who are leaving in the upper grade levels. This hypothesis is of particular concern because of the implication that poor students are leaving in the middle of high school, possibly without a diploma. The second possible conclusion is that students and families are not applying for free lunch as much in the upper grade levels.

Third, I reviewed the data on Black male high school students' enrollment in special education classes. The special education data are summarized in the following table and graph:

Trend Data Special Education Status

| Grade | Number Not in Special Education | Percentage Not in Special Education | Number in Special Education | Percentage in Special Education | Total |
|-------|---------------------------------|-------------------------------------|-----------------------------|----------------------------------|-------|
| 9 | 113 | 53.81 | 97 | 46.19 | 210 |
| 10 | 101 | 53.72 | 87 | 46.28 | 188 |
| 11 | 81 | 68.07 | 38 | 31.93 | 119 |
| 12 | 62 | 65.96 | 32 | 34.04 | 94 |
| Total | 357 | 58.43 | 254 | 41.57 | 611 |

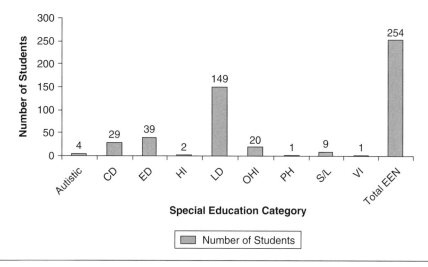

NOTE: CD = Cognitive Disability; ED = Emotional Disturbance; HI = Hearing Impairment; LD = Learning Disability; OHI = Other Health Impairment; PH = Physical Handicap; S/L = Speech and Language; VI = Visual Impairment; EEN = Exceptional Educational Needs.

The data indicate that 41.57 percent or 254 out of 611 Black male high school students are currently enrolled in a special education program, with the majority (149) of these students falling in the category of learning disabled. The overall yearly average for enrollment in special education in the school district is 14 percent. Given that 55.49 percent of MMSD Black male students are in poverty, I decided to take a closer look at the percentage of students in poverty who are in special education. The percentage of male high school special education students in poverty is 33.29 and the percentage of Black male high school special education students in poverty is 63.00. This tells us that almost twice the number of Black male students in special education are in poverty compared to the total population in special education. Last, the special education data indicate that the percentage of students enrolled in special education decreases in the upper grades, while the percentage of regular education students increases. Two possible hypotheses are that special education students are leaving in the upper grades or that students are not enrolling in special education as frequently in the upper grades.

I was also interested in Black male students' achievement level, so I collected and organized the tenth-grade WSAS data for current juniors and seniors. The following graph depicts trend data for Black male students' performance on the tenth-grade WSAS:

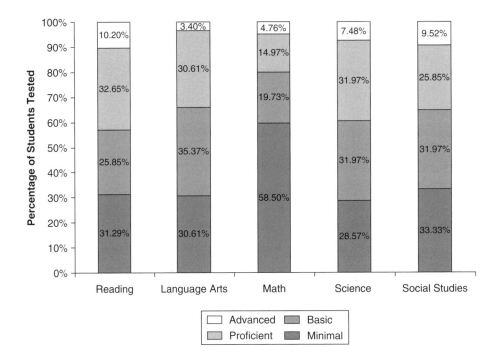

During these two school years, 69 percent (147/213) of Black male students took the WSAS test. The percentage of Black male students who scored in the proficient or advanced category ranges from 20 percent in math, 34 percent in language arts, 36 percent in social studies, 39 percent in science to 43 percent in reading. This indicates that Black male students are showing the highest level of competency in reading and the lowest level of competency in math. The competency in reading, however, accounts for less than half the number of Black male students who actually took the test. In other words, the majority of Black male students had a score in the basic or minimal categories in each subject area. The percentage of students who scored in the basic or minimal categories ranges from 57 percent in reading, 61 percent in science, 64 percent in social studies, 66 percent in language arts to 79 percent in math. These WSAS results imply that the majority of MMSD Black male students are not at the appropriate achievement level for academic success by the tenth grade.

Finally, I collected and cross-referenced Black male students' tenth-grade WSAS data and GPA scores. The following table is a summary of my data analysis:

Black Male Students' Tenth-Grade State Test Data

| Proficient/ Advanced | Number With < 2.0 | Percentage With < 2.0 of Tested | Number With > 2.0 | Percentage With > 2.0 of Tested | Total Number Proficient/ Advanced | Percentage Proficient/ Advanced of Tested |
|---|---|---|---|---|---|---|
| LA | 18 | 12.24 | 32 | 21.77 | 50 | 34.01 |
| Rdg | 23 | 15.65 | 40 | 27.21 | 63 | 42.86 |
| Math | 5 | 03.40 | 24 | 16.33 | 29 | 19.73 |
| SC | 17 | 11.56 | 41 | 27.89 | 58 | 39.46 |
| SS | 18 | 12.24 | 34 | 23.13 | 52 | 35.37 |

NOTE: Not Tested = 30.99% (66/213); Tested = 69.01% (147/213).

The data show that approximately 20 percent to 43 percent of Black male students who took the test had a score of proficient or advanced depending on the curricular area (language arts, reading, math, science, social studies). In addition, of the students who had a score of proficient or advanced, 17 percent to 36 percent currently have a GPA of less than or equal to 2.0 (depending on the curricular area). In other words, approximately one fifth to one third of students showing competency on the WSAS test are not showing academic success according to their GPA status. This is obviously not a cause-and-effect relationship because of the many factors that play into and influence test scores and GPA, however—at a minimum—it is a reason for some discussions. These data are especially alarming, however, when they are coupled with the fact that the majority of Black male students had a score of either basic or minimal on the tenth-grade WSAS. I conducted the student interviews to better understand why some Black male students succeeded while others were unable to succeed in the school district.

## INTERVIEW DATA AND ANALYSIS

### Characteristics of Interviewees

I asked 11 Black male high school students to tell me their stories and to talk about their school experiences. All my interviewees are non–special education students from high-poverty backgrounds (as determined by their receipt of free or reduced-price lunches) whose WSAS test scores indicate that they exhibit the potential for academic success. In addition, I collaborated with school staff members to confirm students' potential for academic success in a majority of cases. Five of the interviewees are currently high achievers (GPAs between 3.0 and 4.0) and six are currently low achievers (GPAs between 0.0 and 2.5). With the exception of two students, all the interviewees have attended Madison schools since kindergarten. The following table provides more specific data on each student interviewee:

Interviewee Characteristics

| Student | Grade Level | GPA | Language Arts | Math | Reading | Science | Social Studies |
|---------|-------------|------|---------------|------|---------|---------|----------------|
| 1 | 11 | 1.65 | P | P | Adv | P | Adv |
| 2 | 10 | 1.03 | P | P | P | P | B |
| 3 | 10 | 2.37 | Adv | Adv | Adv | Adv | Adv |
| 4 | 11 | 1.81 | P | B | P | P | P |
| 5 | 11 | 1.56 | P | P | P | P | P |
| 6 | 12 | 2.39 | P | B | Adv | Adv | P |
| 1* | 10 | 3.42 | P | P | P | Adv | P |
| 2* | 11 | 3.19 | Adv | P | P | P | Adv |
| 3* | 12 | 3.20 | P | P | P | P | B |
| 4* | 11 | 3.22 | Adv | Adv | Adv | P | Adv |
| 5* | 12 | 3.46 | Adv | Adv | P | Adv | P |

NOTES: * High-achieving students.
GPA is cumulative through January 2001.
Data is from eighth- or tenth-grade WSAS Test.
Adv = Advanced, P = Proficient, B = Basic, M = Minimal.

## SUPPORTIVE FACTORS

### High Achievers

I asked students who were high achievers to talk about their school experiences, including factors that have supported their school success, as well as barriers to their achievement. First, I would like to focus on the supportive factors. According to the five high-achieving students, the following are factors that have helped them to be successful in school (next to the statement is the number of students who mentioned the factor):

### External Factors

- Having a teacher or mentor (and also a parent for some) with whom they connected (5)
- High expectations (5)
- Supportive siblings
- Supportive friends who provided competition
- Supportive community
- Upward Bound Program

### Internal Factors

- Drive or motivation (4)
- Having a goal or focus (3)
- Attending school and doing homework (2)
- Being active and involved in school activities

The factors that have been an especially positive influence for the high-achieving students are the presence in their lives of a supportive individual (teacher or mentor or parent), high expectations, and drive and motivation. All the students stated that having a teacher or a mentor with whom they connected has greatly impacted them. Student 4 talked about "being discovered by Ms. G in first grade," who was a great support and who also helped connect him with many opportunities, such as making a presentation to the school board as an elementary student. Student 1 described one of his elementary teachers as someone who "was willing to help me out at any time." This student went on to further describe how the connection with his teacher has helped him to make better choices and to stay out of trouble.

All the high achievers mentioned that high expectations served a major role in supporting them to be successful in school. For example, Student 3 shared that his fourth-grade teacher "told me that I could be anything I wanted to be and do anything I wanted to do, and I believed her!" The message Student 3 received from his teacher left a powerful impact on him, which in turn has positively influenced his school career. Student 2 talked about being pushed by his parents, by his teachers, and by his counselor to continually take more and more challenging courses that matched his potential. In particular, he spoke about being counseled to take advanced classes that he later greatly appreciated because of the doors that eventually opened to him. Student 4 talked about being told over and over again by his mentor that "you are intelligent and you need to keep going." This student had taken to heart his mentor's message to succeed and said that he intended to achieve great things and hoped to become a positive role model for other Black male students.

Four of the high achieving students stated that having drive and motivation helped them to be successful in school. When discussing this factor, students shared about their responsibility of being a Black male or their responsibility to contribute to changing the negative stereotype of the Black male, their will to succeed against the odds, their strong determination and positive mind-set, and for several, their goal to be the first in their family to attend and graduate from college. Students emphasized not having the "luxury to fail" because they could not afford to contribute to the deterioration of the Black male population.

## Low Achievers

I then asked students who were low achievers to discuss factors that have helped them in school. They mentioned the following as supportive factors (next to the statement is the number of students who mentioned the factor):

### External Factors

- Supportive parent (2)
- Relevant course work (2)
- Tutoring (2)
- Sports (provided motivation) (2)
- High expectations
- Supportive friends who provided competition
- Relationship with the teacher

### Internal Factors

- Drive or motivation (3)
- Having a goal (2)
- Flexibility

Several factors that have been a positive influence for a number of the low-achieving students include having a drive, having a supportive parent figure, relevant coursework, tutoring, and sports. Three of the six students mentioned that having drive helped them to achieve in school. For example, Student 1 stated that "if I put my mind to something, nothing can stop me." This student also talked about the importance of not succumbing to the negative stereotypes of Black males but rather proving the stereotypes wrong by working hard in school. Student 5 felt that his determination helped him to keep going, especially when things got tough in school. This student also felt it necessary to "let go of the little things" in order to be able to succeed.

Two students mentioned that having a supportive parent was very important to them. Student 6 stated that "My mom is a major contributor . . . she tells me I can do better than her . . . she tells me she wants me to be able to do what I like most in life later." Student 6 talked repeatedly about how his mom has always been there for him and said that she even meets with his teachers to get him back on track when he's having problems at school. Student 4 also felt that he had very good support from his parents, and that they always want the best for him.

Two of the six low achievers felt that relevant coursework has helped them to be successful in school. For instance, Student 3 said that taking courses that relate to his future goal helps him to achieve in school. For this student, it was very important that he could connect his daily school work to his future profession. It motivated him and also helped him to stay focused in school. Similarly, Student 3 felt that he did best in the classes such as economics, social Studies, and contemporary world issues that were interesting to him and in which he could relate to the material being studied.

Two of the low-achieving students stated that having a tutor or mentor is extremely valuable. For example, Student 4 talked about greatly benefiting from a tutoring lab. This Student felt that his tutor "matches the way that I learn, which helps me to do better." In addition, Student 6 talked about taking advantage of afterschool help and how that has helped him to be successful in school.

Two students also mentioned sports as being a factor that has supported their academic achievement. For Student 2, sports motivated him to do well because he wanted to be able to play in the games. As a result, this student pushed himself to do well in his classes in order to be able to play on the field. Similarly, Student 3 pushed himself in school in order to be able to participate in sports.

## Comparison

I have presented the supportive factors for the high-achieving students, as well as the low-achieving students. In summary, I would like to point out some key differences and similarities:

- All five of the high achievers had a supportive individual (a teacher or mentor or parent) in their lives, compared to two of the six low achievers (who mentioned parents being supportive).

- All five of the high achievers stated that having high expectations helped them to succeed, compared to one of the six low achievers.
- Four of the five high achievers and three of the six low achievers spoke of having an internal "drive" or motivation to succeed.
- Three of the five high achievers and two of the six low achievers stated that having a goal helped them to achieve (high achievers' goals seemed to be more specific and challenging, while low achievers' goals seemed to be more general).
- Two of the five high achievers said it is extremely important to attend school and to do homework.
- Two of the six low achievers spoke of being motivated by sports.
- Two of the six low achievers felt that tutoring supported achievement.

## BARRIERS TO ACHIEVEMENT

### High Achievers

I also asked the Black male high school students to speak about any factors that have been barriers to their academic success during their school experiences. According to the five high-achieving students, the following are factors that deterred them from school achievement (next to the statement is the number of students who mentioned the factor):

#### *External Factors*

- Family issues (2)
- Low expectations (negative perceptions of Black males) (2)
- Peers (negative influence) (2)
- Hard courses
- Mobility

#### *Internal Factors*

- Interpersonal skills
- Low motivation (loss of motivation)

The main factors that have been deterrents for the five high-achieving students include family issues, low expectations (related to negative perceptions of Black males), and negative influence from their peers. Two of the five students expressed that family issues have interfered with their academic endeavors. Student 1 talked about his dad being incarcerated and how that nearly destroyed all sense of hope for him. He stated: "I lost all will to go on

... what would be the point?" Fortunately, this student's dad convinced him to be strong, to go on, and not to make the same mistakes that he had made. Regardless of the fact that he may never again see his dad free, Student 1 has chosen to work hard and currently has a 3.42 GPA. Student 3 spoke of his parents' divorce and his mom's remarriage as major deterrents. In addition to the emotional roller coaster that he went through during his parents' divorce, the fact that his family also moved several times throughout his senior year made it very difficult for him to focus and feel connected. Family issues made academic achievement difficult for two of the five high achievers.

Two high achievers mentioned that low expectations (related to negative perceptions of Black males) have served as barriers to their achievement in school. Student 4 expressed that it is extremely difficult for him to be at his high school because he is a Black male. He went on to say that it is difficult because there are few role models among the students and staff and because negative perceptions of Black males are quite pervasive. Speaking about low expectations, Student 4 stated:

> Teachers don't expect as much ... they have seen many Black males fail, so it is hard for them to tell the difference. On the first day, they expect me to be in the lower-level classes. I get looks when they hand out books (not from all but from some). Only when I get an A on the first test do they recognize my abilities and begin to expect more. . . .

Student 1 shared that he has become more conscious of the difference in expectations that Black male students experience compared to other students. For instance, although Student 1 knows that he is capable of "A" work, he is quite often praised for getting B's on his tests. Fortunately, this student has a mentor who stresses that it is extremely important not to settle for less than what one is capable of doing.

Two of the five high-achieving students stated that negative-influencing peers can interfere with academic achievement. For example, Student 5 talked about how hard it is to have to choose between being with friends and staying focused on his studies. Similarly, Student 4 shared that peers can set him back by picking on him and by offering him unhealthy alternatives. Evidently, these two students have been able to make choices that allow them to strike a balance between school and peers.

## Low Achievers

The six low-achieving students also talked about factors that have deterred them from academic achievement. They mentioned the following as barriers to school success for them (next to the statement is the number of students who mentioned the factor):

### External Factors

- Lack of connections with teachers (4)
- Irrelevant classes (3)
- Perceptions and low expectations of Black males (2)
- Family issues
- Hanging out with the wrong crowd (poor choices)
- Presence of security personnel or police
- Lack of time
- Drugs

### Internal Factors

- Organization, attention, and memory (2)
- Not having goals
- Refusing to ask for help
- Low motivation

Several factors that have been barriers for a number of the low-achieving students include feelings of disconnectedness with teachers, irrelevant classes, and low expectations (related to negative perceptions of Black males). Four of the six students mentioned that feelings of disconnectedness with teachers have deterred them from achieving in school. For example, Student 5 spoke in detail about an incident involving a teacher that left him feeling "hopeless and wanting to quit." He talked about having a medical condition that interfered with his academics, and how the situation only got worse when his teacher refused to assist him after he had repeatedly asked for extra help. Student 5 ended by saying that since that situation occurred, he has not put in the same effort, and that his motivation has greatly decreased in all his classes. Student 4 shared about trying to build relationships with teachers for academic purposes. This student unfortunately has also been unable to get extra help, even though he has requested assistance several times from different staff members. Student 4 is quite discouraged due to his negative experiences. Student 2 stated that feelings of disconnectedness with his teachers have made it very hard for him to achieve. He emphasized that it is especially difficult when he is struggling and his teachers show little concern for where he is academically and whether he is learning at all. Disconnection with staff members has left these students feeling very frustrated, less motivated, and more hopeless.

Three low achievers stated that irrelevant classes make it difficult for them to learn. Students emphasized that they do best when the class curriculum has relevance or can be applied to their lives. Student 6 shared that when classes are irrelevant and unchallenging he quickly loses interest in the learning process. More specifically, Student 6 feels that too much of his class time is spent reviewing old material and not enough time is spent learning new material, which leaves him very unchallenged. Additionally, this student believes that he would be more engaged in learning if his teachers incorporated more visual aids and interactive activities. Student 2, on the other hand, expressed his concern about being rushed through the curriculum and not being able to learn how to apply what he was learning to his own life. Similarly, Student 3 prefers "a teacher who can interpret and explain well over a teacher who cannot explain well but knows everything." Both Student 2 and Student 3 explained that they understood that teachers have curriculum that they must get through, but for these two students at least, "learning to learn" is a lot more important than learning without clear understanding and without clear knowledge of relevance to their lives.

Two of the low-achieving students shared that low expectations (related to negative perceptions of Black males) have served as barriers to their academic achievement. More specifically, Student 1 and Student 3 shared that there are negative stereotypes of Black males in society, in the community, and at school. Student 1 went on to share that because of these negative stereotypes he continually has to work hard, to push himself to do better, and to demand that others have high expectations for him. This student wanted to tell younger Black male students to be aware of low expectations and to continue to challenge themselves to live up to their potential. Student 3 also felt that it is important to challenge the stereotypes and to do the best that one can.

## Comparison

I have presented the barriers to achievement for both the high achievers and the low achievers. In summary, I would like to point out some key differences and similarities:

- Four of the six low achievers felt that disconnectedness with teachers deterred them from academic success, compared to none of the five high achievers.
- Three of the six low achievers stated that irrelevant classes served as a deterrent to high achievement (material versus meaning).
- Two of the five high achievers and two of the six low achievers (four students from the total of 11) stated that low expectations (negative perceptions of Black males) deterred them from academic success.

- Two of the five high achievers and one of the six low achievers (three students from the total of 11) stated that family issues interfered with school success.
- Two of the five high achievers and one of the six low achievers (three students from the total of 11) stated that peers can be a negative influence (pressure, intolerance).

## TEACHER CHARACTERISTICS

During the interview, I asked students to identify an individual at school with whom they felt connected. Each student named at least one staff member; some students named two or three individuals. I also prompted the students to describe the individuals, including why they felt connected with the staff members. The characteristics listed by the low achievers and high achievers are quite similar. Black male students feel most connected with staff members who exhibit the following characteristics:

- Knowledgeable about the curriculum
- Has good classroom management skills and holds students accountable
- Makes learning interesting and fun
- Makes learning relevant and practical
- Likes teaching and has a positive attitude
- Takes time to listen to students' viewpoints and respects students
- Takes time to get to know students, is interested in students' goals, and is not afraid to share about himself or herself
- Truly cares about how all students do in school and wants all students to succeed
- Challenges students to do their best and expects excellence
- Is willing to provide extra help to students and connects students to tutors and/or mentors
- Is open-minded and willing to try new things
- Does not "mark students when they first come into their classes"

As is evident by the statements made by the Black male students, the interviewees feel most connected with staff members who have strong knowledge of their curriculum and use instructional strategies that engage learners, who have high expectations of all students, who are truly interested in students' opinions and goals, who are not afraid to take risks, and who enjoy teaching. Every one of the interviewees mentioned that he works harder and in turn does better in the classrooms of teachers whom they respect and who give them respect. Connections to teachers seem to play a major role in interviewees' academic achievement.

## REFLECTIONS AND NEXT STEPS

This has been an extremely powerful action research project for me. The process through which I conducted the study has left as powerful an impact as the results and conclusions I have drawn (from both my data and my interviews). My research project will certainly have a great impact on me as a leader, an educator, and a role model for all children.

I have several "next" steps as I complete this journey and begin a new one. I have already had the opportunity to share my research with several groups, including a Memorial High School study group and two Minority Student Achievement principal study groups. My plan is to continue to share my research with interested administrators, as well as MMSD staff members. I especially hope to share the stories and insights from the students I interviewed. I am also currently preparing a letter to send to the student interviewees and their families summarizing my findings, as well as my next steps. This is important because I want students to know that their voices have been heard and are impacting their educational system. Finally, I plan to continue researching the factors that have had a positive impact on minority student achievement. More specifically, I intend to focus on the Search Institute's 40 Assets (Search Institute, 2006) as well as the resiliency research. I see great potential in focusing on students' strengths, talents, and assets as we continue to examine how to best support all students in achieving to their individual potential.

One suggestion I have for future research is to duplicate the action research project I have conducted here with parents and with teachers. It is important to continue to gather data, stories, and insights from parents and teachers in order to get a full picture and understanding of how to best support Black male students in MMSD. This additional research will give a more complete picture and understanding of the struggles of Black male students. It is important that we continue to ask questions and conduct research that supports positive growth within the area of student achievement. Each one of us can make a difference.

## EPILOGUE

Four and a half years have passed since I conducted the action research project titled Understanding High School Black Male Students'

Achievement and School Experience. During that time, I have had the honor to serve as an elementary school principal in two large school districts. I worked in the first school district for three years before I moved to my current school district. The action research project inspired me to (1) share the research data and findings with other professional colleagues in the field of education; and (2) keep equity at the forefront of my work as a school principal so that all students have an opportunity to receive a quality education. Equity has been a primary goal for me during the last several years due to the action research work.

The results of the research project motivated me to share the knowledge and insights that I learned from the Black male high school students with educators within and outside the school district. I have had the opportunity to speak with several prominent groups, including two school district principal groups, staffs of two elementary schools, a Minority Student Achievement principal study group, and participants in the Minority Student Achievement Network. Each group found the student data to be disturbing and the recommendations to be helpful. It is evident that more student voices need to be shared and that school districts need to listen to them. I have embraced opportunities to share the Black male high school students' voices whenever possible in my work. I anticipate the opportunity to have further positive impact on minority student achievement by sharing the voices of the students with more professionals.

It has also been a privilege for me to be able to directly impact school staffs and students. As an elementary school principal, I led a school staff through two years of equity training with the goal of being able to better serve more children in the school. Before leading the staff, I went through a year of training myself with an equity consultant as part of my job as a principal in the district. With support from the school district, I created a school equity team consisting of a district coach, two teachers, and myself. Together, the four of us led the equity work at the building level. We provided general training on equity for the staff, as well as created opportunities for staff to have courageous conversations about race and equity. As a school, we began to examine achievement data and school decisions through an equity lens. Grade-level and team discussions included conversations on race and equity. Although it was challenging and slow work, the training and actions taken as a result of the equity work positively impacted all students in the school environment. The results were evident in the school achievement and climate data, as well as in positive comments from parents and students. In addition, teachers developed and facilitated book study groups focused on race and equity. Students directly benefited from the work of the staff.

I have also been involved with numerous secondary-level student forums addressing diversity issues. The student forums had several purposes, including listening to the students' voices and building leadership in the minority student population. Students, district administrators, school board members, and parents felt that this past year's forum had an especially powerful impact on the community and provided great hope for the future. As part of the forum, students had an opportunity to share their concerns about the current achievement gap and provide suggestions about what students, schools, and staffs can do to support minority students. The information that the students shared was extremely powerful and helpful to district educators. After leading the highly successful student forum this year, I was asked to colead the diversity work for the school district for the following year.

As coleader of the diversity work, I am in charge of facilitating (1) the equity training for all district administrators; (2) a mentoring program for minority staff; (3) the student forum (including continuing to build student leadership within the school district); and (4) the Parent Diversity Committee. District administrators have already had an opportunity to hear from a panel of students who participated in the student forum. In addition, administrators will have an opportunity to discuss race and equity this year during meetings of principals. A team of district administrators will also be going to the National Staff Development Conference to talk with a consultant about providing more intensive equity training for staff throughout the district. As a coleader of the diversity work, I have helped to develop a mentoring program for minority staff. We have provided each minority staff member with a mentor, and we are meeting quarterly to discuss and solve problems that arise throughout the school year. The hope is to be able to retain more minority staff by providing support and an avenue for discussing and dealing with concerns. We are also in the process of organizing a team of leaders across the secondary schools who will help to plan the student forum for this year. We will be meeting monthly with the school leaders to plan the forum and to develop plans for supporting minority students that the school leaders can take back to their respective schools and implement. My final responsibility is to coordinate with the Parent Diversity Committee. I meet monthly with the Parent Diversity Committee to support it in accomplishing its mission of supporting and embracing diversity in the school district. The diversity work is difficult because of the many facets of the task; however, I continue to embrace the opportunity to positively impact minority students, particularly the Black male students.

As evidenced by the work that I have been involved with over the last several years, the action research project has profoundly impacted my daily work with children. I have purposely chosen to take on administrative leadership roles to address issues of equity in the field of education.

I intend to continue to accept opportunities to educate and lead education leaders on equity issues. I feel strongly about the work and am committed to doing my part in helping others understand the importance of addressing inequities in the educational system in order to support all students to be successful. I hope to be able to connect with other leaders across the country who are doing similar work in order to strengthen my ability to impact greater numbers of minority students. My next step is to communicate on a greater scale about the work that I am doing in my current school district and collaborate with other leaders. I believe that it is essential to build a network to continue the important work that we are all doing.

The research project continues to shape me as an administrator, educator, and role model daily. I often think of the Black male students whom I interviewed. I hear their voices in the students with whom I currently work. I hope to continue to help more students through all that I am doing with social justice and equity.

## APPENDIX: SURVEY INTERVIEW/QUESTIONNAIRE

---

Name _____    Date _____

1. How would you describe yourself? Peers describe you? Parents describe you?

2. a. Tell me about your elementary school experience.
   b. Tell me about your middle school experience.
   c. Tell me about your high school experience.

3. a. You have demonstrated excellence in academics (or the potential) . . . what factors have contributed to your success? Describe them briefly.
   b. What factors have made it difficult for you to be successful? Deterred you from success? Describe them briefly.

4. What are your goals? What do you need to do to achieve your goals?

5. Describe your peer group. Who are they? What kinds of things does your peer group like to do?

6. Describe your relationship with your teachers, counselor, coaches, and/or mentors.

7. Describe your relationship with your parent(s) or guardian(s).

8. Describe any community involvement you have (job, church, community center, and so on).

9. What advice do you have for younger boys who may be struggling to achieve in school? (What difficulties have you encountered in school and how did you overcome them?

10. Do you have any questions for me?

# REFERENCE

Search Institute. (2006). Retrieved January 5, 2007, from www.search-institute.org/assets/

# 6

# *What Teacher Behaviors Encourage One At-Risk African American Boy to Be a Productive Member of Our Classroom Community?*

Barbara Williams

## EDITORS' INTRODUCTION

In her study, Williams examines the ways in which Davonte, an African American boy new to the school, is affected by her efforts to incorporate him into the classroom community. In order to meet Davonte's educational and social needs, Williams uses a variety of teaching strategies, including differentiated instruction, consistent routines, and "sacred time," in which Davonte receives her undivided attention. Employing a unique narrative style, Williams examines her own philosophies of teaching, acknowledges the importance of knowing every student as an individual, and offers readers a glimpse into the realities of classroom life.

\* \* \* \*

## DAVONTE: SEPTEMBER

He arrives at school several weeks after the school year has begun.

He is rather small for a seven-year-old second grader. His hair is braided and tied tight at the nape of his neck. His brown eyes are densely lashed and his expression is one of indifference. He is sullen but when he smiles those first weeks, his face lights up, his left eye focuses on that which pleases him, and his right eye, referred to by the school nurse as his lazy eye, drifts in a different direction. Sometimes when I look at him hard I am uncertain which is the focusing eye and which one is adrift.

His blue jeans are way too big. They fall off his waist and slip down his hips, often scooting to a resting place somewhere above his knees. There are times when the jeans take his underwear along with them on the ride down, and he's baring his bottom to his classmates. This appears to bother him not at all. He clumsily accommodates walking about in the ill-fitting pants even as they alter his gait and restrict his movements. The school nurse rigs up a pseudo-solution, using a piece of string to tie together two belt loops, which reduces the circumference of the waist so that the pants fit better on Davonte's narrow hips.

He does not sit quietly on the blue rug at instruction time. He sprawls and twists and turns. He sighs loudly and talks out frequently. When his restlessness becomes too much he walks away. What we do on the blue rug—read stories, have conversation, recite poems on the easel, and do math problems—interests Davonte not at all. He does not contribute, even when invited. His fuse is short and he is easily frustrated, dropping out of learning to wander, or worse, to leave the room.

The other kids keep their distance. Davonte is unpredictable and often uncommunicative. It seems the other students are not sure of him and do not trust his outbursts. He gives the impression that he is uninterested in them.

He does not have many academic skills just yet. He does not recognize all the letters in the alphabet and can do math problems only if adding two single-digit numbers with manipulatives. His social skills are unsophisticated. He is easily angered, expresses his feelings in the raw, and seems unmotivated to become an accepted member of our classroom community.

In many ways, he is much younger than his classmates. Strangely, however, his attitude is older; he shows the sort of negative resistance that I usually associate with upper elementary and middle school kids.

His father, whom I later learn is called Red (Davonte's brown skin has reddish hues, and I presume that is where the father's nickname came from), is allegedly serving a life sentence in prison. His mother, Kelly, has left Davonte with various relatives who live in the Allied Drive community. In September he is living at his auntie's apartment. His mom is homeless and goes back and forth to Chicago. She is trying to find a job, but it is clear that her life is hard, and that she struggles.

These were my first impressions of Davonte and how he began his school year in Room 102.

## THE QUESTION

I knew I had to significantly alter the curriculum and classroom rhythms, which had worked so well for the rest of the children, in order to make Davonte feel a member of the group, and I needed to "socially engineer" the way others were perceiving him. As I began to tweak and change my approach to Davonte, struggling to accommodate his academic, social, and emotional needs, I was invited to become a member of the Equity Action Research Group. I am not certain that being a member of this group of six inspiring, thoughtful, and intelligent educators changed my agenda. I do know that spending part of a day each month talking about this research with them cemented my commitment to altering my practices. My goal was to increase Davonte's success in my classroom.

The question that frames my efforts is: **What teacher behaviors encourage one at-risk African American boy to be a productive member of our classroom community?**

By teacher behaviors I mean verbal (the words I choose to use and the tone of voice in which I deliver them) and nonverbal (body language) communication. I also wanted to be more deliberate about the curricular choices I made and the expectations I have for Davonte. Not only did I hope for Davonte to become a productive member of the classroom, I also aimed to assure Davonte's general happiness and contentment in Room 102, his academic progress, and his relationships with his classmates.

To succeed with Davonte, I had to become a more deliberate teacher. My choices in teaching had to become more thoughtful. I needed to change what I chose to pay attention to, and I had to invest my energy and time in this little boy while still trying to meet, as best I could, the needs of the other children in the class.

## PAYING ATTENTION

I rely heavily on my Daily Kidwatching Notes. I have for a time utilized these notes to force myself to reflect on my day and my students' learning. On most days, I carry a clipboard with a list of my students' names. I jot down pertinent information regarding academic progress (e.g., Michael solved on his easel a two-digit addition problem involving carrying) and other relevant information (e.g., Meredith is sad because her aunt is seriously ill). These are my Daily Kidwatching Notes. I am also engaged in an ongoing quest for knowledge about closing the achievement gap, which led me to read books and articles and to watch the 4-hour PBS documentary *Beyond the Color Line* with Henry Louis Gates.

This description is based on my perceptions, observations, and reflections concerning one at-risk, seven-year-old, African American boy who lives in poverty and his experiences over the course of his second-grade year in Room 102. My purpose is to make public my efforts, successful and not so successful, and Davonte's progress, academic and social. It is more a portrait than a photograph, an interpretation in which I simply try to be faithful to the evidence I see, mindful always of trying simply to tell the truth.

## THE CITY AND ITS SCHOOLS

Madison, Wisconsin, is both a capital city and home of the University of Wisconsin, a large research university. Our public schools are considered successful by nearly every measure but one. Our African American students' standardized test scores lag significantly behind the scores of their White peers. This problem is not unique to our state, but a recent study showed that Wisconsin ranks near the bottom, compared with other states, in the graduation rates of its African American students.

The Madison school district has begun to take the problem seriously enough to hire a consultant, Glenn Singleton, to study and facilitate changes in the way we do school so that more African American kids might have a better chance of success.

## HENRY DAVID THOREAU ELEMENTARY

The school where I spend my days is about four miles from the Capitol and downtown. It is on the city's west side, situated in a grove of oaks on a busy street that runs through an upper-middle-class neighborhood, Nakoma. Nearly half our students come from Nakoma. About 10 percent come from the Monroe Street area, which has slightly more modest homes but still is solidly middle-class. We also have students who live on or near Doncaster Street, at the other end of Nakoma, a small neighborhood with apartments and homes that might be described as lower-middle-class. The rest of our kids, nearly half, come from the Allied Drive neighborhood. This is described by many as a troubled community of subsidized housing, street drugs, and the unemployed and disenfranchised.

Our city's morning newspaper, the *Wisconsin State Journal,* did a series of articles about Allied Drive. The area was portrayed as a drug magnet, crime-ridden and isolated. The series noted that as other troubled areas in the city have improved, Allied Drive has slid deeper into despair as it absorbs the drug trafficking from other, now improved, areas. The city's mayor appears determined to help the neighborhood, in which the Boys and Girls Club recently has become active. It seemed pretty clear, after reading the series, that this neighborhood needs more opportunities and initiatives. It is packed with school-age children who are bused to many different schools, at which many of them struggle. The life experiences that each of these different socioeconomic groups brings to the classroom present a particular set of challenges to teachers at Thoreau School. Davonte is one of a group of children in my classroom who live in the Allied Drive neighborhood. The others have thrived with the rhythm in Room 102. They are full participants and are progressing academically. As in years past, I realize that most of the children from the Allied neighborhood do pretty well in elementary school even though it appears they have much less academic support at home than do their classmates. It is true, too, that every few years there is one child who seems much more troubled and for whom school is a much greater challenge.

## ROOM 102

My classroom is a rectangle. One side is a strip of windows overlooking the spreading limbs of a big old oak. The other walls are lined with low shelves that hold books—lots and lots of books—and math manipulatives. On a sunny day, the room is filled with natural light. Because I have come to favor a simple and uncluttered work environment, the classroom is centered on the rectangular tables that take up most of the floor space in the center of the room. Near the door are a couple of computers and shelves for games and an old wood wardrobe, which holds construction paper and my jacket in winter. Nearer the window at the opposite end are the blue rug and an easel. On the windowsill are avocados, which we've been waiting for weeks to sprout, and an amaryllis in full flower. Both taught us patience. (In the spring, it is the hyacinths and tulips that we planted last autumn, and which wintered in a basement refrigerator, that are now blooming on the sill.) The walls are decorated with various maps and children's work, though there is not as much "stuff" on the walls and bulletin boards as there is in most of the classrooms in the building. On the white-board, which stretches along one wall, is a number line that I put, for Davonte, at kid height. The room might be considered a bit sparse for an elementary classroom.

In his book *Being With Children,* Phillip Lopate writes about what he perceives as the happy consequences of an uncluttered and austere class-room. He gave me the courage to make my classroom simpler. Visually busy classrooms now strike me as too distracting.

## THE TEACHER

I have taught for 20-some years, at levels ranging from second grade through graduate school. I have felt fairly successful in my efforts, and I take a good deal of pleasure from my work. I am pretty much myself with kids, I don't alter my voice, and I treat my students with respect. I have high academic expectations because I have come to realize that grownups, too, often underestimate kids. But I also think that adults often fail to pro-vide kids with what they need to succeed.

I have a lot of energy and get into our studies with enthusiasm, but I have the tendency to be disorganized and I lose papers frequently. When I misplace my coffee mug, I announce a search. Someone invariably locates it, and amazingly the class goes straight back to the business at hand. Rather than keep a grade book, as other second- and third-grade teachers in my school tidily maintain, I have a fat file folder with work samples for each of my students. Instead of planning my year's units in advance, we often study a topic about which we have become spontaneously excited from a previous unit. For example, when we studied Thomas Jefferson the week of his birth, the kids became fascinated by Lewis and Clark. We then studied Lewis and Clark, and the kids became enamored of Sacagawea. And so it goes. This style has its advantages and disadvantages, but that's another subject.

I look at teaching as a profession that can foster social justice. I believe that teaching is full of moral and ethical opportunities and that the choices we make as teachers can go a long way toward helping children imagine their own possibilities. I am convinced that education is liberation and that it is the last best hope for children who live in poverty. As I have come around to these opinions, I have acquired a sense of urgency in teaching some of the kids in my classroom.

I expect good manners and civility, and most often the children are quite capable of meeting these expectations. When not, we problem-solve together. I am emphatic about kids getting playtime and outside recess time to balance classroom work.

The single attribute that is important and prevalent in my classroom is humor. We laugh together every day.

In agreeing to join the Action Research group, I knew that I had to examine an issue that had to do with the children I teach every day, an issue that is directly linked to their academic success and sense of belonging to our classroom community. I have, over the course of my teaching career, had several students with whom I felt unsuccessful. I wanted to become more deliberate in my choices of words, actions, expectations, and reactions, so that I might more positively affect one child's learning and sense of belonging.

## INFLUENCES ON MY THINKING

The first time I taught a large group of African American kids was 10 years ago at Cherokee Middle School. A group of eighth graders refused to take a foreign language and so the school created a class, world literature, for them. There was some difficulty finding a teacher for the course. Someone working at the school knew I was in the process of completing a dissertation and asked if I'd be interested. I began teaching the class a few weeks after the school year had begun.

The students were resistant and not at all interested in the idea of world literature. They did not do well in school. Their attitude could be summed up as "Screw this!" I decided to turn the class into a study of African American literature. We read Walter Dean Myers (*The Young Landlords*) and Alice Childress (*Rainbow Jordan*) and the *Autobiography of Malcolm X*. At first I read aloud to the students. After some time they began taking turns reading. We began to have spirited discussions. We ended the year with *There Are No Children Here* by Alex Kotlowitz. Many of the kids in the class were familiar with the Chicago gangs and projects that Kotlowitz describes in the book. This book, too, provoked animated discussion.

What I learned from the school year was how smart these kids were. Despite their refusal to take a foreign language class and despite their generally low academic performance, they were engaged in a whole lot of critical thinking and connection making and thoughtful articulation of ideas. The books had engaged many of them and prompted discussions that allowed the kids' intelligence to be seen despite their slouchy resistance to school.

My thinking also has been influenced by the book *The Envy of the World*, in which Ellis Cose describes the forces that shape the lives of young Black men. He mourns the number of Black men in prison and the impact of popular culture and the messages it sends. He points to programs that allow young Black men to excel and become successful despite the odds against them. He worries that too many Black kids grow up without a supportive father in their lives and that gangs too often take on the role of family. I have also recently read and been deeply affected by *The Color of Water* (James McBride), *Growing Up Literate* (Denny Taylor and Catherine Dorsey-Gaines), *Parallel Time* (Brent Staples), and the fiction of Toni Morrison, Ernest Gaines, Gloria Naylor, Dorothy West, and Z. Z. Packer.

In the PBS series *Beyond the Color Line,* Henry Louis Gates, like Cose, describes the forces working against Black kids growing up in poverty. He also points to programs that work. He interviewed people who, despite the odds, have carved out for themselves creative, purposeful lives. Years ago I read Gates's *Colored People,* a sort of coming-of-age story in which Gates details his childhood in a West Virginia mill town. He recalls thinking of himself as Colored, then Negro, then Black. He describes well the transformative power that reading had on him.

I listened to and then ordered the transcripts of a National Public Radio (NPR) show about the achievement gap and schools that have closed it. The show highlighted one district in Ohio that had high standards but also had a system in place to help students achieve their potential. For example, the district adjusts high school class times to students' work schedules, and teachers modify their curricula so that more kids succeed. The district tries to make up for the fact that some kids receive academic support at home while others do not. Tutoring programs and before- and afterschool study groups were emphasized. The adults in the school went to extraordinary efforts to reach students most at risk for failing.

In addition to Cose's book, Gates's program, and the series on NPR, I also have been influenced by *Other People's Children,* in which author Lisa Delpit bemoans that too many teachers come from mostly White, "progressive" university programs that fail to effectively confront the achievement gap. In her own first years of teaching, she moved quickly from learning centers and other more progressive methods to desks in rows and structured lessons. She observed that White kids from middle-class backgrounds do fine in the more progressive classrooms but that children of color fare far better with structure and clear expectations.

This brought to mind my student teacher, who, along with other student teachers from UW–Madison, visited a highly successful Milwaukee school in which about 90 percent of the African American children come from impoverished backgrounds. She described a classroom that sounded much like what Lisa Delpit promotes—lots of structure, clear expectations, and, though I don't know if Delpit would go this far, teachers who were nearly robotic in the delivery of the Direct Instruction curriculum. Every child would be on "the same page," getting their pencils ready at the same time, or listening to a story with good posture and hands folded in their laps, all eyes on the book. My student teacher and her peers were impressed with the combination of the students' serious learning and the staff's firm friendliness. The school was one of the most successful in Milwaukee as measured by standardized test scores. I couldn't help but wonder if Davonte might be more successful in such an environment.

## THE CHILDREN

Seventeen of us spend the morning together in Room 102. Because our school is a Student Achievement Guarantee in Education (SAGE) school, a state program that allows for smaller class size for the teaching of language arts and math, each second-grade classroom at Thoreau has an average of 16 kids in the morning, and 24 kids in the afternoon for social studies and science. In the afternoon I teach language arts and math to third graders, whose schedule is opposite that of the second graders.

For the last several years I have taught all subjects and looped between second and third grade, which allowed me to be with the same children for two years. This school year, I am teaching language arts and math to a group of second graders in the morning and to a group of third graders in the afternoon.

The morning second graders are an especially bright group. Half of them read well above grade level. They are a particularly curious bunch, which has precipitated many spontaneous research questions. We have a Chinese American girl, a Chinese American boy, a boy who was born in Colombia, a girl whose mother is from Mexico, four African American children, and eight Caucasian children.

Though half the students are academically successful, the others struggle a bit to acquire skills. In this latter group are children from the Nakoma neighborhood as well as those from the Allied neighborhood. Some of the more critical thinkers are from the group that has the least sophisticated skills. The class divides itself neatly into two to three instructional groups—except Davonte. Davonte is just beginning to read consonant-vowel-consonant words, and he becomes frustrated when working in a group.

## ADJUSTING THE CLASSROOM FOR DAVONTE

To try to better meet Davonte's social, emotional, and academic needs, I needed to change the kind of teacher I'd been. What follows is a description of my attempts and Davonte's responses. Though I organize my observations into two sections—socioemotional and academics—really, the two were decidedly intertwined.

## Davonte's Social and Emotional Life in Room 102

One of the first things I learned about Davonte was that he had a very, very low threshold for frustration. If he was asked to exert effort toward a goal that was not his own, he became frustrated. For Davonte, frustration was directly linked to anger. He expressed his anger loudly and frequently, turning his body away, and often stomping off from the instructional area. Sometimes, if left alone, he'd return and we'd adjust the task. Other times he'd keep going, right out of the room. On the worst days, he'd grab the door on his way out and slam it hard.

For example, one morning in November I introduced a writing idea to the kids. We had talked about and were learning how to add more detail to our writing. I told the kids they were going to use their new descriptive writing skills to describe a *National Geographic* magazine photograph. I explained how they would each receive a photograph, placed in a folder so that only the writer could see it. When the children had finished writing and editing the descriptions, each child would give his or her writing to a classmate to illustrate. The illustrator would not see the photograph until the artwork was complete. If the kids wrote with detail, we figured, the illustrations would resemble the photographs.

As with most assignments, the kids were anxious to get started. They left the blue rug with their photos tucked in folders and began writing in earnest. I approached Davonte, who was wandering around the room, and told him we'd do the project together. He grumbled and groaned but sat down at a table with me. When I asked him to describe with his words what he saw in the photograph I gave him, being certain that my tone was sincerely friendly and inviting, he pushed away from the table and walked out of the classroom, yelling, "I ain't doin' no stupid writing!" As he stormed out, the class collectively held its breath. Davonte didn't slam the door this time. The students sighed and resumed their work.

I had learned to let Davonte go rather than confront him when he was so full of anger. I had also learned not to blame myself. Something other than writing was deeply troubling him. I'd also learned, in our weeks together, how short-lived Davonte's anger could be, and how easily he came back to us even if the required apology was difficult.

As was the routine, I called the office to let whoever was "on discipline" know that Davonte had left the room. The staff member on discipline knew well the drill. Davonte could return to Room 102 when he apologized to us and when he was ready to work with me.

The thing I had in my favor was that Davonte always wanted to come back, usually sooner rather than later. There were only a few times when I wasn't ready for his prompt return and needed more time. Most times Davonte made his apology. He knew he was required to look at his classmates and identify what he was sorry for. On this particular morning, about 16 minutes passed between Davonte's departure and his return. He made his apology, with some support. The kids accepted it ("We forgive you," they said sincerely before returning to their writing), and Davonte sat down next to me, took a few breaths, and began describing the photo. Thirty-five minutes later he'd written six sentences, which he'd copied from his dictation to me, about a striped fish he called "Nemo." It was descriptive and he was clearly proud of his work. He couldn't wait to find a classmate to illustrate his words.

This routine became fairly typical—Davonte's unprovoked anger, his leaving, his return and apology, his getting down to the business at hand, and finally and most important, the pride he felt after academic effort and work were completed. He was usually the first to share his work on the blue rug, and his classmates always showed their admiration for his effort.

When Davonte had joined us in September, he lacked social skills. He did not know how to be a polite listener when another child was speaking. He constantly blurted out and interrupted other children when we were on the blue rug. His classmates were clearly annoyed with his rude behavior, but this did not seem at first to affect Davonte. My admonitions also had little effect. ("Davonte, please show Rose respect. She's sharing now and I noticed she showed you respect yesterday when you shared.") We learned, as a group, to ignore the blurt-outs, or to invite Davonte to read with someone or to leave the blue rug to listen to a book tape. I tried to use a friendly tone when I'd say, for example, "Davonte, I notice it's really hard for you to be a polite listener on the blue rug just now. Would you like to listen to a book tape or choose a classmate to read with you?" I'd learned to delete from my voice any trace of annoyance or hint of punitive consequences. For example, I did not say, "Davonte, you are being rude, you are excused from the blue rug." The civility we were working so hard to establish would be further diminished if Davonte slammed the door or pushed over chairs on his way out. I learned that rather than asking Davonte to leave the blue rug when he'd lost his manners, a strategy that worked so well with the other children, it was better for all of us if I stopped instruction, looked at Davonte, and spoke with him slowly and deliberately but with kindness. I would ask him to choose something different to do or to be more polite. This seemed to interrupt what I believe would have become a tantrum. We used these times as an opportunity for Davonte to read with a classmate. If I could stay calm and rational myself no matter how Davonte was acting, he had a better chance of saving face and making a choice that would be good for him and for our group.

As the weeks passed, I wanted to get a handle on what made Davonte mad. I paid closer attention to his moods. I suspected that much of his emotional life had less to do with school than with what was happening outside of school. Indeed, school may have been the most stable part of his life. I learned to be more sensitive to Davonte's mood when he came into our classroom in the morning. Making the effort to connect with him, to check in one on one, often helped me know how to adjust for his day.

Too often Davonte's day began badly. He frequently got into trouble a lot at breakfast. More than once the woman in charge of food service had him escorted to the principal's office before the school day had even begun because Davonte had been physically aggressive toward another child. At other times he'd get into a ruckus with another student in the hallway and come into class angry. His bad temper was clear when his jaw was set and he refused to meet my eye when I greeted him in the morning. This negative start began to occur much more frequently as Davonte got himself into trouble before school in the mornings. My job, no easy task, was to try to turn him around.

One tactic seemed to help. When I was at the classroom door greeting kids in the morning, I'd pull Davonte aside before he entered the room. I'd ask him to repeat, after me, positive affirming sentences such as, "I am smart," "I will write today and become a better writer," "I will do math today and become a better mathematician," and "I will respect this room and myself." As with most of my schemes, Davonte at first resisted but as I stayed with it he warmed to the idea and even became compliant.

By paying close attention to Davonte's anger, I found that when I expected too much of him, he'd react negatively. Whether in response to a dictated sentence that was a few words too long, a blue rug conversation that went beyond his attention span, or math problems that were bumped up too soon, Davonte, when frustrated, became angry. Over and over I was reminded of the critical importance of providing Davonte with lessons or activities that were finely calibrated to his level. Davonte's Vygotskian zone of proximal development was ringed by an invisible fence that zapped us when he bumped into it.

Despite what I thought was my sensitivity to what set off Davonte, I came to realize that I'd never know how to completely rig the morning to avoid Davonte's unpredictable and seemingly unprovoked anger. So I decided that he and I might learn the best ways for us to handle the anger once it happened. I not only wanted him to learn ways to manage his emotions, but I wanted to prevent his anger from holding the rest of the class hostage or sabotaging our learning. I also wanted Davonte to know that just because he drew more attention to his angry emotions than the rest of us did to ours, he was not alone in experiencing them. The rest of us got angry too.

Davonte, in a calm mood after recovering from a tantrum, was receptive to his classmates describing what they did when they were angry. Davonte called on kids to tell him what they did when they got mad. He liked listening, and they seemed to like telling. Emily told him how she slowly counted backwards from the number 20. She confessed that she used to start at 10 but found that this didn't give her enough time to cool down. Jake told Davonte how he did the "lemon squeeze," and he then demonstrated with his fist and mock anger. Tyrone told Davonte that what worked for him was to walk away from anger. Desiray described how she would talk it out, beginning with the words, "I'm angry because . . ." I told Davonte that I thought it was important to name the emotion and try to understand its source. I gave him some examples I thought he could relate to.

When he was calm and anger-free, Davonte gave us the impression that he understood better the ways he might choose to relieve and express and use anger. But when he became angry, as he often did, his emotions ruled.

Sometime in the second quarter of the school year, I discovered a quieter way to derail Davonte's anger. If I gently put my finger under his chin or my arm around his shoulder or knelt so that we were eye to eye, Davonte would more likely listen to me and adjust his behavior. There was a very narrow window of opportunity from Davonte's initial show of frustration to his bailing out by leaving the room. I learned to exploit that window. As long as Davonte hadn't moved to full-blown rage, there was hope that I could turn him around. Along with the techniques described above, I also found it useful to change the task requirement, or even the subject. ("So, I see you don't want to write just yet. Would you like to solve those math problems on the board instead?") My goal was to keep him in academics, to keep those skills growing, to allow him the feeling of work well done. With other students, I'd take the attitude, "If you don't want to do it now, I'll help you with it at recess," because it was effective. With Davonte I took the approach that "If I can't adjust this task to your liking, let's try a different task altogether."

## Academics

Davonte could not read well at the beginning of the school year, and I noticed that he was the only student who never raised his hand when we talked about and read our weekly classroom poem, which also provided us a means for word study. Early in the year, I decided to ask Davonte if he'd like to come up to the poem (written in large letters on easel paper) and point to and read for us some of the words he knew. He reluctantly sounded out several consonant-vowel-consonant words. The rest of the class was clearly proud of him, and it turned out that he rather liked the attention. (I want to make clear that the rest of the class did not belittle, pander to, or patronize Davonte with their praise; they sincerely felt proud of him. I understand that difference.)

We began making a habit of having Davonte contribute to our poem. I was aware that this was one way he could be part of the group even when what we were doing seemed over his head. I noticed that Davonte paid attention a bit longer when he was involved than when he was not participating. Also, getting Davonte up in front of his classmates to demonstrate his growing knowledge and skills began to spill over into other areas of our curriculum. I appreciated Davonte's need to be recognized, not as the naughty kid with the temper tantrums, but as a student who was acquiring skills and whose progress the rest of us could celebrate. In short, Davonte could become someone different than who he had been in our classroom in September. Providing Davonte with opportunities to define himself differently was, I think, critically important.

Because Davonte was restless and could be expected to sit for only a very short time when working, I began to put his math on the whiteboard. I wrote problems that took up nearly half the length of the room and taped a number line at Davonte's eye level. He began to enjoy choosing a marker and using the number line to solve single-digit addition and subtraction problems. Soon we moved to single-digit and double-digit problems. Presently we're working on problems with a missing addend (e.g., _____ + 5 = 10). In this way, I get Davonte to do math, and another child can go over his answers with him. I was afraid that Davonte's classmates would claim that it was unfair that Davonte got to do his math on the marker board. I am reminded of how humane this group of children is. They forgive, are always ready to offer another chance, and seem to accept that Davonte needs something different from our classroom than the rest of them do.

I have worked to get Davonte to see himself as a capable learner and as someone whose intelligence his teacher and classmates believe in. I am adamant about pointing out to my students the difference between intelligence and skills—how children can be lacking skills but be quite bright. We have studied important people for whom school was hard, such as Thurgood Marshall, Thomas Edison, Langston Hughes, Marian Anderson, Jacob Lawrence, and many others. We talk about how each did something important with their lives even though school was rough for them when they were young. I believe the discussions these studies provoke go a long way toward children rethinking their ideas of who is smart and to imagine possibilities for themselves. I can't be certain of the effect of our studies on Davonte. Sometimes he would choose to leave the blue rug at the very moment I thought he would relate to a topic. He did like our charades (when one of us acted out a person we'd studied for the rest to guess) and always chose Hank Aaron or Duke Ellington when it was his turn. Whether this was because those two men had inspiring stories or because they were easy to imitate (pretending to hit a baseball or pound on an imaginary piano) I couldn't tell.

We studied African Americans in American history. We read about George Washington Carver, Wilma Rudolph, Sojourner Truth, Harriet Tubman, Frederick Douglass, and many others. We wrote haikus to express our admiration of their lives. Sometimes Davonte seemed genuinely interested in the person we were reading about, but at other times he was disengaged from our work during this unit.

One strategy that I found worked well with Davonte was to focus on the positive, to find something to say that validated Davonte's learning. I admit that there were days when I felt beaten down by Davonte, when I didn't feel like trying once again to tweak the routine just for him, when I longed for him to be the one who would adjust a little. Those were my bad days, and my inflexibility did little to help Davonte or myself feel better. Fortunately, there were few days during which I'd insist he follow a routine that worked for the others but clearly not for him, because I learned that when I did, too much precious time was wasted.

## Sacred Time

Davonte needed more than his classmates did. He needed more instruction, more individualization, more patience, more thoughtful responses to his behavior. He needed more time with me to trust me. Sometime during the first quarter, I began to use the last 15 minutes of the morning as a time for Davonte and I to read. Nearly every day at 11 a.m., as the other students were completing their math work and moving into free choice, Davonte and I would take two chairs, pull them to the side, and read together. I did not allow others to interrupt us. No other child had privilege to such an arrangement.

Davonte liked this time, even though he had to exert effort. I read every other page of whichever book we had chosen so that he'd feel as if the burden was shared. But the fact is that once Davonte warmed up to the process, he liked reading to me. And the best part was when he would talk about a character or make predictions or comment on the story. He proved to be a thoughtful reader, and his decoding skills became stronger by the week. We progressed from Dr. Seuss's *Green Eggs and Ham* to Cynthia Rylant's *Henry and Mudge* by second semester.

In my view, reading brought out the best in Davonte. He was patient, he problem-solved without losing his temper, his voice was gentle and unaggressive, and he continually signaled his awareness of me, my ideas, and what I thought of the story as well as giving his own opinions. The time was sacred.

Two important things resulted from our sacred time. One was that Davonte was progressing at an incredible rate with his reading. I was told that he had become the top performer in his Title I group. The second was that Davonte was beginning to trust me. He became openly affectionate with me, throwing his arms around me when waiting for the bus after school. He continued to be moody and unpredictably angry, but there was another layer in our relationship that made all the difference, and I can only name it as trust. I began to trust Davonte, too. As I got to know him, I began to respect him more than I might otherwise have done if I hadn't carved out the time we spent together each morning.

My dad died in March, and I missed a week of school. I had told the kids stories about my dad, with whom I was very close, and the oldsters at the nursing home where he spent his final year. The stories were mostly funny ones, and the kids knew a little about my dad's life and our "wheelchair adventures."

When I returned after being away, my students carefully greeted me, telling me that they'd missed me and that they were glad that I was back. Most looked at the floor rather than at me. I was musing once again on our culture's weird attitude toward death, when I spotted Davonte out of the corner of my eye.

Davonte spotted me at my usual morning post, outside the classroom door greeting kids as they entered. He broke into a run and threw his arms around my waist tight. "Take me with you to the funeral!" he said.

## Two Steps Forward, One Step Back

Rakeem transferred to our classroom from another school at the end of the first semester. His former school had begun a building team on him because of behavior problems. Rakeem seemed to bring out the worst in Davonte and vice versa. It began with under-the-breath insults and escalated to physical aggression. If one or the other of the boys was absent, the day was invariably more peaceful. The tension between them seemed to erode much of the progress that Davonte had made.

I decided to keep the boys apart from each other (whether on the blue rug or in an instructional group) whenever I could, while at the same time encouraging smart problem solving. I modeled for them ways to express anger and resolve conflict. We worked on tone of voice and looking each other in the eye respectfully.

All this, or just the passage of time, helped defuse the tensions between Rakeem and Davonte. Rakeem continued to wrangle with Davonte on occasion, but he also did so with Robert and Jasmine and several others. In many ways he was more aggressive and felt slighted more easily than did Davonte ("What you lookin' at?"). As a class, we became more skilled with problem solving, asserting ourselves respectfully, and resisting bullying. Though we certainly didn't become perfectly well-behaved, we were becoming more savvy in our reactions to discord. Mostly this was done through group discussions and modeling and acknowledging good choices. When someone had hurt feelings or a sense of injustice, we processed the feelings rather than dismissing them.

School was especially hard for Davonte after a break. When he'd seem to have made such good progress (more participation, fewer outbursts, and so on) a break would come and, with both winter and spring break, Davonte did not return for more than a week after school resumed. When he did return, it was as if we did a rewind back to the beginning of the year. Fortunately, the progress we'd made was more quickly gained than the first time around. Yet, as with Rakeem's arrival, it would seem that just as things were looking pretty good, with better established habits and patterns, there'd be something that would sabotage our progress.

One indication that Davonte had backpedaled from the progress we'd made before a break was his relationship with a volunteer, Mary. She was a gentle woman who brought Davonte books and treats, and they read together twice a week. Over the course of the first semester, Davonte learned to trust Mary and only after a time went with her to the library without protest. After winter and spring break, he refused to read with her. As I write this, nearly a month since he has returned from spring break, he still refuses to read with Mary.

## SPRING

Most days now, Davonte joins us on the blue rug in the morning. He still interrupts, some days more than others, but he is also more likely to contribute, whether to the poem or the conversation. He still has trouble remembering to raise his hand, but the other kids cut him slack on this. His attention span is longer than it used to be, but after a quarter hour or so, restlessness sets in. Davonte will need something different, just when the other kids are getting deeper into discussion of our poem or the date in history or a math problem.

This is when I tell him he may invite someone to read with him. Often he does, and Davonte and a classmate will go to his bin of books to select something to share. At other times Davonte will listen to a book on tape or he'll park himself in front of the computer to do a math or word game.

More recently, he has come to school exhausted. He will sit at a table, put his head down, and fall asleep. Some days I ask the office to send someone to help him down to the nurse's office, where he can lie down and get a proper nap. Other days we simply let him doze.

Davonte has become a stronger reader and a better mathematician, and he can write a few sentences. He participates more in discussions, and kids are more willing to work with him than they were in September. He is working significantly below grade level (according to assessments) but he has made more progress than perhaps any of his classmates. Equally important, he interacts a little more with his classmates as he has gotten to know and trust them better through his one-on-one work with them. They are no longer as intimidated by his anger, which is expressed much less frequently than it was at the beginning of the year.

Not long ago Davonte read an entire stanza of our most recent poem, *The Song of Hiawatha* by Henry Wadsworth Longfellow. He raised his hand when we were dividing the long poem to read it aloud, and he read his part well. It was an important moment for us.

This is not to say there aren't still bad days; there are. Davonte still becomes angry when frustrated, and he continues to express his anger in destructive ways. Yet he is much more willing to process an incident with me and the class after he has calmed down, and he has not resorted to physical aggression in our classroom, as he sometimes does outside the classroom. He smiles more and stays with a task longer.

## WHAT I'VE LEARNED

I have learned how important it is to communicate daily to Davonte, in sincere ways, that I believe in his intelligence. It has been equally important to find positive things to say to him about his work or effort or himself. Corrections, I have learned, are best delivered gently, saving my most firm approach only when others' learning is disturbed. When correcting or redirecting Davonte in the group, I found it effective to stop, pause, get his attention gently, and tell him plainly why we don't like what he is doing (e.g., interrupting, being rude to another child, disrespecting the classroom). After a time, he appeared to recognize when his behavior was unfair to his classmates, because he would make quick and seemingly sincere apologies. Perhaps this was more potent after he had slowly built a relationship, through reading and math, with so many of the students in Room 102.

Spending one-on-one time with Davonte nearly every day for 15 to 20 minutes seemed to be the single effort that made the most difference in Davonte's academic progress and in his relationship with me.

I learned to not give up when Davonte was giving me all the messages that he was not interested in learning. While the class is working on a writing assignment, I will escort Davonte to the easel with markers and ask him about his day. He may turn away from me or grump at me, but when I make as if to go ahead anyway with the writing and ask him to help me spell a word, Davonte, body still turned away, head lost in his sweatshirt hood, will begin spelling the word. If I stay with it long enough, Davonte will rotate his body, his hood will come down, and he and I will be writing about his weekend.

I became better at knowing when enough is enough. For example, when the lower-skilled group and I sit around a table and practice the week's dictated sentences, Davonte can often do some but not all of the words. I praise him for what he's done, knowing he's at the end of his effort, and give him the rest to copy so he'll stay with us. Another way to keep him with us, I learned, was to give him the dictated sentence to read slowly for the group to write. Because this was a teacher role, the kids would, with amusement, call him "Mr. Davonte." "Mr. Davonte, would you repeat that please?" "Mr. Davonte, would you slow down some?" Davonte enjoyed this role immensely, and the group he was with seemed untroubled by the fact that Davonte was giving them their dictated sentence. Even Rakeem was okay with it, something I didn't expect.

Sometimes before school, after a bad day especially, having Davonte repeat a mantra seemed to have good effect. I'd say, "I'm here to learn. I will do math and become a better mathematician. I will read and become a stronger reader. I will write and become a better writer. I will respect this room and the people in it. I will do my best. I am smart. I will learn." Sentence by sentence, Davonte will half smile and repeat these sentences, and it seems to have a positive effect on the mood with which he approached his morning work.

Shortly before this writing, at the end of April, I decided that Davonte needed an incentive to accomplish more work in writing and math. He was doing well in reading but had made less progress in the other two areas.

Overcoming my own stubborn opposition to overt bribery, a brown bag with some reward inside that Davonte earns if he's completed his math and writing, as well as reading, has served the purpose to motivate him to accomplish more work. The more problems he has solved or sentences he has written, the better his work habits have become. If he has a bad day, the bag is there, with his name on it, for the next day he completes his daily work.

The apologies that I have required of Davonte over the course of the school year were not meant to humiliate him; rather they were meant to help him begin to own his own behavior. The apologies also helped Davonte's classmates know that he is trying, even as he messes up, and that when he is rude he takes responsibility for his behavior. They tell him, after every apology, that they forgive him, and I sense his apology helps them do that.

Preserving the dignity of this small boy in the classroom was paramount. I've long subscribed to the notion that the humanity of a classroom can be measured by how the least powerful are treated. I was mindful of this in the way our class embraced Davonte, but also held him accountable.

But it is also true that, as much as I tried to remain calm with Davonte, there were several times over the school year where I was just plain angry and I let Davonte know. For example, one morning in late March when Davonte returned to the classroom after being at Title I reading, he slumped over the table of an instructional group. We politely asked him to join us or go somewhere else, at which point he began angrily barking and growling at us. The kids repeated their pleas for him to stop. At this point, I decided to intervene. I picked him up and carried him down the hall. There, I met with the school counselor, who had been alerted by another teacher to help with a fight she'd witnessed between Davonte and another student in the hallway. Davonte had come to our classroom fresh from that "fight," which explained his aggression. My anger seemed to surprise him, and perhaps had the effect that he learned to recognize he had stepped over a boundary.

In the area of academics, it was important for me to know the sensible next step instructionally and to be always mindful of how easily Davonte became discouraged with schoolwork.

I learned that it also was helpful to offer Davonte many opportunities to share with the class what he'd learned. Though he got more attention than any of the other students, they seemed to understand his need, and they celebrated his accomplishments. He often read his writing (which he would dictate to me, I would write, and he would copy) to his classmates. The pride he took in sharing in such ways convinced me that he believed in himself as a learner, in his worth to our group. This was what was important to me, this was what I worked to have come about. This change from the beginning of the year was what pleased me most.

A student teacher, Ms. K., joined Room 102 for the second semester. Davonte avoided working with her and sometimes was disrespectful toward her (not following her directions, subverting her attempts to work with his group). He did not begin to trust her until well into second semester. I remember clearly the day we took the kids to the arboretum, pretending we were all Lewis and Clark recording unknown plants and animals west of the Mississippi River. That day, Davonte worked with Ms. K without resistance. She helped him draw a plant, measure it with a tape measure, and look at it through a magnifying glass. She recorded his words describing it as the two hunched over the plant together in the morning sun in the arboretum. It was near the end of April, and Ms. K had been with our class since the middle of January. Finally Davonte had begun to trust her.

## CONCLUSIONS

From my school year with Davonte, carefully observing and reflecting on what I could do to best help him learn, I concluded that:

1. Davonte's needs required that our classroom allow him more latitude. He had privileges that the other children did not, but they knew and I knew that he needed something different from the rest of them.

2. Davonte excelled when he could make his efforts public to the rest of the class, whether it was reading words from the poem we were studying or reading his story that he dictated to me and then copied.

3. Davonte viewed himself as a part of the group when he was given a role that empowered him in reference to his classmates. Allowing him to choose someone to read with or selecting a classmate with whom to go over his whiteboard math problems were particularly effective techniques. Later in the year, I found that asking Davonte to read the dictated sentences for his group made him feel academically powerful. The more academic power he felt, the less he seemed to need to get his power by tantrums or sabotage.

4. As the year progressed, I found that if I could set apart a time every day to spend alone with Davonte, our relationship became more successful. I grew to admire his intellect as he grew to trust me. When he did have his messy expressions of frustration-turned-to-anger, he was, as the year went on, more likely to want to rejoin the classroom sooner and apologize to our group more appropriately.

5. It helped to have Davonte repeat positive, affirming sentences before entering the classroom in the morning. At other times I reminded him of the purpose of school and of why we were here, hoping to catch him before he completely withdrew from an academic effort.

6. Requiring Davonte to take some responsibility for his choices was helpful. He could then bask in the glow of his classmates admiring and appreciating his work or accept their forgiveness if he had made the classroom feel unsafe.

7. I am quite sure that I would not have been able to work as I did with Davonte if I had 20 some kids in a classroom, rather than the 17-member SAGE group. I am familiar with working in a classroom of 25 or so kids, and have had much trouble finding the time to individualize for one, or creating the sort of community our class of 17 was able to make.

8. I have come to believe even more deeply in a kind of teaching that might be best called "relentless teaching." Relentless teaching is described as just that: teaching that is relentless (Borsuk, 2004). It works best, I think, for those who truly believe that every child is capable of learning and that learning is ultimately liberating.

## EPILOGUE

Looking back on my year with Davonte and considering how that year and my research shaped my teaching convinced me once again that each child is an individual and that my responses to my students should have more to do with their particular academic and social needs than with my general agenda. If there is one thing that Davonte taught me, a lesson relearned every time I pay close attention, it is this notion of each child having his own particular needs. In education we are so earnest to generalize from past experience to make our teaching lives better informed and more successful. The danger, for me, is that taking what I have learned with one child and applying it to another seemingly similar child does not give the next child the room to show me his or her particular needs.

That said, there are ways in which my year with Davonte has affected the way I teach. I am ever more aware of my power to redefine children's perceptions of themselves and their classmates. Making public a child's clear thinking or admiring aloud a student's work truly can alter the way a child sees himself as a learner. Acknowledging the thought that went into a response, even if—or especially when—the response did not accurately answer the question, also goes a long way to preserve the child's pride and show a child and his classmates that he is indeed an intelligent, competent learner. I have found this to be especially true for students who have been reluctant learners or not particularly successful in school. As important as this is for the child, it is equally important for the child's peers. When they begin to see their classmate in a way that causes them to respect him more, the old roles that kids assign to themselves and one another are rearranged and even upended. I saw how this deliberate approach gradually changed Davonte's belief in himself as a learner and his investment in our classroom community, and I have since seen how it has a similar effect on others.

I also have become more diligent about making certain that all my students are participating in their learning. If we are on the blue rug (in whole-group instruction, when it is easier for kids to tune out if they are so inclined), talking about a topic we have been studying, I am sure to call on those who might not be paying attention. I used to allow students with raised hands to carry the discussion forward. Now I tell my students that "checking out" is not an option. If they choose not to pay attention, then I will teach them individually at recess. And I follow up on this. After several recess tutorials with students who tended not to involve themselves in our class conversations, I now have much better participation and involvement. They know I will call on them even if they are not raising their hands. No longer am I the polite teacher who avoids inflicting discomfort on a child by calling on her when she doesn't know the answer. If she doesn't know, I find another way to teach or explain. Students become involved in this, often doing better than I in getting at an idea from another angle. Not knowing is not something to feel bad about, but not paying attention is. I like how this approach has transformed learning in my classroom, and I am aware that Davonte was the one who caused me to rethink the pattern of my instructional approach with reluctant learners.

The way in which I invest time in my students' learning has altered. If a child needs more time for learning place value or writing a sentence or reading a book, I am more likely to find that time. During silent reading, game time, or when a busy lull has settled in the classroom, I will make it my business to sidle up to a child who needs extra support on a skill or piece of work and give my time and attention. This is like the idea of relentless teaching that I refer to in my study, and it can be exhausting, because as a result there is less "downtime" for me in my classroom. The upside is that the students I am likely to spend the extra time with know that I believe in their capacity to learn. It is likely exhausting for them, too, but the effect has been that more of my students seem to be completing projects they are proud of or acquiring the skills they need to know.

Reading novels is one of the more important experiences in my life. To better appreciate the circumstances and forces that affect those with lives very different from my own, I have been reading more books by authors who I believe may help me better understand another view of the world. Recently I finished *The Known World* by Edward Jones, which examines the life of a former slave. Because Jones's book examines the life of a Black slaveholder in the Antebellum South, the story offered me yet another fascinating prism from which to view race and power. Presently I am reading Zadie Smith's books *White Teeth* and *On Beauty.* Her novels, particularly *On Beauty,* take on the culture wars from the perspective of those whose lives are directly influenced by them. I have recently read Geoffrey Canada's *Fist Stick Knife Gun,* which reveals the escalation of urban violence and offers a hopeful response to it. *The Fortress of Solitude* by Jonathan Letham explores a friendship across race, and the course two boys' lives play out, in part because of the color of their skin. Letham's book gave me yet another opportunity to question the ways in which people are assigned roles and to consider the possibilities of interrupting the patterns and habits that help create those roles. Books like *The Curious Incident of the Dog in the Night* by Mark Haddon and *The Discovery of Slowness* by Stan Nadolny have allowed me to consider the world from the point of view of a child who seems out of step with his peers.

Finally, I have been thinking more and more about the effects of poverty on the lives of my students. *The American Dream* by Jason DeParle speaks forcefully on this topic. I am frustrated that a parent can work full time yet still not significantly improve the circumstances of his or her life due to the disgrace of minimum wage and lack of opportunity. I am angry that we have neighborhoods in our city where children's lives are hemmed in by drugs and crime. I am ever more aware how difficult lives can be and how unfair it is to judge those who struggle daily with finances, transportation, health, and family challenges.

I am reminded again and again that the battle of the achievement gap ought to be fought on many fronts: housing, jobs, training opportunities, child care, living wage . . . I have recently read an article in *The New York Times* that describes a study that concludes that a child in a dysfunctional family living in a healthy neighborhood has a better chance of success than does a child in a functional family living in an unwholesome neighborhood. I am once again reminded that as we try to counter the effects of poverty on children's learning in the classroom, we are fighting for a civil right on but one front of a battle that needs so many advocates on so many fronts.

## SUGGESTED READING

Borsuk, A. J. (2004). Cavalcade of ideas. *Milwaukee Journal Sentinel,* May 22. Retrieved January 9, 2006, from www.jsonline.com/story/index.aspx?id=231173

Childress, A. (1988). *Rainbow Jordan.* New York: Avon Books.

Cose, E. (2003). *Envy of the world: On being a Black man in America.* New York: Washington Square Press.

Delpit, L. (1996). *Other people's children: Cultural conflict in the classroom.* New York: The New Press.

Gaines, E. (1997). *A lesson before dying.* New York: Vintage Books.

Gates, H. L. (1995). *Colored people: A memoir.* New York: Vintage Books.

Gates, H. L. (2004). *America beyond the color line with Henry Louis Gates* (PBS, February 3 and 4, 2004). (DVD at www.shoppbs.org)

Hall, A., & Mosiman, D. (2004). Life and death in Allied Drive. *Wisconsin State Journal,* April 19. Retrieved January 9, 2006, from www.madison.com/wisconsinstatejournal/allied/72613.php

Kotlowitz, A. (1992). *There are no children here: The story of two boys growing up in the other America.* New York: Anchor Books.

Lopate, P. (1996). *Being with children.* New York: The New Press.

McBride, J. (1996). *The color of water.* New York: Riverhead Books.

Morrison, T. (1987). *Beloved.* New Yok: New American Library.

Myers, W. D. (1989). *The young landlords.* New York: Puffin Books.

Myers, W. D. (1990). *Scorpions.* New York: Harper Trophy.

Naylor, G. (1992). *Bailey's café.* New York: Vintage Books.

Rylant, C. (1996). *Henry and Mudge.* New York: Aladdin Paperbacks.

Seuss, Dr. (1960). *Green eggs and ham.* New York: Random House.

Staples, B. (1994). *Parallel time: Growing up in black and white.* New York: Pantheon Books.

Taylor, D., & Dorsey-Gaines, C. (1988). *Growing up literate.* Portsmouth, NH: Heinemann.

West, D. (1996). *The wedding.* New York: Anchor Books.

X, Malcolm. (1987). *The autobiography of Malcolm X: As told to Alex Haley.* New York: Ballantine Books.

# 7

# But Then It Got Real

Jane Hammatt Kavaloski

## EDITORS' INTRODUCTION

Hammatt Kavaloski, a teacher at an alternative high school, attempts to increase students' engagement with schoolwork, improve students' perceptions of themselves, and positively impact academic achievement by implementing a service-learning project. Through interviews and observations, Hammatt Kavaloski captures her students' impressions as they prepare and implement lessons to teach sixth graders in a traditional middle school about Malcolm X. This study, an examination of the ways in which the teacher researcher uses reflective practice to develop and improve a curricular unit, provides readers with an example of the ways in which classroom inquiry can lead to sustainable change.

\* \* \* \* \*

## FIRST QUARTER—THE EXPERIMENT

I walk around the room, astonished at the hum of energy and activity that radiates from the clusters of middle and high school students scattered throughout the space. I hear the two Shabazz High School students in each group discussing the life of Malcolm X. They use stories, photos, timelines, and games to reinforce the main points of their lesson. I see looks of curiosity and concentration, as well as shyness, on the faces of the two or three sixth graders in each small group.

These small discussion groups are part of a "service-learning" project that is integrated into the curriculum of our orientation class for new students at Shabazz. The "service" for these high school students is teaching sixth-grade students who share our building about Malcolm X. We hope that this service-learning project will not only inform these middle school students about our school's namesake but also help bridge the gap between these two different programs—a public alternative high school and a traditional middle school.

But more important, we introduced service learning as a pedagogical technique. This service-learning project is an experiment in trying innovative ways to get new Shabazz students interested in studying Malcolm X (Shabazz). My Classroom Action Research project begins with the question: **Does service learning enhance academic achievement?**

My joy and satisfaction come from the sounds and sights before me that Friday morning in late October. Malcolm Shabazz City High School students, many with years of academic frustration and failure behind them, are successfully teaching sixth graders about Malcolm X!

It is exciting to know that we may have found a way to bring relevance and vitality into an academic assignment that Shabazz students have historically met with resistance or nonparticipation. Today these students are reinforcing their learning through the service of teaching!

## THE HISTORY OF OUR SCHOOL

Malcolm Shabazz City High School, a public alternative high school in Madison, Wisconsin, opened its doors in January 1971 for students who are not comfortable in their traditional high schools. A large proportion of the students have experienced harassment in their previous schools; many have significant academic or personal problems that interfere with their learning; and most are behind in credits before they come to Shabazz. The student body consists of a wide range of students who vary in academic skills, learning styles, race, disabilities, ethnicity, socioeconomic levels, and sexual orientation. At Shabazz, these students find a welcoming academic environment that promotes the values of nonharassment and community.

I am the school social worker and coordinator of service learning. Kate, an English teacher; Susan, our nurse and liaison with the middle school; and I team each quarter to teach the Shabazz Experience class. The purpose of this required orientation class is to introduce new students to the history and philosophy of Shabazz. As a final class project, we expect students to read *The Autobiography of Malcolm X.* Many years ago, the school's first class of students named the school for this articulate, self-educated, powerful African American leader.

Although we thought that reading *The Autobiography of Malcolm X* was an important assignment, the three of us were continually frustrated by the lack of student enthusiasm and interest. Some quarters, many of the chapter assignments were not turned in. Most students were unwilling to do the necessary preparation outside of class to adequately lead a discussion when it was their turn to teach a chapter. Others did not come to school on the day their presentation was due. Because the student-taught units were interdependent, when students were absent or unprepared the staff had to fill in the missing information as background for the next student presentation.

The dilemma at the end of each quarter was how to award credit for the class. Should we give credit when students made a serious effort to get to school and complete 80 percent of the work, even if they didn't finish the Malcolm X assignment? Or should we withhold credit if the Malcolm X work was not completed because we see that as the culminating assignment of the class?

We had tried many things. We offered varied reading materials and writing assignments. We experimented with cooperative groups and peer teaching. We changed the emphasis to a research project on Malcolm X, with his autobiography being one of several resources that could be used. But something was lacking. Many students were still failing to complete this assignment.

One fall when Kate, Susan, and I met to plan the class, I suggested that we experiment with a service-learning component. I wondered what would happen if we asked our students to teach the life and times of Malcolm X to the sixth graders at Sherman Middle School after the Shabazz students completed their research. My research question was: **Can service learning enhance academic achievement?**

## THE SERVICE-LEARNING PROJECT

These will be our academic expectations for this service-learning project.

1. Students must complete a research project about the life, work, and influence of Malcolm X.

2. Students must develop educational materials that demonstrate their knowledge of Malcolm X (essay, collage, timeline, game, and so on).

3. Students must use their educational materials to teach sixth graders about Malcolm X.

The new students are introduced to the concept of service learning by a group of students who have been at Shabazz for several semesters and have been involved in a variety of service-learning projects. These experienced students show a video, facilitate a discussion, and then share their own experiences.

Initially some of the new students express great anxiety about the expectation that they will teach sixth graders. To address these worries, Kate explains that the Sherman students will be divided into small groups. In addition, after students complete their individual projects, they will be grouped with other students with complementary personalities and learning styles. For example, a highly verbal student who has written an essay might team with a more visual learner who has created a timeline. Or a student who has created a board game about the stages of Malcolm X's life could team with a student who has made a colorful children's book.

After weeks of preparation, the day of our teaching experiment finally arrives! Small groups of high school and middle school students huddle together in small study circles in the sixth-grade classroom. Shabazz students who have created projects that necessitate using audiovisual equipment form circles in the library media center.

As I look around the classroom, I become aware of ways we can make this project better. A small number of the Shabazz students are not well prepared, which is evident as I watch them teach. In addition, these sixth-grade classes have some students who have great difficulty staying focused because of their special educational needs. This is a teaching challenge for which we did not prepare our students. I also wonder if the groups are too small. Most of the groups have two Shabazz students and two sixth graders, a ratio that seems uncomfortable for the younger students.

Despite these concerns, a sense of excitement and satisfaction predominates on that October morning. I remember how difficult it has been in the past to get new students involved in this assignment. Now, before me, is a testimonial to service learning as a means of increasing academic achievement. With only a few exceptions, these students have completed their research projects on Malcolm X, developed educational materials that demonstrate what they have learned, and are now using them to teach the life of Malcolm X to these sixth-grade students.

## THE REFLECTION PROCESS

A central part of service learning is reflection. Reflection can take various forms, and it needs to permeate the service-learning experience. We have three reflection sessions for each service-learning project. During the first reflection, we explore the methods that the students might use to demonstrate the knowledge they will acquire about Malcolm X. From the previous spring quarter, when Kate introduced Gardner's idea of "multiple intelligences," we gather a wide variety of sample projects created by the students in that previous Shabazz Experience class: collages, timelines, essays, children's books, and board games.

During the first reflection process, students are given time to analyze their own learning styles. They then brainstorm how they will use this information about themselves to approach the task of demonstrating their knowledge of Malcolm X. The educational materials that they create, after they complete their research, will be their teaching tools when the Shabazz students work with the sixth-grade classes. (See Appendix A.)

After the first reflection session, each student meets with one of the staff and completes a form that identifies the type of educational materials that he or she is planning to create. Although we are flexible about allowing the students to change media as their projects evolve, we feel that this early identification of project approaches is a good way to get students thinking about their learning and teaching strategies.

During the second reflection time, later in the quarter, the students have the opportunity to get feedback from their classmates about the project they have created. All the students present their projects on Malcolm X and demonstrate how they will use them as teaching tools with the sixth graders. Feedback is then solicited from other class members and the teachers.

Some typical suggestions include adding more information to a timeline, expanding a collage, or shortening an oral presentation. Questions about content help clarify what information students should be certain to include in their presentations. The teachers encourage the students to consider ways to make their presentations more interactive and participatory.

For the most part, feedback is extremely supportive. Students take delight in the creativity of their classmates. This trial run is a great way to bolster self-confidence and to finalize preparations for the actual teaching experience.

The third reflection session occurs after the teaching, when the students share their opinions and feelings about the experience. Because my colleagues and I have been experimenting with service learning this quarter, we are very interested in these students' reactions. We know that the academic expectations have been raised significantly from previous quarters. Not only are students expected to do a research project about Malcolm X, but they also are expected to create educational materials and then use them to teach sixth graders about Malcolm X.

I place felt-tipped pens, Play-Doh, and paper in the middle of our circle. I ask students to write, draw, or sculpt their answer to the question, "How do you feel about the teaching experience that you had on Friday?"

During the ensuing silence, reflective essays, vividly colored drawings, and sculpted figures emerge. We have learned from experience that providing a variety of ways to engage students in reflection increases the quality of the analyses.

## STUDENT REFLECTIONS

Among those who feel negatively about this experience are five students who did not prepare well for their presentations. It is interesting that their reflections do not touch on their own lack of preparedness. Here are some of the comments:

Jake creates a skull with Play-Doh: "I made a little skull because all they cared about was the death. I sort of felt it was a waste of time. But thinking about myself in sixth grade, I was pretty messed up."

Amy holds up a drawing and says: "I drew a smiling face because it was fun. Our kids were kind of stupid because they just sat there and laughed. I just read the stuff to them. They made us feel stupid because we were trying to teach them stuff they were not interested in."

Another group of 10 students was well prepared but raise concerns about the relevance of the activity for sixth graders. Some of them had students who had difficulty concentrating. Others did not get sufficient feedback from the sixth graders to know if they understood the lesson. And still others of this group wonder if what they taught would be remembered. Here are some of their comments:

June, whose mother had told me that her daughter hadn't been so excited about a project since fifth grade, wrote about her difficulty in getting the sixth graders interested in her excellent presentation:

> My feelings about our presentation to the sixth graders are mixed. Henry and myself had a lot of good ideas but the two kids weren't very interactive. I felt like we were on two different wavelengths and the kids weren't getting all the information. I was kind of disappointed.

At that point another student offered her support: "You can't blame them. They're in middle school."

The most negative comment came from an African American young man, who had worked very hard on this presentation.

> I think it was dumb because the kids didn't want to be there and I didn't either. They didn't know who Malcolm X was . . . It was worthless for sixth graders. They didn't care. Seventh or eighth graders

would be better. A waste of our time and theirs. In sixth grade they don't really care about Malcolm X or learning things—just care about playing football or whatever. I'd rather spend the time in class writing about the project—that's how much a waste of time I thought it was.

However, the remaining 11 students who participated in this final reflection said that the service-learning experience was very positive. Here are three of their reflections:

Ben, a Latin American student who had come to live in the United States this fall, shared his written reflection.

I felt really good. I thought I was going to be nervous but I wasn't. I also thought that I wasn't going to be able to express my thoughts and what I wanted to say in English, so I really felt very good and comfortable. What really felt good was when they [sixth graders] said what they had learned. It was nice to see what they said because I saw that they really paid attention to what Dan and I were saying. I was glad that I was able to teach someone. I liked it very much. It was a good experience.

Jeff, who previously had been in a class for emotionally disturbed students, read his reflection:

The way I felt was kind of important because they didn't know that much about Malcolm X. And thanks to me and Jill they hopefully know more about him. I feel very good about opening up their minds a little bit to what Malcolm X went through in his life. And teaching them why Malcolm matters today.

Darrell, who felt he was "treated like cattle" in his previous high school, wrote perceptively about his teaching experience. Although we did not know it at the time, Darrell and his partner had the only emotional disturbed student in the class. The extremely withdrawn girl appeared frightened by the two Shabazz students who became her "teachers" in this activity. Darrell's comments capture for me the frustrations, challenges, and joys of being a teacher:

Teaching was, well, interesting. When I walked into the room, I thought it would be a breeze—we were prepared, excited, and confident. BUT THEN THINGS TURNED REAL! There weren't any desks for us to sit in, so we sat around a cluttered table. The student was basically terrified of us. (I don't even know her name

because she couldn't speak past a mumble.) As we talked, I realized we had no real way of knowing whether or not she was listening, whether or not she understood, or whether or not she
cared. It was unnerving. But when we finished, and the [middle
school] teacher asked for the kids to tell him what they learned,
she raised her hand to make a comparison between Martin Luther
King, Jr., and Malcolm X. It was extremely satisfying. Maybe I would
like to be a teacher!

## LESSONS LEARNED

As I reflect on this feedback, I am very pleased with these initial results.
We seem to have broken through the resistance that the Malcolm X assignment had previously created for many students. Certainly the creativity,
energy, and commitment to learning exhibited within this service-learning
project surpassed any we had previously witnessed in this orientation
class.

Despite the heightened academic expectations, there is an increase in
the number of students who got credit for the class. Of the 42 students in
Shabazz Experience during the first quarter, 34 received credit. (We always
have a double class of new students in the first quarter to replace the
students who have graduated, been dropped, or transferred in June.) Of
the eight students who didn't get credit, four did not get credit because
they did not meet our attendance requirement. So of the 42 students, only
four did not get credit for academic reasons alone!

We are pleased to see that service learning seems to be increasing the
academic achievement rate of our students. Despite the fact that we have
intensified the academic expectations, more students are completing this
final assignment. However, I realize that there are ways we can make this
service-learning experience even more beneficial.We need to make certain
that students are adequately prepared. Those who had not completed their
presentations in time to share them with their peers during the second
reflection session generally did not have their projects done later when the
day came to teach.

We need to talk more about strategies for teaching students with special
needs. Some of the sixth graders had learning needs that were extremely
challenging for high school students. These students' inattentiveness and
lack of responsiveness were a source of disappointment for some Shabazz
students, who had worked hard on their presentations.

We also need to talk about the importance of the Shabazz students creating a supportive atmosphere before they begin teaching the sixth graders.

Many of our students didn't introduce themselves or ask the sixth graders for their names.

We need a higher proportion of middle school students to Shabazz students. The smaller groups appeared intimidating to some of the younger students.

We need to have a regular feedback mechanism that will show the Shabazz students how much the sixth graders understood of the lesson. Some of our students were left wondering if the sixth graders understood anything about their presentations.

But most important, our students need another experience with service learning before they teach the Malcolm X unit. When that is the only service-learning opportunity in the class, the Shabazz students cannot fully benefit from the final reflection session.

I want the students to have an opportunity to integrate their insights from the first teaching experience into their preparation for teaching the Malcolm X unit.

## DEEPENING THE PRACTICE

### Background Information

The biggest challenge this quarter is the Shabazz students themselves. As a staff, we are used to students who have become alienated from formal schooling, who have little confidence in their ability as learners, and/or who have personal issues that make it difficult to experience academic success. Generally, curiosity or desperation draws students to investigate Malcolm Shabazz City High School. These students come in for an interview and, if selected, usually are willing to give this alternative school a try.

But in the first week, three of the new students are dropped for lack of attendance, and one decides to stay at her previous school. The majority of the remaining students struggle to make it to school on a regular basis. Without a doubt, this is one of the least engaged groups of new students we have encountered in years.

However, I am determined to continue the service-learning dimension of the class. It will be interesting to see if the teaching responsibility will propel this group of students to achieve greater academic success. Since we have made a commitment to work with every sixth-grade class this year, we will be with a different sixth-grade teacher this quarter.

As Kate, Susan, and I review the lessons from the first quarter, we want to make certain that we integrate our suggestions into this new service-learning project. We definitely want the students in the Shabazz Experience class to have two service-learning experiences. The Shabazz students will then have the chance to learn from their first teaching experience before they undertake the challenging assignment of teaching about Malcolm X. In addition, the sixth graders will have two opportunities to spend time with Shabazz students.

## First Teaching Experience

To make this added teaching responsibility feasible in the time we have, Kate, Susan, and I want to have our students teach a topic that is already in the Shabazz Experience curriculum. Because developing conflict resolution skills is an important goal at both the middle school and Shabazz, we decide to experiment by having our students teach a session on "alternatives to violence."

As we did during the first quarter, we introduce the concept of service learning before we begin preparing the students for their first teaching experience. Instead of having other Shabazz students help with this presentation, we decide to use written handouts. Attendance is a problem, and handouts can be given later to any students who might be missing on the day we discuss service learning. We distribute and discuss the overall model of service learning. We feel that it is important that students understand the rationale and dimensions of the big picture of what they are doing.

Next we spend several days having students study various learning styles as well as analyzing their own. We have them brainstorm the teaching strategies that were the most effective for them when they were sixth graders.

Then the students study the Shabazz nonharassment policy. They also hear from older students about the importance of conflict resolution in our own educational community at Shabazz. At the end of the week, we ask our students to plan a presentation on alternatives to violence for the sixth graders. The high school students are to utilize the information from our previous conversations about learning styles and to create activities for teaching conflict resolution. The Shabazz students will have approximately 40 minutes to present alternatives to violence in a way that is understandable for the middle school students.

An initial reflective brainstorm is used to help students clarify the task and the various activities that they might use. We also talk about the importance of being well prepared so that the sixth graders stay interested. We then divide the students into pairs, again taking into account their variety of personal skills and learning styles. Each pair can design its own lesson plan for this topic.

We schedule a second reflection so that students can give feedback to their peers about the quality of the projects they have created. As before, we hope to provide the class with an opportunity for peer review before they do the actual teaching. However, when the day for the second reflection arrives the students are either absent or have not completed their projects, so this opportunity for feedback is missed. True to our original observations about this class, they remain a challenge!

Because we had overlooked the special education needs of the sixth graders last quarter, Susan interviews the sixth-grade teacher with whom we will be working this quarter to gain insights into the learning needs of her students. Susan then offers this description of the sixth-grade class:

> There are no children who should present discipline problems. However, there are four cognitively delayed students, who will be with their educational assistants. You may not be able to identify these students, except that they may look like they don't care.

This is helpful feedback because one of the biggest frustrations last time was that the Shabazz students did not know if the middle school students understood what was being said. We encourage our students to ask questions of the sixth graders throughout their presentations. That way the Shabazz students will know if they need to repeat information or present some ideas in another way.

We also remind the Shabazz students that it is important to create a comfortable and supportive atmosphere. We suggest that each group begin by having the members introduce themselves.

When the day comes, our original pairs have to be rearranged because several Shabazz students are absent. There are two groups with the original pairs of students and two newly formed groups with three Shabazz students. This time there are five or six sixth graders in each group, making it a less intimidating ratio for the younger students.

As before, after this teaching assignment, I ask the Shabazz students to reflect on their experience by writing, drawing, or sculpting their reactions.

## Student Reflections

The tone of the reflections once again varies and largely depends on how well the Shabazz students prepared for their teaching. One team of three students whose presentation was didactic and uncreative complained about the students.

Amy, who said nothing during the presentation and looked as if she wanted to escape, holds up a white blob of Play-Doh and explains: "I made this because I thought it was boring and dull. Kids didn't listen very well. It was hard to get them to, except for one kid."

Mary shows her collage-like picture with faces and quotes from the students. "Ingrates" is written on the bottom of the paper. "The kid with teeth," she says, pointing to one of the faces, "said that all this talk made him want to go out and fight."

At this point, we could ask these students to think about the relationship between the quality of their presentation and the sixth graders' lack of interest in the topic. However, Kate and I decide to postpone this discussion. Teaching these sixth graders involves extensive risk taking for most of our students. We want the reflection process to be a safe place to honestly express feelings about the experience. Later we will share our concerns as the Shabazz students plan for teaching about Malcolm X. It is important for our students to see the relationship between their being prepared for the teaching responsibility and the sixth graders' interest in the lesson.

Although the previous, small group of students was negative about the experience, the rest of the students were pleased.

Ellie's written reflection shows her satisfaction:

When I was working with the sixth graders, it made me feel very good because I knew that out of those six kids I was talking with, at least one or two of them will think about what we talked about. When they get into a problem they might think about what we talked about and how to avoid fighting . . . It just makes me feel good I did something good.

On the day of the teaching I found Paula, a Latin American student who had not attended school for more than a year, hiding in another room of our building. She had to be coaxed to go to the sixth-grade classroom with the other students. Since she had nothing prepared, I told her that for today I just wanted her to sit with one of the groups and listen. For her reflection, she creates a teacher made of Play-Doh. "We got through to those kids. They were sitting and listening. It wasn't as bad as I thought it would be."

After these reflections, we show the students the thank-you notes each of the sixth graders had written. They all express positive feelings about the Shabazz students. Our students acknowledge that the middle school students seem to look up to them.

Kate expresses how proud she is that, despite some frustrations, they all stayed "professional" during this first teaching experience. I share with the students my impressions that it appears to work best when they, as teachers, are well prepared, have interactive activities, and have a back-up activity in case they finish the lesson early.

## Second Teaching Experience

As we anticipated, this group of students had a difficult time preparing for the Malcolm X teaching experience. In a preservice reflection, they identify the approaches they might use to teach the information about Malcolm X, such as collages, essays, timelines, comic books, and puzzles. However, they have difficulty organizing their time and materials. As usual we give them time in class, but we also tell them that some of the preparations will have to be done as homework.

When the day for our "peer review" reflection arrives, many students, again, are not ready to share their projects and others are absent. Needless to say, as the day of our second teaching experience approaches, Kate, Susan, and I wonder if we are going to be able to follow through with our commitment to the sixth-grade teacher.

To our relief and surprise, as the teaching day nears, projects begin to appear. Several students are working frantically on their final touches until the moment we leave our classroom and go to the other side of the building. As we walk down the hallway, I look around and realize that our students are much better prepared than we could have imagined several days ago. Several of the extremely shy students insist that they will not say a word during the session but will offer their visuals to be used as teaching tools by the more verbal Shabazz students in their groups.

When we enter the room, the sixth-grade students seem happy to see us and call out: "The Shabazz students are back!" Since this is our second visit to this class, the transition into small groups is easier. Again, there are four groups with five or six middle school students and two or three students from Shabazz. The sixth graders are excited to see the materials that the Shabazz students have created for them.

Andrew, who said nothing last time and doesn't want to say anything now, carries his large, complex, and beautifully designed timeline and collage. He puts it in the middle of a circle of desks and tells the sixth graders to read it. Eagerly they huddle together—bodies balanced on the tops of their chairs, heads touching, with legs radiating out from the center like the spokes of a wheel. Several students begin reading different sections at the same time. At first Andrew looks bewildered. Amy, who was extremely uncomfortable last time, moves in closer and says a few things. When I suggest that the sixth graders take turns reading the collage out loud, Ellie, the third Shabazz student, easily moves into a leadership role and facilitates the discussion.

In another corner, Shabazz students Carrie, Jodie, and Mick have a group consisting of cognitively delayed and regular education students. Jodie and Mick do little talking, but Carrie, who 15 minutes earlier had been crying about a family crisis, rises to the occasion. Carrie is the only student who, after reading *The Autobiography of Malcolm X,* answered all the chapter questions for double credit. She obviously enjoys sharing her knowledge. Carrie had created a puzzle but it was not completely finished. Mick made a timeline but left it in his locker. Jodie, who also refuses to talk, holds up her enormous timeline, on which she has written the significant events in Malcolm X's life. Though Jodie and Mick are silent most of the time, they do get involved minimally.

Joan and Arnie sit in a circle on the floor. Joan has created an enormous timeline and collage using copies of photographs of Malcolm X, his family, Elijah Mohammed, and Dr. Martin Luther King, Jr. Joan talks about the life of Malcolm X, pointing to the photographs to illustrate her points.

In the fourth corner of the room, Annalisa talks to the sixth graders in her group, using a timeline created by Neal. Just moments before we left the classroom, Annalisa was frantically writing down important dates in Malcolm X's life. Her dual responsibilities as mother and high school student often make keeping up with assignments difficult. At the last moment, Annalisa asked if she could take some of the candy from my office. She had the idea of making her group's presentation into a quiz game, with candy as prizes for the right answers. Now she has the rapt attention of the students because they know the reward for remembering the facts. Later, squeals of glee are heard as Annalisa and Neal hand out the treats.

Because the Shabazz students from last quarter were so concerned about Malcolm X being too difficult a topic for sixth graders, I ask the sixth-grade teacher to spend a few minutes at the end of the session asking each group what they have learned about this man. To the delight and surprise of the Shabazz students, the sixth graders have little difficulty answering their teacher's questions about Malcolm X's life and work.

As we walk back to the Shabazz side of our building, it is obvious that these students are proud of what they have accomplished. Susan, Kate, and I look at each other—so are we! Again, service learning has pushed these students to meet our academic expectations. I seriously doubt that this group of students would have completed the Malcolm X assignment without this added service-learning responsibility. The Shabazz students felt accountable to the sixth graders and, for the most part, they wanted to do a good job. With these students, I doubt that a traditional research project or final examination would have resulted in their wanting to do this well.

## Student Reflections

Here are two student comments from our third reflection. Amy, who had been so withdrawn during the first teaching experience, shares her insights: "Teaching about Malcolm was easier and it made me understand about his life better. I enjoyed it more than the 'resolving conflicts.' The children listened better." She then added, "I think they were interested and they did understand. I felt better than I did last time."

Joan holds up a Play-Doh model of a sixth grader's face, with mouth open. "They didn't seem too excited—either they were really tired or maybe I was tired and bored them. But I liked the kids." Then she said that having this as a service-learning project had helped her planning:

> It does change how I went about the assignment. You have to think about what would grab their attention and make it interesting. It made it easier to keep in mind what I was supposed to do. With other papers or things I have to do, there's a big gap about what's expected or if the final product is right. With this, you know exactly what is expected.

## THE LESSONS FROM OUR SECOND QUARTER

As I think about our experiences over the past nine weeks, I wonder how well we integrated our lessons from the first quarter into the second quarter's experience.

Although we stressed the importance of being well prepared, this group had more difficulty getting ready than the last group. However, when the day came for teaching about Malcolm X, *everyone* had a project.

It worked well to talk more about teaching strategies for students with special needs. Although for the most part this was an attentive group of sixth graders, the cognitively delayed students did present a challenge.

The ratio of two Shabazz students to five or six middle school students was much better. This was a much less intimidating atmosphere for the sixth graders and made the discussion easier for the high school students.

It was valuable for the sixth-grade teacher to ask her students questions at the end of the session. This feedback helped the Shabazz students know that they had been understood. It is interesting that this time there were no complaints from Shabazz students that the topic of Malcolm X was too difficult for sixth graders.

Having two teaching opportunities gave our students the chance to learn from their first teaching experiences. Feedback from the first post-teaching reflection was integrated into the preparations for the Malcolm X assignment. This made the second teaching experience more rewarding, both academically and personally.

Despite our reservations about the motivation and academic skills of this particular group of students, they far exceeded our original expectations. The majority of them met our increased academic expectations for this quarter, which were to: complete two research projects (the second far more extensive than the first); create two sets of educational materials to demonstrate what they had learned; and teach sixth graders, incorporating their assessments of the first teaching experience into the planning and implementation of the second.

Of the 15 students who continued with the class after the first week, six did not get credit because they failed to meet the attendance requirement.

Despite the fact that this was an unusually challenging group to motivate, every student who attended regularly also completed the Malcolm X assignment. In the past, it was usually this final research project about Malcolm X that was not completed and thereby jeopardized students' getting credit in the class. The service-learning responsibility of teaching the sixth graders motivated these students to higher levels of academic accountability. Learning through teaching has enhanced their academic achievement!

However, as we plan for third quarter, we ask ourselves if there are still ways to improve this service-learning experience to foster even greater academic success. I feel that I need to develop a checklist for monitoring the various steps in implementing this service-learning class. We have found that it is important to follow certain sequential steps in our teaching to assist the students in meeting these higher academic expectations. In addition, Kate decides that next quarter, she would like to develop "rubrics" for the class so that students have clearer expectations about how they will be evaluated. Because rubrics were the focus of Kate's Classroom Action Research project two years ago, it is exciting to see our two research projects merge.

## THIRD QUARTER:
## BECOMING MORE INTENTIONAL

Because of the success of our service-learning experiment during the first and second quarters, I am interested in identifying the sequence of teaching strategies that reinforce academic success in this service-learning class. Since this class now includes two service-learning experiences, the necessary steps in the preparation and reflection have become somewhat complex. I create a "service-learning checklist" for Kate, Susan, and me to follow (see Appendix B).

It is apparent during the first few days of the third quarter that this new group of students in the Shabazz Experience class is very different from the previous group. By comparison, these new students appear more motivated and excited about being at Shabazz. There is a positive, inquisitive energy as they gather each morning. Kate distributes the course expectations and the rubrics (see Appendix C) that she has created. Instead of developing rubrics for the entire course, she has developed a set solely for the Malcolm X service-learning project.

In contrast to last quarter's students, who barely had their educational materials ready by the day they had to teach, this group of students begins working on the Malcolm X projects right away. With minimal prompting from us, some begin to do the necessary research and create their projects in their spare time. Students periodically ask if they can have time in class to work on their "Malcolm project." Since we see this project as their end-of-the-quarter assignment, we continue to follow our sequence and post-pone this classroom planning time until later in the quarter. However, we distribute *The Autobiography of Malcolm X* and other materials to help students begin their independent research.

## Preparation

As usual, Kate, Susan, and I use group-building activities with the Shabazz Experience students during the first week of the class. Since the students are new to Shabazz and may have negative feelings about their previous school experiences, it is important to build a sense of community from the beginning.

By the second week, we begin formal instruction about the definition, components, and steps of service learning. Initially this teaching is done by showing a video, holding group discussions, and distributing handouts. However, the most effective method is to have students who have already taken service-learning classes come in and talk about their experiences. For example, some students have taken an English class in which they did advocacy work for political prisoners through Amnesty International. Other Shabazz students built a greenhouse to expand the science program last spring. Two classrooms teamed up to create personalized children's books for kindergarten students as part of their Children's Literature or Graphic Art assignments. African Studies students created learning centers for younger children to learn about Africa. Social Studies students did service-learning projects in Mississippi and Appalachia. These stories intrigue and inform the Shabazz Experience students, many of whom have never heard of service learning.

Then we move to an exploration of "learning styles" and "multiple intelligences." Since many of our students have experienced academic frustration and failure in other settings, identifying their personal learning styles is an important strategy for taking responsibility for their own learning. Students are given a variety of inventories that they can use to decipher their own intellectual strengths and learning patterns. This information can then be used to help them approach future academic assignments.

The students are reminded of the attendance policy and academic expectations for this course. In order to receive credit, they must meet the attendance requirement. In addition, they must complete two research projects (one about "alternatives to violence" and the other about Malcolm X), create educational materials that demonstrate their knowledge of these topics, and use their educational materials to teach sixth graders.

Several weeks into the quarter, we begin preparing the Shabazz students to teach the "alternatives to violence" lesson to the sixth graders. Again we present information about the conflict cycle and have them analyze their personal responses to conflict. Then we study the school's nonharassment policy and have a student panel discuss why a harassment-free environment is important at Shabazz. The panel also explains that a student can be dropped from our program if he or she repeatedly violates the nonharassment policy.

## First Teaching Experience

Kate, Susan, and I facilitate a discussion of conflict resolution strategies. After that, we have our first reflection. Again students brainstorm about possible ways to teach "alternatives to violence" to a small group of sixth graders. The students create two lists: one of points they might emphasize in their presentations and the other of media that might be effective for accommodating the sixth graders' various learning styles.

The second reflection is the "peer review." At first we thought it was adequate that the pairs of students simply give an overview of their activities. However, we have learned that we need to break the large group down into several subgroups so the students can actually practice their presentations. It is clear that we also need to develop rubrics for these "alternatives to violence" projects. These rubrics could then be used by the students to assess each other's work.

Before the actual teaching experience, students need to know if there are any special learning needs among the sixth graders. Whenever possible, we have the sixth-grade teacher come to our class to describe his or her students and to answer any questions from the Shabazz students.

For the third reflection (after the students have taught "alternatives to violence"), students use colored pens, pencils, or Play-Doh to share their reactions to the initial teaching experience. The question they are asked to respond to is: "What did I learn from this first teaching experience that will help me plan for the next one?" Here are two responses.

Vince, an African American boy who had previously dropped out of school, thoughtfully analyzes how he wants to improve his teaching:

I learned that I should give something more fun and active because they would be more into such activities than they were with ours. They were listening and answering questions, but I noticed that they were looking at George and Lenny's skit [in another group] and it caught a lot of their attention. I feel good because there were students listening to what I was saying and I got to teach them about harassment.

Mary easily recognizes one of the challenges of teaching:

I learned from the sixth graders' discussion that we needed to have planned more questions for discussions—or things to say. We had to just ramble on at the end. We are lucky that we didn't have a group that was not talkative. We would have died.

Kate and I record the feedback from this reflection and then incorporate it into the students' plans for teaching about Malcolm X.

## Second Teaching Experience

As we prepare for our second service-learning project, we follow the pattern we had established earlier. The first reflection concerns the possible ways the Shabazz students can teach about Malcolm X. Again, we show the class previous projects. Then, using a form that Susan created, students identify what media they might want to use for their projects.

Kate develops step-by-step guidelines (see Appendix D) for creating the Malcolm X projects. Since the majority of our students this quarter learn more from reading printed materials than from hearing information, it is important that we give them written directions.

As before, final preparation includes the integration of student and teacher feedback from the first teaching experience. We learned that some of the sixth-grade students read at a first-grade level, so they had difficulty with some of the handouts that our students had created. These students will need to be paired with another sixth grader if there are worksheets again. In addition, the learning disabilities teacher suggested that the Shabazz students not sit together, but space themselves at intervals around the circle. This helps to keep the sixth graders more focused during the presentation.

The Shabazz students also acknowledge that the sixth graders were most interested in participatory and hands-on activities, as opposed to more didactic presentations. This is helpful information for planning their teaching strategies.

As the projects are completed, Kate forms pairs or trios to be teaching teams. As before, these groupings include a variety of learning and teaching styles.

The important addition in the third quarter is the introduction of the evaluative rubrics (see Appendix C) for assessing student achievement in three categories: their knowledge of Malcolm X, the quality of the project, and their teaching ability.

After the students' planning is completed, the rubrics are used during the second reflection. The students are divided into small groups, and the teaching teams practice their presentations with each other. After each presentation, their peers rate the team members using the evaluative rubrics. Experience has shown that, with some preparation, most students are honest in assessing each other and themselves. If anyone falls below the "achieved" level in any category, the student is encouraged to make the necessary improvements to reach the required standard. Credit will be given to students who reach an "achieved" level in all categories.

Again, the quarter ends with the students teaching the sixth graders about Malcolm X. This activity remains the culmination of our Shabazz Experience class. Many of the students in this class have been preparing for this day for six weeks or more. They have created beautifully designed posters, games, books, and timelines. On the day of the Malcolm X presentations, all the teaching teams participate. Kate, Susan, and I divide ourselves among the different groups so we can observe and assess the groups according to the rubrics for the assignment. To our delight, all but one pair of students reach the "achieved" levels! Many of the students even reach the "exceeded" level! Again, service learning has enhanced academic achievement!

I decide to change the final reflection question this time. I want to know how this group of students feels about service learning as a methodology. Therefore I create a scale for this third reflection. First I ask the students to rank service learning on a scale of 1 to 5, with 1 meaning "I don't like this style of learning," 5 meaning "I like this style of learning very much," and 3 meaning "I am neutral." I then ask the students to write, draw, or sculpt why they chose the numbers they did. Here are some of their responses:

Amy, a student who had had problems with truancy in her former school, spent hours creating an elaborate and interesting game about Malcolm's life.

> I think, referring to the scale, service learning would be a 4 or 5. I think it's a great way to learn and teach, and everybody gets involved. The result is usually successful and beneficial, from what I know.

Jake clearly improved in his teaching skills from the first experience.

> I liked teaching this group of kids. Everything went well; they were very attentive and asked lots of questions. They also retained the information well. They liked watching the video. I gave service learning a 5 because it helps the teachers [the Shabazz students] retain the info, and getting up in front of groups is good experience.

To my delight, all the African American students (six males) in the class rank service learning as a 5. Because I have seen their enthusiasm and commitment for this project, their responses do not surprise me. I wonder if service learning is a pedagogical strategy to reengage these students for whom American public education has been the least responsive!

Here are two responses from these students. Conrad writes:

> I think service learning is the best thing that has happened to me since I've been in school. [My other] high school didn't take out time to see that people are different. They called it "learning disabilities," but here at Shabazz it means "learning differently."

Dan, who admits that in his previous school he attended only his weight training class, takes pride in his teaching responsibilities.

> I like doing service learning because you don't just sit in class and take notes or read out of a book. It seems like it gives a reason for what you learn. Also, while I'm expanding my knowledge, I make something that will teach other kids too, whether it be a speech, presentation, or book. Also, I like doing presentations in front of a crowd. I am good at it.

The 16 students who participated in this reflection gave service learning an average ranking of 4.5. To me this is a remarkable rating when you consider that we are asking students, many of whom had previously felt extremely alienated from formal schooling, to become "teachers" of younger students within the first quarter of their being at Shabazz.

The ability of these new students to get credit in this first hour class continues to be hampered by attendance and tardiness problems. Out of 22 students, two young women eventually dropped out of school. Of the 20 remaining, 12 received credit for the class; three received "in progress" and complete missing assignments later; and five did not get credit. However, four of these five did not meet our attendance policy.

Only one student who met our attendance policy did not get credit for the class this quarter. A bright and capable young man, he thought he could "wing it" when he did his service-learning projects. His preparation and teaching were not at the "achieved" level on our evaluative rubrics, and so he did not receive credit despite having good attendance.

## THE LESSONS FROM THIRD QUARTER

Again I reflect on the lessons we have learned from this quarter.

The service-learning checklist helps staff members keep track of the steps in this form of teaching. We have found that it is important to follow these sequential steps in order to empower students to achieve the higher academic expectations of this service-learning class.

The evaluative rubrics provide students with the standards by which they will be evaluated. In addition, these rubrics help with peer review and with the teachers' evaluation of the service-learning projects.

We seem to have developed a style of teaching and learning that meets the needs of a wide range of students. (The students gave this form of learning an average score of 4.5 on a 5-point scale, with 5 meaning "I like this form of learning very much.") I am especially interested in the response of the six African American males, who all give service learning the highest rating of 5.0.

## SUMMARY

The year began with a service-learning experiment in the Shabazz Experience class. For some time, the three teachers in the class had been concerned about the large number of students who do not get credit in this orientation class. Aside from attendance concerns, many students did not complete their Malcolm X assignments. Because the Malcolm X project was the culminating project for the class, it weighted heavily in the students' final evaluation. Since this class is designed to be an introduction to Shabazz, we wanted it to be a successful experience for as many students as possible. But at the same time we did not want to compromise our academic standards.

For the first quarter, we initiated a service project in which the students taught what they had learned about Malcolm X to the sixth graders who share our building. We immediately saw an increase in motivation and preparation with this service responsibility. After that experience, however, we realized that we needed to add another teaching opportunity, so that students would be able to benefit from their reflections after their first teaching experience.

For the second and third quarters, we added the responsibility of teaching "alternatives to violence" midway through the quarter. We also integrated more reflection time, information about teaching strategies, and rubrics for evaluating the projects.

The two service-learning projects that were integrated into the Shabazz Experience class added a new relevance and importance to the academic work. Service learning met the needs of students with a wide variety of learning styles and cultural backgrounds. It helped students further develop their research, planning, assessment, and communication skills. Through this teaching and learning experience, all our students have had the opportunity to assume leadership roles. Students who have greatly disliked school now experience the frustrations, challenges, and joys of being teachers themselves.

My Classroom Action Research question was: "Can service learning enhance academic achievement?" Overall I am very excited by the change that I have witnessed this year. Of the students who met our attendance requirements, only five did not complete the Malcolm X project and therefore did not receive credit. (The other students who didn't receive credit simply did not attend school enough to meet our minimal attendance requirement.) Even though we have significantly increased our academic expectations for the Shabazz Experience class this year, service learning has made it possible for the vast majority of our students to receive academic credit. Learning by teaching has made the difference!

Malcolm Shabazz (X) once said, "Education is our passport to the future, for tomorrow belongs to the people who prepare for it today." I think our project would please him!

## EPILOGUE

All educators are confronted with the challenges of meeting the diverse academic needs of their students. In the alternative high school where I worked, for 23 years, most students have a long history of academic failure and disillusionment with formal education. Many are victims of racism, homophobia, family and personal problems, boredom, and/or poor lifestyle choices. The ultimate goal of Malcolm Shabazz City High School is to reengage these students so that they eventually graduate from high school.

Two important goals of the Shabazz Experience class were to establish good study habits in the students as well as to build their confidence by helping them to successfully complete academic tasks. But I was not certain what pedagogical strategy would be most effective in promoting academic achievement within this alienated and often marginalized population.

I was curious to see if service learning could add meaning and relevance to the students' classroom work. In short, I wondered if service learning could enhance the academic achievement of our students.

I brought these questions to my Classroom Action Research (CAR) experience. As I participated in the yearlong group discussions and planning, I realized that the greatest gift of CAR is the fostering of reflection and mindfulness. Through a continual process of individual reflection and discussions with my teaching colleagues and the members of my CAR group, I became more aware of what was happening in my classroom. I also became more intentional about the curricular choices I was making.

As a result of my participation in CAR, I conscientiously observed the students and collected data on how they responded to the variety of modifications that we initiated. I was fortunate to work with a talented team of educators who, like myself, were interested in questions of equity. Since the Shabazz Experience class lasted only nine weeks, I had the opportunity to study three different groups of students. I wanted a pedagogical approach that not only promoted equity but also did not become less effective when student groups varied in academic skills and motivation. CAR was the constant prism through which I observed multiple teaching strategies and various levels of student engagement. My research kept me focused on the goal of finding equity in academic achievement through the introduction of service learning into an existing curriculum.

Because our professional lives are so busy, it is difficult to take the time to be reflective and mindful about our educational practices. CAR was of paramount importance for me in sorting out the many variables to be considered when addressing equity issues. I was grateful that the Madison Metropolitan School District had the foresight to realize that educators need time and support to continually improve their teaching. Educators involved in CAR were given a half day a month to meet together. At each meeting, participants not only shared their latest findings with the group but also acted as "critical friends" in reviewing the research of others. In the spring, educators had the opportunity to take time from their teaching to write their final reports. The professional challenge of conscientiously addressing equity deserves that level of organizational support!

My CAR findings helped validate and legitimize service learning as a pedagogical tool that enhances academic achievement for our diverse student body. With that information and our shared commitment to equity, I encouraged more teachers in our building to integrate service learning into their teaching. Within a few years, service learning permeated the curricula. There were service projects in English, social studies, science, physical education, computer science, and Spanish courses. Many of the projects involved Shabazz students teaching younger students about what they had learned, as the students were doing in the Shabazz Experience class. But other new service-learning projects include students performing a play about the assassination of Harvey Milk and then facilitating talk-back sessions with students from other high schools; interviewing African American elders and writing their personal stories to share with the wider community; rebuilding computers for distribution to low-income families; playing recreational games with developmentally delayed students; assessing local businesses for wheelchair accessibility; and developing a K–12 curriculum to teach the history of Mound Bayou, Mississippi, one of the few remaining historic Black townships.

Because of our award-winning service-learning program, Shabazz students experience the opportunity to work with a wide variety of students and staff throughout our school district; to give many presentations for university students majoring in education; to do workshops at local and national conferences; and to team with a wide range of community agencies. My data on the number of people served by Shabazz students within the first 10 years reached well into the tens of thousands. The service-learning program not only continued to enhance academic achievement, but it also changed the public image of our school. The Shabazz service-learning program became so successful that it won local, state, and national recognition. Shabazz was recognized as a National Service-Learning Leader School in 1999 and as a National School of Character in 2002. In 2004, I was named the Service-Learning Practitioner of the Year by the Corporation for National Service.

I am no longer working at Shabazz, but my CAR project continues to shape my practice. After retirement, I took a part-time job coordinating a mentoring project for "initial educators" in the Madison Metropolitan School District. The purpose of this project is to provide every new educator with a mentor (a retired teacher) who will help foster reflection and mindfulness about educational practices. Needless to say, educators who have been involved in CAR are very comfortable in this mentoring role. From their experiences with CAR, they understand the importance of reflection in their professional work. They are comfortable posing questions and exploring alternatives with their mentees. These experienced teachers know the importance of providing support and encouragement as initial educators explore their own issues of professional development.

Equity remains a prism through which I view this new responsibility. I am convinced that the academic achievement gap among ethnic and racial groups does not have to exist. It is the ethical and professional responsibility of educators to explore pedagogical strategies that enhance academic achievement for *all* students. The mentors assist new teachers in pursuing that goal. Through this mentoring project, with its emphasis on reflection and equity, we are striving to improve public education, one teacher at a time!

## APPENDIX A

| What you need to know about Malcolm X | Where you can get the information | How you might demonstrate your knowledge |
|---|---|---|
| 1. The basic biographical data and the important details of his life and times. | *The Autobiography of Malcolm X*, especially chapters 1, 3, 10, 13, 17. Watch part of the video *The Life and Death of Malcolm X*. Interview someone who has read the *Autobiography* (make sure they know what they're talking about, though!). Read one of the easier biographies in the library. Form a group and divide the chapters of the autobiography; share the information with the rest of the group. Read the entire autobiography. Double credit. | Construct a timeline of important dates and events. Write a summary biography. Enact a scene or scenes from his life. Create and perform a rap or ballad about Malcolm's life. Rewrite Malcolm's biography for middle school or younger students. Create an illustrated biography (comic book format). Tell Malcolm's life story orally (to staff, friends, parents). Write/perform a play based on his life. |
| 2. The stages of his life. | Same sources as above, plus magazine articles available in the classroom. | Create a chart or timeline or diagram. Make a collage or mural depicting the stages of Malcolm's life. Write a quest/hero tale, taking him through the stages (requires some knowledge of archetypal myths). |
| 3. Malcolm's beliefs. | Same sources as above, inculding newspaper and magazine articles available in class Film: *Malcolm X Speaks* | Write and deliver a monologue that includes a variety of Malcolm's ideas. Create an oral interpretation of one of Malcolm's speeches—or parts of several. Make a collage. |

# APPENDIX B

Distribution and discussion of "Course Expectations" and "Rubrics"

Mystery Game - with brainstorm about "Important Components of an Effective Collaborative Project" (i.e., communication, cooperation, respect, participation, clear understanding)

Introduce Malcolm X Assignment Sheet

Training in Service Learning - using video, student panel, or handouts

Exploration of Learning Styles - theirs and sixth-grade students'

Study of Conflict Resolution Techniques - using handouts, student panel, activities

**Reflection I** - possible ways to teach "Alternatives to Violence," keeping in mind the variety of learning styles among sixth graders

Project Preparation in Pairs

**Reflection II** - Peer Review of conflict resolution projects

Preparation to Teach - (i.e., reminders about introducing group members, review of teaching strategies and introduction to the class by Sherman teacher)

**\*TEACH\***      "Alternative to Violence"

**Reflection III** - process first teaching experience

Re-introduce Malcolm X Assignment Sheet

**Reflection I** - possible ways to teach "Malcolm X"

Individual Project Preparation

**Reflection II** - Self Assessment using Rubrics and Peer Review of Malcolm X Projects

Review "What we learned from past teaching experiences"

(Encourage Shabazz students to nurture curiosity by asking questions: Have you ever wondered why our school is called "Shabazz"? Do you know why I find Malcolm X an interesting man?)

**\*TEACH\*** "Malcolm X"

**Reflection III** - process second teaching experience

## APPENDIX C

The Malcolm X project—learning about and teaching the life and times of El-hajj Malik el Shabazz (Malcolm X)—is the major project for this class. We want you to do your best possible work on it. You have many choices of how to learn and how to present the information; pay attention to your own best learning styles. No matter what form your presentation may take, these are the things we will be looking at as we assess the quality of your work.

### I. KNOWLEDGE OF MALCOLM X

Exceeded expectations: You went beyond the resources available in the classroom or LMC, finding more information than was readily available. You showed great initiative and research abilities.

Achieved expectations: You knew the important facts about Malcolm's life, times, and beliefs. You understood and were able to clearly relate this information.

Developing knowledge: You knew some of the important information, but not as much as we expected. Or you had some misinformation about important details/events/beliefs.

Emerging knowledge: You know a few things but not enough to satisfy this assignment.

### II. PROJECT

Exceeded expectations: You did an exceptional job! Your approach was unique; the presentation was very creative and carefully done. Very high quality work. People will learn a lot and respond to this project.

Achieved expectations: Your project was carefully planned and executed; you used your skills to the best of your ability. From this project, people will be able to understand the basics of Malcolm's life, times, and beliefs.

Developing knowledge: You made an attempt at a project, but it was not done as fully or as well as it could have been. Your effort isn't in line with your skills.

Emerging knowledge: You started a project.

### III. TEACHING SIXTH GRADERS

Exceeded expectations: You are a natural teacher! Your presentation was extremely well organized, clearly presented, and planned around the learning styles of sixth graders. You had a variety of approaches and anticipated questions or problems ahead of time.

Achieved expectations: You presented your information clearly, with some variety of methods and enough confidence to hold the interest of your listeners. They learned something through your presentation.

Developing knowledge: Though you made an effort, you were not clear enough or organized enough to hold the interest of the students. Materials were not made well enough (or not used well enough) for your purpose.

Emerging knowledge: You showed up, but you took very little part in the teaching.

| TIMELINES | |
|---|---|
| Introduction to service learning | Monday, Feb. 10 |
| Overview of learning styles | Tu–Thurs, Feb. 11–13 |
| Nonharassment policy | Friday, Feb. 14 |
| Teaching conflict resolution: planning | Mon–Tu, Feb. 17–18 |
| Peer Review of plans | Thurs, Feb. 20 |
| Teach 6th graders | Friday, Feb. 21 |
| Work on Malcolm X projects | Feb. 10–March 7 |
| Plan teaching; finish projects | March 10–12 |
| Peer review | March 12–13 |
| Teach 6th graders about Malcolm | Friday, March 14 |

## APPENDIX D

As a group, you are overwhelmingly visual in your learning styles; the great majority have *auditory* as your least accessible mode. This sheet is intended to give you some directions for getting started on your Malcolm X project, along with some ideas for making the best use of your learning strengths.

### Monday, February 17–Sunday, February 23

If you haven't already begun, find the resources that will best help you learn about Malcolm. Read, view, or listen—and get down the information in a form that will be most useful to you.

RESOURCES:

Rent the film *Malcolm X*—maybe several of you could get together to watch it (it's three hours long, so you'll need an evening or a weekend). If you need money for the rental, let us know.

Read chapters 1, 3, 7, 10, 13, and 17 in *The Autobiography of Malcolm X* (you won't be able to read the entire book in one week, unless you're an exceptional reader).

—ALTERNATIVE: Get together with several other students and divide the chapters, then share the information with each other.

Find information on the Internet: get addresses from Dave Odenweller's poster (in the classroom).

If you have enough time and good organizational skills, you might make a rough timeline and fill in information as you read. A *double-entry form* can also work well:

| Early life, 1925–1939 | What happened, in your own words |
|---|---|
| 1939–1946 | |

Or you might use organizing blocks:

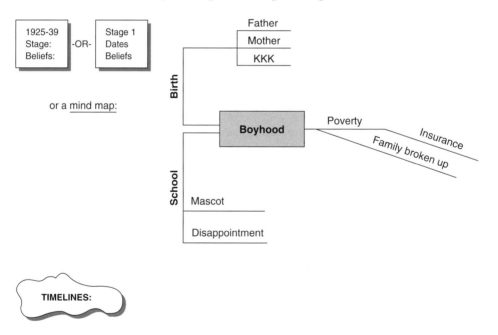

or a mind map:

TIMELINES:

| By Sunday, February 23 | Finish collecting information |
|---|---|
| By Monday, February 24 | Decide on how you're going to present what you've learned |
| February 25–February 28 | Rough drafts, planning, first steps on project |
| March 1–March 7 | Final drafts, polishing of projects |
| March 10–12 | Present your project to the class |

**SAMPLE WORK PLANS:**

| | | | |
|---|---|---|---|
| Mon., 2/17 | Read Chapter 1<br>Double-entry notes | Wed., 2/19 Watch *Malcolm X*<br>(no school that day) | |
| Tues., 2/18 | Read Chapter 3<br>Double-entry notes | Depending on learning style,<br>take notes as you watch or | |
| Wed., 2/19 | Read Chapters 7 & 10<br>Double-entry notes | write down the main parts after<br>watching. Write down questions, | |
| Sat., 2/22 | Read Chapters 13 &17<br>Double-entry notes | too, that still need to be<br>answered or made more clear. | |
| Sun., 2/23 | Read over notes and<br>make a list of<br>Malcolm's stages<br>and beliefs in a<br>three-column<br>format. | Fri., 2/21 Get answers to questions<br>Sun., 2/23 Because the film is done<br>in flashback, you'll need to<br>reorganize your notes. The stages<br>& beliefs will be clearer than the<br>dates. | |
| Mon., 2/24 | Decide on project<br>format: visual &<br>written | Mon., 2/24 Decide on project<br>format: visual & oral | |
| Tues., 2/25 | Thesis & plan for<br>paper | Tues., 2/25 Start looking for poems<br>or speeches by or about Malcolm | |
| 2/26–3/2 | Rough draft of paper | Thurs., 2/27 Decide on three pieces | |
| 3/3–3/5 | Work on poster | Fri., 2/28 (no school): Work on<br>painting. | |
| 3/6–3/8 | Final draft of paper | 3/1–3/7 Divide time between<br>painting and practicing oral<br>interpretation. | |

You will have some class time to work on these projects: probably 3–4 periods during the weeks of February 24 and March 3. You also have two days without school—February 19 and February 28—as well as weekends to do some major blocks of work. If you encounter difficulties, make sure you ask for help as soon as possible . . . don't put it off!

## BIBLIOGRAPHY FOR SHABAZZ EXPERIENCE CLASS

Aquina, B. (1992). *Malcolm X.* New York: Writers and Readers, Inc.

Auerbach, S. (1994). Malcolm X. In S. Auerbach (Ed.), *Encyclopedia of multiculturalism* (3rd ed., Vol. 4, pp. 1098–1100). North Bellmore, NY: Marshall Cavendish.

Haley, A. (1964). *The autobiography of Malcolm X.* New York: Ballantine Books.

Myers, W. D. (1993). *Malcolm X: By any means necessary.* New York: Scholastic.

# 8

## *We Want to Work With Our Friends*

### Diane Coccari

### EDITORS' INTRODUCTION

In her sixth-grade classroom, Coccari notices several disturbing patterns. Students begin to sort themselves academically and socially, and classroom discussions and activities become dominated by a faction of the boys in the room. Wary of these tendencies, Coccari embarks on an action research project to create a more equitable classroom for all students—many of whom are English language learners (ELLs). Through analyses of videotapes, student work, and her teacher research journal, Coccari provides an engaging account of her attempts to create an educational learning environment that capitalizes on the strengths of all members of the class and requires students to move beyond the comfort of working solely with their friends.

* * * *

### BACKGROUND

I am a sixth-grade regular education teacher at Black Hawk Middle School on Madison's northwest side. This is my third year of public school teaching, the result of a midlife shift from an academic career in South

Asian studies. I lived, studied, and did fieldwork in Banaras, India, for 3 years and spent 13 years as a student, teacher, and researcher in this field. When my children started school, I began many years as a volunteer in the public schools, becoming increasingly focused on culturally appropriate teaching and on children who appeared to be slipping through the cracks. I was struck by the difficulty and importance of teaching as a profession and wanted to be part of the effort to help respond to the increasing diversity of the student population in the Madison public schools and the dramatic increase in the number of children with special needs. Fortunately, I was able to obtain teaching certification relatively quickly through University of Wisconsin–Madison Teach for Diversity Masters and Certification Program.

Black Hawk Middle School receives students from six feeder elementary schools. The student body is diverse—yes, that word—socioeconomically, racially, and ethnically. The school's immediate neighborhood is largely middle class, but the attendance area includes six separate neighborhoods that contain low-income housing. These neighborhoods are located in several directions and are some distance from the school, and the children living in these areas ride the bus.

During the school year in which this study took place, the total population of Black Hawk Middle School was 565 students. The school population was 59 percent Caucasian, 20 percent African American, 13 percent Asian (Hmong, Laotian, Vietnamese, Cambodian, Tibetan, and Chinese), 7 percent Latino (mostly Mexican), and about 1 percent other minorities. Twenty-eight percent of the students had certified special needs, and 41 to 42 percent came from families earning low incomes.

The school's enrollment had increased by 185 students in three years, making it more than 100 percent of capacity, and everyone—staff and students alike—felt the squeeze. Every available cranny was being utilized, and many spaces were serving multiple functions. Teachers shared classrooms and had to negotiate the crowded hallways with carts packed with books and materials that they pushed from a central teacher planning room. Others conducted their "Super Study" programs (supervised study times for those needing extra help) in the library or in "specials" rooms. The school had been forced to shift to a complex double lunch and recess period to accommodate the presence of so many people.

In addition to the overcrowding, almost every special needs category had seen an exponential increase in students being served, especially the English as a second language (ESL) and learning disabilities programs. The number of at-risk students had also rapidly increased. Each grade level handled this increase in a different fashion. In the sixth grade, each academic classroom unit (three paired, or double, classrooms and two self-contained classrooms) included a special program that served children who spoke English as their second language, or those with emotional, cognitive, or learning disabilities. The students considered at risk (not fitting into one or more of the above categories but behind grade level) in the sixth grade were mainstreamed in all the classrooms, because there were too many of them to fit in one program.

This year, my own self-contained classroom was created to accommodate a larger incoming sixth-grade class in general, as well as a sharp increase in children needing ESL services in the sixth grade. After the first-quarter hiring of an additional sixth-grade teacher, my class of 27 became a group of 23, 10 of whom were recent immigrants or refugees or the Madison-born children of the same. The racial and ethnic breakdown of my students was this: 12 Caucasian students, including a child of Albanian refugees (seven boys and five girls); one African American boy; two African American–Caucasian biracial students (one boy and one girl); four Hmong students (three girls and one boy); two Cambodian students (one boy and one girl); one Laotian boy; one Vietnamese girl; and one Honduran girl. I mention these demographics because they played an important role in the classroom dynamics that inspired my Classroom Action Research question.

## MY QUESTION

My question emerged out of what I understood to be problematic classroom dynamics that surfaced immediately at the beginning of the year. For one thing, eight boys—six Caucasian boys, most of whom were from the same feeder school, one biracial boy, and one Cambodian boy—dominated the classroom, especially during all-class discussions. They did this by waving their hands in the air constantly and vigorously, expecting to be called upon. Of more concern to me, these same boys constantly interrupted, commented, and made noises and remarks without the formality of waiting their turns to speak. This had a powerful dampening effect on the other students in the room, both male and female. Not infrequently, direct girl-baiting remarks were made with the intention of getting a rise out of some of the girls in the room. Several girls were visibly angered and insulted; a few were willing to jump into the fray and trade insults, leading to a divisive and unpleasant atmosphere.

It was also interesting to me that when class members were invited to share or read something in front of the class—writings from journals, and so on—it was always the same boys who eagerly volunteered, working the crowd and relishing the attention they received at the front of the room.

I noticed how these boys would unselfconsciously share what was often mediocre work, while other students sat quietly, some with brilliant and creative work lying in front of them on their desks.

Some of these behaviors were more problematic than others. I welcome students' pride in their work and enthusiasm for what is being done or discussed in the classroom. But what does a teacher do when only a minority of the class is empowered to participate freely in this way? Some of the behaviors clearly angered, insulted, or shut down the other children. Gender domination by the boys occasionally had a very sharp edge, and the bloc of boys from our sister elementary school clearly felt the most empowered. Yet looking out at me were the faces of the majority of the children in my classroom who were inhibited in their participation, among these extremely shy Caucasian girls and most of the Southeast Asian students. They were extremely still, attentive, and reserved, and I feared that, without help, their voices would not be heard in front of the entire class.

A second interesting pattern emerged. Whenever I asked the class to voluntarily form groups, line up, or make a circle, they did so in exactly the same fashion, sorting themselves neatly, first by gender, then by ethnic and racial affiliation. This happened over and over again. The pattern generally went like this: biracial boy, African American boy, Cambodian boy, Laotian boy, Hmong boy, Albanian boy, Caucasian boys and then a gap, and then Caucasian girls, biracial girl, Honduran girl, Cambodian girl, Vietnamese girl, Hmong girls. This, I knew, was perfectly natural. "Look at the way we sit in the teachers' lunchroom!" my Classroom Action Research buddies said. But the voluntary reproduction of this identical arrangement over and over again seemed so outrageous to me that it made me laugh out loud! I really had to see if I could help increase the comfort level of these students so that they might eventually choose to broaden their voluntary selections of groups and partners. At the very least, I wanted everybody to get to know each other and to feel comfortable enough to work well with one another, regardless of the particular configuration.

Thus my concerns were twofold: (1) How could I defuse the domination of one group while encouraging the participation of other students; and (2) how could I help my class get to know one another better so that they could work comfortably together and maybe even begin to voluntarily expand their choices of partners? My official question remained in two parts and in early October was as follows:

1. **How can I increase participation in all-class discussions by those less willing or able to risk and share?**

> 2. **How can I help the students in my classroom feel comfortable working with diverse groupings of classmates and ultimately overcome, at least part of the time, their desire to always be with their friends?**

Awkwardly stated, but there it was. The essential nature of this question changed little over the course of the following months. Here is what I attempted to do about it.

## WHAT I DID

I knew that my approach to this problem had to be multifaceted. I wanted to build a sense of community and ownership in the classroom and to increase everyone's comfort level so students might feel more free to take risks. I wanted to teach openly and positively about the differences among the children in the classroom. I wanted to deal directly with problematic issues and behaviors as they arose, and I wanted to experiment with a variety of class formations and cooperative groupings.

## DATA

To initially get a handle on the problem and to document change over time, I recorded several types of data. I made videotapes of cooperative group activities, and I made notes about the composition and outcomes of all cooperative groups—voluntary, modified choice, and teacher-selected. I had my practicum student create many checklists that kept track of class participation (who raised their hands, who spoke out of turn, who got called on, and so on). This turned out to be *very* interesting and useful information. I included questions about class participation and working with partners on student self-evaluations. I copied all relevant written student feedback (journals and other writing) and attempted to record in my journal all discussion and verbal feedback on this topic.

During parent conferences, I spoke with the parents of the more reserved children (especially the Hmong and Vietnamese girls) about my desire to have their children become more assertive. In each case, the parents assured me that they wanted this for their daughters. In one case, a Hmong father, acknowledging the stereotype, stated that it simply is not true that Hmong families raise their daughters to be submissive.

Finally, I had the class fill out an inventory listing (1) those classmates with whom they already knew they worked well; (2) those classmates with whom they knew they did not work well (some of these being good friends with whom they became distracted); (3) those classmates with whom they felt they could work well but had not yet done so (a very important category, because it became the pool of classmates they were frequently asked to choose from); and (4) a classmate of the opposite gender, if they had not included one already in their list.

## CLASS PARTICIPATION:
## DEALING DIRECTLY WITH THE ISSUES

From the outset, I called attention to some of the issues as they occurred. For example, I might say to the class, "Did you happen to notice who is always willing to come up and speak in front of the class? I love it that these boys always participate, but what about the rest of you? What about the girls in this classroom?" Some girls were eventually able to articulate why they held back: they did not want to be laughed at, made fun of, or teased. For the ESL students, language was always an issue, as well as "not wanting to give the wrong answer and be laughed at." I realized that two different things needed to happen: some of students needed to be asked to practice greater restraint, while the others had to be encouraged and challenged to participate. The put-downs were unacceptable in my Stress/Challenge classroom (see below), and so I dealt with this behavior immediately and became increasingly stern with those who habitually and impulsively made inappropriate comments. I privately coached others on their people skills (for example, what do kids usually think about showing off, and what behaviors shut others down?) and challenged the heretofore silent to speak out. Rather quickly, when they saw that I would not tolerate inappropriate noises and remarks, a new group of girls (Cambodian, Caucasian, and biracial) found their voices. For others, full participation would come more slowly.

## COMMUNITY BUILDING:
## STRESS/CHALLENGE PROGRAM

From the first day—if not the first minutes—of the school year, I introduced and initiated the Stress/Challenge (S/C) program in my classroom. What I pull under the S/C umbrella includes bona fide Stress/Challenge activities, presented in a sequence from "ice breakers" to "deinhibitizers" to "trust builders" to increasingly sophisticated group challenges or "initiatives"; Odyssey of the Mind–type challenges; and conflict resolution/peer mediation activities as needed. I cannot say enough about the value of this program for bringing a diverse classroom together. For one thing, the student buy-in is almost total. As educators, we see a lot of sophisticated and important learning happening. For the kids, the activities are almost always seen as a lot of fun. Stress/Challenge, which, after daily activities in the beginning, settled into a last-hour-on-Friday activity, was for most of my class the favorite part of the week, something they looked forward to enthusiastically. This program has clarified for me the role of teacher as facilitator: one who clearly sets up the challenge and the parameters but who then backs off to allow the students to work together and learn from their own successes and mistakes. The sequence of the Stress/Challenge activities is very important. A group cannot be successful at a more challenging level until it has pretty well mastered the earlier levels, and a group cannot accomplish some of the more complex challenges until total focus and cooperation are achieved.

Stress/Challenge activities and concepts set the tone for my classroom. We became a Stress/Challenge classroom, one in which I did not have to repeatedly ask students for attention but could quietly wait for the class to quickly settle. The students gained a more sophisticated understanding of group process and saw what could be accomplished by working together. They noticed the different impact that "put-ups" versus put-downs made on their energy and spirit, and we learned a format for processing our experiences. The extension activities available in this district—the low and high ropes courses at the School Forest, spelunking at Popp's Cave in Richland Center—were extremely motivational. Furthermore, it was often the case that the most valuable and successful participants were children who struggled in academic areas. One student, who was the most behind in grade level of all the children in my class, was a key player in many Stress/Challenge activities and all Odyssey of the Mind activities. He was extremely and visibly proud of his key role in his groups' successes, and this transformed his defensive and adversarial posture to a full and willing participation in classroom activities. I could not come up with a better advertisement for these types of activities for *all* children than that.

## DEALING WITH DIFFERENCES: GARDNER'S SEVEN INTELLIGENCES

Another framework that fits in well with the other orientations of my classroom is Howard Gardner's delineation of the seven intelligences. I have on the wall a large poster with Gardner's terms along with their simplified forms (word smart, body smart, music smart, and so on) and illustrations for each category. We do a number of activities during the first weeks to understand Gardner's model and to explore what people's obvious talents are and what their unrealized talents might be. The power, however, is in using Gardner's model as a touchstone throughout the year. One must refer back to this scheme again and again, pointing out how smart the children are—as individuals and collectively—recognizing strengths as you see them, nudging the nonbelievers into acknowledging their own talents, encouraging students to recognize and praise these talents in others. I am always so pleased when I begin to hear from some members of the class, "Wow, that's really word smart!" or some such comment. Reference to this scheme is also useful in explaining differences in abilities and therefore urging tolerance and patience in peer tutoring and other activities. Everyone shines at something; no one is perfect in all areas. We can use our diversity to help and support others. And, of course, the teacher must strive to provide a curriculum that speaks to all abilities.

## DEALING WITH DIFFERENCES: THE CURRICULUM

An "ancient civilizations" social studies curriculum is an easy one in which to include many lessons about cultural differences, both historical and modern. I choose the ancient cultures that we explore in response to the ethnicities of the children in my classroom: ancient China, India, Southeast Asia, Africa, Egypt, Mesoamerica, and Greece. Integrated with this historical study is our reading of myths, legends, folktales, or historical novels that relate to each cultural group. This provides us with many opportunities for cross-cultural comparison and finding connections to our own lives and experiences.

Before we launched into the study of ancient civilizations, I had all the children write extensive autobiographies and family histories. It is very important to me that my students have a clear sense of who their classmates are and why their families came to live in this country. Because of the makeup of my class this year, I added a short unit on Southeast Asian cultures, the Vietnam War, and the resulting immigration. An Indonesian staff member and a Hmong parent told their stories of escape and resettlement, and my class became involved in a service project raising money to purchase reading glasses for elderly Hmong villagers living on the Thai border. We were able to send a photograph album and drawings to the children of Huai Ku (the village where the relatives of two students live) and we received an album in exchange. Such efforts, I believe, contribute greatly to the feelings of connectedness and belonging of immigrant and refugee children. I overheard one Hmong girl tell another: "Ms. Coccari understands us." In fact, I find that I have to watch carefully for feelings of alienation and backlash from my other students, who may be unused to so much emphasis on foreign cultures in the classroom. One White male student asked me, "When do we get to study about *us*?" I am still trying to convince him that our study of human origins, Indo-European migrations, and the culture of ancient Greece is, in fact, about him, but he remains skeptical.

## EXPERIMENTS WITH COOPERATIVE GROUPS

I launched into all kinds of experiments with cooperative groups. I tried all types of configurations and alternated among my careful choices of group members, to modified choice of different sorts, to free choice of partners. The aforementioned inventory turned out to be very useful. I would often ask the students to choose as partners classmates in category #3—people you have never worked with but with whom you feel you could work well. This method of choosing a partner became, for many, a source of new potential partners and, in some cases, friends. My most controversial request (which I eased into gradually) was to ask the students to work with a partner of the opposite gender. This was and still is a very big deal for some children but is not such a big deal for others.

## RESULTS

Well, my students *still* (on May 6) line up in almost exactly the same order as they did at the beginning of the year, and they still would rather work with their friends! At the recent Action Research of Wisconsin (AROW) conference, a psychologist who heard my presentation suggested that this behavior is totally appropriate developmentally for children of this age. The identities of sixth graders, she said, are not settled and secure enough for them to easily and readily take on the kinds of risks that I was expecting. In another two years, apparently, it will be a different matter. This certainly resonated with my observations of the students in my class, many at a seemingly shy, fragile, tentative, or protective place with regard to their images of themselves. Further reading in this area would be extremely interesting. The tenacity of these choices notwithstanding, I feel that there has been some progress, which I will detail as follows.

### Male Dominance

The male dominance that had existed at the beginning of the year, and the atmosphere created by the freedom that certain boys felt to speak out and make sharp, critical, sometimes taunting and girl-bashing remarks and noises, abated almost immediately. As certain behaviors were named and discussed—and it became clear that they would not be tolerated—some of the girls were able to be as free in their participation as the boys. There is still a lot of male exuberance, and certain boys still want to be first in many circumstances (e.g., exploring rooms in the cave) and still flock to and dominate certain activities (e.g., microscopes and manipulatives), but they are much less aggressive about these behaviors and much more sensitive to the group and more amicable about backing off if necessary. The unsafe feeling that pervaded the classroom at the beginning of the year went away.

## Cooperative Groups

The largest strides can be seen in the way this class performs in cooperative groups. Quite some time ago, the students became a class able to work well together as a whole group and in almost every cooperative group configuration, so much so that I almost forgot why I was so worried about this issue in the first place! In fact, I couldn't ask for better group work. I was heartened to see solid working relationships develop, and even friendships form out of new partner choices. More mixed-gender partnerships were initiated, but most of the students still preferred partners of the same gender. I find that I have been dealing less with whole-group process issues and more with fine-tuning interactions when subtler issues, conflicts, and misunderstandings arise between individuals. As kids get to know each other better and become more familiar with each other, new conflicts and issues appear. I still stop and mediate these issues the moment they come to my attention, and try to model positive mediation and active listening techniques.

## All Class Participation

This has been the most problematic area. While an initially reluctant few have begun to find their voices, speaking in front of the whole class remains a challenge for many. What I increasingly began to tune in to were individual differences. Different things hold back different people. For example, one student has low self-esteem, another is almost pathologically shy, and a third is thinking about lunch or daydreaming about Leonardo DiCaprio! Many students are sensitive about their English. Some were able to jump in as soon as they saw that their feelings and opinions were going to be protected. Others have come around more slowly. Even when individuals agree in principle to full participation, doing so with each still takes some time.

I was conflicted at the beginning of the year about how much I should restrain the more exuberant students in certain circumstances, and how much I should push the shy ones. What about cultural issues? Don't some people have a right to be shy? Parent conferences resolved some of this for me, as did experiences like participating in a professional development experience where it was expected that everyone contribute their voices at least once a session. I think all students should be required to participate. I think everyone should be encouraged and challenged to ask for what they need and to freely express their views. I eventually became unequivocal about this requirement. Presenting to the class was painful at first for many students but eventually became more routine. Observations and checklists both reveal that voluntary participation has increased. But the instruction needs to continue. My Hmong and Vietnamese girls are now asking, "What will we do next year if we don't have a teacher who will help us?" I tell them that everyone *deserves* the help they need. Teachers are busy, preoccupied people. Sometimes they overlook students, sometimes they forget. You must ask. If you don't get what you need, you ask again. We practice the language that they might use. I've even acted as a voice coach! We practice speaking louder, from the diaphragm, finding that deep and powerful voice. "How loud are you when you yell at your little brother? Okay, now say it that loudly!" Hey, I wish that someone had done this for me when I was young!

This is not to say that the students who are quiet in front of the whole class do not feel uncomfortable in the classroom or when expressing their opinions or telling their stories at other times. The classroom is a place where most of the kids want to be before school, during lunch and lunch recess, during study halls, and after school. The girls take over the classroom during lunch and recess periods, when they are much more relaxed, expressive, and uninhibited. "Lunch bunch" grew from a small group of the shyest girls to all the girls and some of the boys. Absent only are the boys who desire the physical activity of the playground and want to be with friends from other classrooms, and those avoiding a teacher who demands too much work of them! In these smaller groups, I hear all about people's lives and am asked endless, probing questions. So the students themselves came up with the missing format—a time and space in the classroom for informal, voluntary gatherings of smaller groups of students.

## Academic Achievement

It's interesting that, while I did not include academic achievement as part of my initial question, I always assumed that a comfortable environment would help to facilitate academic success for the majority of my students. To quantifiably assess student achievement, I have only two objective measures: a comparison of class grades between the end of the first quarter and the end of the third quarter, and scores from the Stanford Diagnostic Reading Test.

At the end of the first quarter, the students had an average grade point of 3.16, with 12 students (52 percent) on the honor roll (earning at least a 3.2 cumulative grade) and six of these (26 percent) on the high honor roll (at least 3.7). At the end of the third quarter, the class averaged a 3.2 grade point, only a slight increase, but 19 students (83 percent) had made the honor roll. The Stanford Diagnostic Reading Test—out of date and culturally inappropriate as it is—revealed an average grade-level increase of 1.2 in vocabulary and 1.8 in reading comprehension. Not everyone in my class achieved as much academically as I would have liked. I have four students who are extremely challenged in their learning, each with individual and complex issues that make learning difficult. But I think these figures are witness to some increasingly focused and hardworking students.

## FINAL REMARKS

Our efforts in the classroom this year resulted in much learning for students and teacher alike. I am very happy to have gotten to know so many wonderful children, and I am glad that so many seemed to be comfortable and successful in my classroom. I cannot attribute any specific effect to any specific effort or practice on my part, yet I feel that all the actions discussed here had value and I will certainly continue the cultural learning and sharing, community building, and experiments with cooperative groupings in the future.

At the beginning of the year, I really thought that I could have a huge impact on the voluntary choice of student partners. My impact upon this factor was, in fact, minimal. I was naïve, it turns out, about the cultural and developmental aspects of identity at this age and profoundly naïve about the importance of gender. But the students did broaden their friendships and were able to work well with almost anyone when called upon to do so.

As the year progressed, more students became more comfortable expressing themselves in front of the entire class, but some continued to remain quiet and reserved. Yet it was this group of shyer students who initiated smaller groups within which they could be more expressive and relaxed. I also became increasingly appreciative of the students as individuals— their humor, talents, quirks, needs, and differences—and I think that the students grew in their appreciation of their classmates as well.

I was far more organized and systematic with data collection concerning these issues than I might have been had I not been involved in Action

Research. I am quite sold on data collection as an initial and follow-up response to problem solving and will try to do this on a regular basis in the future. I have seen how the results of data collection may sometimes be surprising or unexpected. This is an important lesson for a teacher—to realize that what may actually be going on is not exactly what you thought, that your perceptions are subjective and limited. I have also seen that it is especially critical to include as an important source of data student perspectives and voices as they relate to any issue.

Last, the time provided by the Action Research process to get away from the classroom and talk and reflect with other professionals was invaluable. Our days are full of performing, acting, and reacting, and there is so little time for the critical and nurturing activities of sharing, supporting, and reflecting.

## EPILOGUE

Several years have passed since I conducted this Action Research project. If anything, the children entering our classrooms are more challenging each year. The lives of many of these children and their families are difficult, the number of children with special needs has increased, and previously extraordinary behaviors have become ordinary. But these children are quite wonderful, and they are who they are. They bring an incredible richness of experience and diversity to the classroom, and they deserve the best we can give. We as teachers need to constantly strive to stay at the top of our game, and we need to be encouraged, supported, and renewed in approaching what we do.

On my best days I continue to use the skills that I learned as an Action Researcher and relearned and reinforced as an Action Research Facilitator. I try my best to avoid personalizing the challenges that I face in the classroom but to focus instead on collecting data that shape my responses to the issues and challenges before me. These practices are part and parcel of what I regard as professionalism as a teacher. The Action Research process is fundamental in serving the needs of every single child in the classroom, and that includes taking into account each child's personal and cultural differences to the extent that we are able. It is important to acknowledge that this is an ongoing struggle, but this struggle is front and center for me.

Beyond our own classrooms, we also must try to encourage reflective practices in our schools and school districts. As part of my participation in school subject-based cadres, leadership, climate, and equity teams, and as a member of districtwide committees and regional conferences, I have tried to learn about, support, and encourage research-driven and reflective teaching practices. But these are, in many ways, top-down approaches to change and reform, or exercises in preaching to the converted. Far more powerful is the impact and example of good teaching. Change is a complex and nonlinear process, and in these days of increasing challenge and shrinking resources, teachers are under stress and under siege as never before. So we have seen periods of progress, but also reaction, regression, and even reversals in the growth of school community, trust, personal and academic experimentation, and risk taking. Often as professionals we do not always model what we expect from our children, and that is a very big and complex problem. Perhaps this is naïve, but if we are to survive and thrive in this crucible of funding caps and growing challenge, it has never been more critical for all school districts to invest in the deep professional development of their teachers. I feel with great conviction that, as struggling professionals, we deserve the time away from our schools and classrooms to reflect and to be nurtured and supported in our attempts to take risks, experiment, grow, and change.

For me, equity is all about each student getting what she or he needs. This is not an easy task, for we are not perfect teachers or perfect people, but if we are to remain in the game we must accept the challenges and appreciate the gifts of every working day.

# 9

# Ribbons, Racism, and a Placenta

## The Challenges and Surprises of Culturally Relevant Teaching

### Kate Lyman

## EDITORS' INTRODUCTION

Building on the work of scholars in the area of culturally relevant teaching, Lyman's study captures the power of attending to knowledge students bring with them as they enter her second- and third-grade classroom. Capitalizing on conversations she overhears on the playground and in the classroom, Lyman builds a unique curriculum that attends to the needs and concerns of her students while meeting—and often exceeding—the standards those same students are expected to master. By examining recordings of classroom interactions, field notes, student work, and district measures, Lyman shows the power of a curriculum that has direct relevance to her students' lives.

* * * *

# PROLOGUE

I was told that I needed to find a framework for how I would study my teaching. I was puzzled. I had put the sweat and tears, the fears and triumphs of a whole year into the writing of it, as well as the political, educational, and humanistic beliefs that have sustained me through 20 years of teaching. For me, my story of this year of teaching was enough. It was my framework.

Academicians and friends made suggestions. Was my framework "action research"? What about "narrative inquiry" or "feminism"? I was tempted to look up some of the articles I had read in my graduate classes, in the hope of discovering a framework that would fit my paper.

Once I started to focus on *why* I wanted to write about my teaching, the framework that emerged from red ribbons, racism, and a placenta was that of culturally relevant teaching. I had found my sought-after framework.

First, I believe in the power of the story. This is, after all, a story. It is a narrative of my teaching experiences. Although it contains aspects of "research"—taped and recorded interactions, extensive field notes, and collections of student work—it is, in essence, a story. That there is more than one version to these accounts is something I realized when I heard my student teacher recount her version of a story that I use here (the one about the student's reaction to the bloody placenta). The facts were different. "Is that how it happened?" I asked her. "Yeah, I was there," she attested. We were both there, but our stories were different. But the differences weren't important. In the telling of the story, the essence of the experience was conveyed. In fact, as Tim O'Brien writes in *The Things They Carried* (a soldier's account of the Vietnam War), "story-truth is truer sometimes than happening-truth" (O'Brien, 1990, p. 204). I tell these stories, in part, simply because they are good stories. Even people who aren't teachers enjoy them. But the purpose of my storytelling is not essentially entertainment.

But when I started putting more of my stories in writing, it became clear that my narratives were often related to the issues of social justice and equity that were a focus in my classroom. As I told or read my stories to larger audiences, such as my narrative inquiry class, my Wisconsin Writing Project group, and my action research cohort, then—when I finally became convinced to submit a story for publication—I became more aware of the political potential of my storytelling.

The second part of my framework brings me to the political aspect of my writing. I wish my politics could fit neatly into a category of social thought. "He (she) is a Marxist . . . a po-mo queen (A what? Oh, a postmodern feminist) . . . a social reconstructionist," I would hear in graduate school classes. But none of the academic papers I have read influenced my political thoughts to the extent that my life experiences have. I was brought up by parents who had advanced degrees in English and positions teaching at a university. My thinking was influenced by my parents, who were "liberal" in politics, at a time that being "liberal" could mean being blacklisted as a Communist. As the "campaign manager" in my eighth-grade class for John F. Kennedy's presidential campaign, I became infused with the era's Camelot idealism, a belief in the possibility of social change that has stayed with me for the last 40 years. Cynicism about and awareness of fundamental flaws within our system came with learning about the civil rights struggles of the late 1950s and the 1960s. While I was a student at the University of Wisconsin from 1964 to 1968, I marched and demonstrated against U.S. involvement in the Vietnam War. This experience moved me much later to become involved in actions and delegations supporting groups struggling for freedom from U.S. control in Central America. My thinking was also influenced by reading feminist literature and attending Equal Rights Amendment rallies. I began to critically review and permanently alter my own views and understanding of social constructions of femininity. Finally, bringing up three daughters—on my own—made me more aware of women's issues, both in relation to psychological and social pressures on girls and women and in regard to economic status. I broadened my conceptions of what it meant to be underprivileged economically, at least as much as my middle-class background and my status as a single mother dependent on Aid to Families with Dependent Children (AFDC) would allow. Coming to some understanding of gender and economic oppression was a factor that helped sensitize me to issues of oppressed groups and move me to work with racial minorities, gays and lesbians, and people with acquired immunodeficiency syndrome (AIDS). So it was my life experiences, rather than one specific train of social or political thought, that led me to my belief that profound social changes must occur before our society can be considered democratic or equitable. I chose to teach, however, not because I thought I could change the inequities of our society through my work, but because through reaching kids and their parents, by working with student teachers, and by planning and talking with other teachers, I felt I could practice my beliefs. Also, I've been realizing lately that reaching other teachers through my writing may be a way to work toward meaningful changes in education.

Why am I telling this story? The more I think about it, the more complicated the answer becomes. However, the easiest part of the answer is that I am telling this story because I was doing action research. Twenty credits' worth of graduate school classes had convinced me that very little in the writings of the academics would help me tell my story. When I tried to understand concepts like "dialogic heteroglossia" or "institutional hegemony," I always found myself looking back to my classroom experiences. Action research enabled me to look to myself and my colleagues, the classroom teachers, as the experts and to my classroom as the source of data. I had faith that, if I closely observed and reflected on the daily interactions that occurred in my classroom, I would find "answers" at least as profound, and certainly more entertaining and easier to read, than those contained in the academic articles. In choosing this particular story, out of all the possible stories, for my action research, I found my topic in my journal. The most compelling narratives in my journal always centered on the issue of practicing culturally relevant teaching with my class. For a while, I toyed with narrowing my discussion to the topic of the work I was doing with poetry. But, although the use of poetry did fit in with my final telling, focusing on the poetry sessions felt like a lie; it wasn't the essence or the "story truth" of the year's experiences.

## BURNING ISSUES

"When you introduce yourself, let me know if you have any burning questions about the human body or birth," requested the mom of one of my second graders. Mary, a nurse in a hospital, had volunteered to speak to my class of second and third graders about an aspect of our current unit. Listening intently to each other, students patiently waited their turns to say their names and articulate their questions. "Can you live with just one kidney?" "How can twins be a boy and a girl?" "Sex . . . well, I know what it is, but I just want to know more about it." "Why do people make so much noise when they have sex?" "How does the placenta come out?"

After answering the questions and talking about her job of assisting with the birth and care of babies, Mary surprised the class with something she had brought from the hospital—a placenta. Anticipating exclamations of shock, possibly disgust, and certainly giggles, I was impressed by the students' reaction. In a single voice, they expressed their wonder and excitement in a slow crescendo: "WHOOOOOA!" There wasn't an inattentive child as Mary held up and explained the function of the umbilical cord, the sac, and other parts of the placenta. With their hands protected by latex gloves, the kids took turns touching the placenta. "Yuck!" exclaimed a girl who was returning from a resource class. "What do you mean, 'Yuck'?" someone challenged, "That's a placenta. You had one, too." "But mine wasn't that bloody," the newcomer protested, at the same time inching over to get a better view.

Looking at the placenta, a human organ, ejected that day from the body of a woman who had just given birth, I felt moved and inspired. The placenta, along with the students' questions and their exclamations of wonder and curiosity during hands-on exploration, struck me as symbols of the power of a relevant curriculum. It was an appropriate and dramatic climax to our unit on the human body, the last of several units that were central to the students' lives, interests, and experiences. For all my effort to measure the success of the curriculum through test scores, journal writing, transcriptions of classroom discussions, and samples of student writing, I realized that the true impact of the curriculum was most simply and profoundly demonstrated by that softly articulated "WHOOOOOA!"

In the early 1970s, when I returned to school to get my teaching certification, I read in *Teacher* by Sylvia Ashton-Warner (1963) that Maori children who had failed to learn how to read or write using traditional methods could achieve literacy by learning words organic to their culture and experiences. The image presented in this book of children reading and rereading battered cards displaying key words like "kiss," "cry," and "ghost" (Ashton-Warner, 1963, p. 67) stayed with me through the 1970s and 1980s, and into the 1990s. As I taught preschool through third grade at Lowell, Lincoln, Midvale, and Hawthorne schools, I learned that, although "culturally relevant teaching" worked well with all children, it was particularly important in motivating low-income children and children of color. My experiences were confirmed by the research of Gloria Ladson-Billings, who studied successful teachers of African American children. Ladson-Billings found that

> . . . culturally relevant teaching attempts to make knowledge problematic. Students are challenged to view education (and knowledge) as a vehicle for emancipation, to understand the significance of their culture, and to recognize the power of language. As a matter of course, culturally relevant teaching makes a link between classroom experiences and the students' everyday lives. These connections are made in spirited discussions and classroom interactions . . . By owning the form of expression, students become enthusiastic participants in classroom discourse and activities. (Ladson-Billings, 1994, p. 94)

"As a researcher," wrote Ladson-Billings, "I am cynical about the potential for change. But as an African-American parent I am desperate for change. I cling to the possibilities held forth by culturally relevant teaching" (Ladson-Billings, 1994, p. 91).

This school year struck me as the perfect time to take a closer look at my practice of culturally relevant teaching. Although I have always worked with diverse groups of students, this year was the first that the children of color would outnumber the White children. At the beginning of the year, I had in my class 22 children (10 boys and 12 girls), including six African American children (pseudonyms are used throughout: Jeremy, Henry, Anitra, Valerie, Tony, and Tonisha), four biracial children (two identifying themselves as "Black"—Kendra and Renee—and two calling themselves "half Black" or "mixed"—Lena and Dana), two Asian American (Hmong) children (Blia and Joel), one Mexican American child (Steven), and nine European American children (Emily, Cassie, Junior, Samantha, Caleb, Sarah, Ian, Jana, and Adam). The students' families were also socioeconomically diverse, with more than half being low-income (as defined by eligibility for free or reduced-price lunches). For the most part, parents had blue-collar or white-collar jobs; only a few were professionals. About half of the students lived at a low-income housing project.

The class also was very diverse in terms of academic achievement. On the districts' primary language arts assessment, the students' reading levels ranged from Preprimer 1 to eighth grade. Two students spent part of the day in a classroom for children with learning disabilities, and three spoke languages other than English at home. I was continuing with 15 students I had taught in a first-grade and second-grade combination the previous year; seven students, including three students who were new to the school, were new to my classroom.

The three second graders new to Hawthorne were of immediate concern to me because of their oppositional behavior, lack of participation in academic activities, and low reading and writing skills. On an initial Running Records screener, Renee and Henry scored at Preprimer 1 level and Tonisha scored at Preprimer 2 level. In practical terms, they were nonreaders and very aware of it. They also had no confidence in writing; they were reluctant even to try invented spelling. Henry's first attempt at writing is unreadable. Renee's is hard to decipher through the erasures (she was trying to get the correct spellings from her friend, Anitra). Tonisha wrote a few words that she knew: "cat" and "dog." When I came over to her table to see her work, she said anxiously, "Are you going to make me erase it all and write it over again?" The moms of all three of the children said that their children were "slow" or "behind" and/or had "bad attitudes." The children's previous report cards showed below-average marks, mainly in behavior and language arts. Comments on their report cards include, "[Renee] is capable of doing better work"; "I would love to see [Tonisha] show more enthusiasm about learning"; and [Henry] has a tendency to take things—very quick—toys, candy, pencils and things that were in the teacher's drawers."

Although I was concerned about these three new students, I had many other children who were lagging academically or whom I knew to have serious emotional or behavioral issues. In this class—unlike others I've had—it soon became apparent that all the African American or biracial students were significantly behind in reading and writing skills and/or had social or emotional issues that were causing them to "act out" in class or that were alienating them from school. I desperately needed to discover a curriculum that would not only lessen the academic gaps but also create the sparks needed to ignite the students' passion for learning. It also soon became apparent to me that if significant learning were to occur, a cooperative classroom community needed to emerge and supersede all the interpersonal conflicts and cultural differences.

I have always had an intuitive faith in the efficacy of culturally relevant teaching, but this year appeared to be the perfect opportunity to take a closer look at my own practice. I decided to collect detailed records of day-to-day classroom experiences by writing in a journal, taking written and videotaped records of classroom discussions, and collecting students' writing and records of their standardized test scores. Looking back at my data, I realize that I have gained knowledge of how culturally relevant teaching looks in action. Each thematic unit that I describe below has taught me something about what works, or doesn't work, in the teaching of relevant issues to a diverse classroom.

# NAME-CALLING

### Some of the Best Lessons Arise From Classroom Incidents.

Because I was continuing with 15 (out of 22 total) students from last year, I was not expecting a difficult first week of school, but I was wrong!

> August 28: First day of school! WOW! . . . Tonisha was a challenge. She defied most of my directions, only complying when I threatened her with consequences . . . Aside from the clique of African American girls, who, if I can't get the upper hand, will try to run the classroom, a Kindergarten temper tantrum from one of the third graders and a kid who wasn't on his Ritalin, something else was bothering me about the classroom dynamics. I couldn't put my finger on it until after school, until I realized that . . . I am missing four of the strongest leaders from last year: Jordan, Calandra, Nathan, and Alexia. Those kids were the ones I turned to when other kids' faces looked blank to analyze a situation in a story, to have a unique solution to a math problem, or to explain the injustices of the world. This class, I realize, now has a big hole.

I had planned a wetlands unit with another teacher, but now I had doubts about it:

> I am worried about this wetland unit. Is it too far removed from these kids' lives to be interesting? But there is a marshy area right across from the projects . . .

On Friday of the second week, 12 kids were involved in a major fight at recess. Eight of the kids were from my class. I spent most of that Friday afternoon piecing the stories together; the physical fight (nine girls cornered and beat up three boys) turned out to be the culminating act of several recesses' worth of angry and bitter incidents of name-calling and threats. After an hour or so of discussion and problem solving, all the kids involved were given in-school suspensions for the rest of the day, and all the parents were reached through notes or phone calls.

Although I regarded the discussions and consequences as necessary steps to quell the violence, I also decided to have a whole class discussion on name-calling the following Monday:

September 10 . . . I knew I had to find a way to stop the fighting, or teaching reading and writing in my classroom would become impossible. I knew I had to let them know in no uncertain terms that verbal or physical abuse would not be put up with, that severe consequences would ensue. I knew that the moms of these kids wanted, above all, even above academic success, good school behavior, I knew they'd back me up . . . I decided to let the kids brainstorm insults. I would write them down and we would discuss why these words make people so angry. I discovered a poem perfect for the occasion, "Coke Bottle Brown" by Nikki Grimes in her 1994 book *Meet Danitra Brown*.

### Coke Bottle Brown

*Dumb old Freddy Watson called my friend "Coke Bottle Brown"*
*(So what if her bifocals are big and thick and round?*
*"Pay him no nevermind, Zuni," is what Danitra said*
*Then hands on hips, she turned away and lifted up her head.*
*"Me, Danitra Brown, I've got no time for Freddy's mess.*
*Can't waste time on some boy who thinks it's funny bein' mean.*
*Got books to read and hills to climb that Freddy's never seen."*
*Then dumb old Freddy Watson called me "Toothpick legs" and spit.*
*I stared him down, and abled my fists and said, "Okay! That's it!"*
*But suddenly I thought about the words Danitra said.*
*I rolled my eyes and grabbed my books and turned away instead.*

September 11: We had our discussion about name-calling today . . . These were the names that they dictated: Fucker; Bitch; Asshole; Whore; Black Nigger; Yo' mama _____!; Back to you; You an ugly mama too!; Cry baby; You're ugly; You look like a boy; Crackhead; Gay bitch; You're gay; Hype; Dummy; Sissy; Idiot; Drug dealer; Sick bitch; Gay bitch; Pistol; Stupid brat; Shut up!; Blackie; Faggot; Jackass; MF; Shithead; Black ass; Let's carjack her!

Kids talked specifically about some names and why they hurt ("I don't like people saying things about my mama 'cause my mama's not that kind of person.") We role-played different ways to handle name-calling and I read the poem, but I realized that we had a long way to go. That this was a relevant topic I had no doubt. Kids who were often stumped at math and reluctant to volunteer ideas about science had their hands up continuously. They felt heard, certainly, and important. They were the experts.

## NAME-CALLING CONTINUED AND STEREOTYPING

### Issues Concerning Oppressed Groups Often Cannot (and Should Not) Be Isolated; Interconnections Are a Natural Part of Culturally Relevant Teaching.

The terms that came up in the discussion on name-calling fell into natural categories. We talked about how the names fell into certain categories, like racism, sexism, and homophobia. We defined and discussed each category.

> Kendra brought up "homophobia" and I wrote it on the board and talked about what it meant and how it's related to words like "faggot" and "gay bitch." There were some negative reactions (among kids new to my class) to the word "gay." Tony said, "I hate gay people." After school he met one of Caleb's moms, Anne. Caleb went up to Tony and said, "Well, do you like my mom?" He said, "Yeah." Caleb said, "Well, my mom's gay, so I guess you don't hate gay people."

That weekend I sent home a copy of the "Danitra Brown" poem and an assignment to write about a time when they were called a name. The stories that the kids wrote were about a range of issues, from physical differences to sexism to homophobia to racism.

> When I was in 2nd grade some Body said I was little (by Jeremy)

> You are drty
> You are drty
> ha ha ha ha
> then I ran home (by Steven)

> When I stand in line to Play tether ball people say "you probably can't beat anybody."
> And I just egnore it. (by Jana)

> A kid at scool made fun of me because I had two moms and thretend me not to tell.
> It made me mad and sad and scard nd I wanted to figt him. (by Caleb)

*My cosint said I couldn't come in the play stor becose I was brown. (by Lena)*

*One day somebody call me and some other peole a neacger and we dod not like that.
(by Anitra)*

Looking back to September, I realize how crucial the name-calling discussions and activities were. They were a beginning to helping bridge gaps of understanding among the kids in the class, a way to help Tony understand how his hurt at being called "Blackie" was linked to Caleb's distress at hearing kids put down gay people and to Jana's struggle to define herself as a girl who defies constructions of femininity by competing with boys at tetherball.

In other discussions throughout the semester, I have been reminded how the problems of one oppressed group are linked to those of other groups. Never have the kids let me get away with isolating them. Typically in November, children receive confused messages about happy Native Americans, who (when they weren't being violent and savage) were helping the Pilgrims have a nice time in America. To counteract those stereotypes, I decided to show the filmstrip "Unlearning Native American Stereotypes." Before the filmstrip, I started a discussion on what a stereotype is. No one seemed quite clear on the definition, so I asked for volunteers to demonstrate the meaning of the word. Jana came up. I said, "Jana is a fantastic tetherball player, right?" The class agreed emphatically. "Jana's a girl, so all girls must be good tetherball players." "No!" protested Samantha. "I'm a girl and I'm really bad at tetherball!"

"But Jana's a *tomboy*," someone called out as if that explained everything. "That's why she's good at tetherball."

I wrote the word "tomboy" on the board and asked what a tomboy was.

"It's a girl who wants to be a boy!" someone said, with conviction. I wrote that down, along with other descriptors, like "loud," "likes to get dirty," and "gets into fights." I checked out this definition of a tomboy with Jana, who, although she loves all sports, from ice hockey to competitive swimming, is one of the most soft-spoken and unaggressive children in the class.

"Jana, do you want to be a boy?" "Are you loud?" "Do you like to get dirty?" Jana answered every question with an emphatic "NO!"

"Well, there you have an excellent example of a stereotype!" I pointed out. I was rather surprised but also pleased that my lesson on Native American stereotypes had turned into a powerful learning experience about gender constructions.

## THE COURT SYSTEM

**Current Events Can Provide the Spark to
Ignite the Classroom; You Never Know What
Hidden Talents Your Kids Might Have.**

I was still struggling with how to make my wetlands unit more compelling when the verdict from a murder involving a well-known African American athlete was announced over the school's loudspeaker. We had a long discussion, not only about the news (almost everybody had an opinion) but also about the court system and how it works. As I noted in my journal:

> Our discussion was a big hit. I couldn't contain the energy and enthusiasm.

I decided to go with the interest and have the class conduct a mock trial of the wolf from the book *The True Story of the Three Little Pigs* by Jon Scieszka. This book, which tells the traditional folktale from the wolf's point of view, is—intentionally or not—relevant to the lives of oppressed minorities, particularly male African Americans. The wolf describes himself as being misinterpreted, unfairly judged by a society in which all the power is held by the pigs (the police are represented as pigs, and the press is also run by pigs). The wolf, who starts off with a bad reputation and then is caught up in a series of unfortunate circumstances, doesn't have a chance to prove his innocence. I asked my husband, Jack, a legal services attorney, to be our resource person for the trial. I warned him about the class, however, telling him that it might be more difficult to control than previous classes.

> October 23: This morning we did the trial of the big bad wolf. This class, which all the "specials" teachers say is so difficult, sat for an hour and a half while Jack explained our legal system and then helped them facilitate a trial. They not only sat still; they were focused, appropriate, attentive. There was not one behavior problem.
>
> Tonisha stole the show. She was a stellar defense attorney. Strutting back and forth, with her hands behind her back, she grilled the witnesses, never once losing her composure . . .
>
> "And where exactly was you at 7:30 a.m.? And what was you doing? . . . Uh huh . . ."
>
> Caleb's (prosecuting attorney) closing statement did not hold a candle to Tonisha's. Looking hard at the jurors, she said,

"And how could he have gone to the store? It's three blocks away. He has no car. There's no bus. He had to borrow the sugar. And he didn't kill the pigs. It was an accident! And what was that third pig doing calling his grandma names!"

The jury found the wolf innocent.

Jack enjoyed the experience; he was very impressed with the class, especially Tonisha. "She's a better advocate than a lot of attorneys I know," he said. I made the mistake of telling Tonisha how much Jack and I liked her performance. "Jack says you should be a lawyer when you grow up," I told her the next day. A few minutes later, when I reminded her to stop twirling around and get to work on her writing, she said to me slyly, "But if I go straight to lawyer school, then I don't need to do this work!" But even when the side of Tonisha that her mom calls the "bad attitude" comes to the forefront, the image of Tonisha the attorney still remains fresh in my mind.

## ALCOHOL AND OTHER DRUGS

### The Students Are Likely to Know More Than You Do. In Addition, You Can't Rely on Prepackaged Materials to Teach Socially Relevant Topics.

The school district supplies teachers with a scripted, prepackaged kit to use in teaching about alcohol and other drugs. The kit, "Here's Looking at You, 2000" (Comprehensive Health Education Foundation, 2000), contains posters, puppets, and videos, along with a script giving students simplified solutions, such as "Just say no." However, as Jonathan Kozol states in *Amazing Grace:*

> If only enough children, we are told, would act the way the heroes do, say no to drugs and sex and gold chains and TV and yes to homework, values, church, and abstinence . . . we could turn this thing around and wouldn't need to speak about dark, messy matters such as race, despisal, and injustice. (Kozol, 1995, p. 154)

I gave the kit to another teacher and instead decided to teach about alcohol and drugs by having students share their own ideas on a "web" and by having discussions branching off of related literature, such as "The Seller" by Eloise Greenfield (1991), from *Night on Neighborhood Street.*

### The Seller

*When the seller comes around*
*Carrying in his many pockets*
*Packages of death*
*All the children go inside*
*They see his easy smile*
*They know his breath is cold*
*They turn their backs and*
*Reach for warmth*
*And life*

November 20: Discussion of the poem: "The Seller"

*Kendra:* The "packages of death" are packages of crack and cocaine. The sentences "Easy smile . . . breath is cold" probably mean they know he's trying to sell crack. He is near death. When it says that they turn their back it means that they go to a family member, talk to them about it.

*Emily:* He is selling alcohol and drugs and cigarettes. Kids don't want to take drugs and get hooked on them.

*Lena:* The line "Seller . . . death" means that people are dead. They're burying them—all the children go inside because they don't want to die, " . . . cold" means he's not breathing. They're trying to get away.

*Junior:* The packages of death are guns in packages. They came to kill.

*Cassie:* "Packages of death" are guns. People are going inside.

*Samantha:* Any kind of thing that would hurt someone. Children think he could sell them to somebody. He's mean inside, but he doesn't show it. He acts like a good person.

*Caleb:* The "packages of death" are bullets and gunpowder.

*Anitra:* They're dead people in packages.

*Jeremy:* It's guns.

*Anitra:* It's little pieces of body.

(I redirected them to the poem several times, reminding them that the packages were so small that they fit in the seller's pocket.)

*Sarah:* It's drugs and alcohol.

*Kendra:* (Still sure of her initial response): It's crack. It can kill you. Is crack the drug that you cut up with that little shaver thing and sniff it up your nose?

*Anitra:* With a straw.

*Jeremy:* That's cocaine.

*Kendra:* Crack you can shoot up with a needle or put it in your mouth.

*Ian:* The packages are guns and bullets.

*Tonisha:* The seller is selling weed and stuff like that. The kids are trying to get away from him. They don't want to grow up like that.

*Cassie:* It's cigarettes and cigars. They can kill you. They plug up your lungs.

(I remind them how you can get cigarettes—by buying them at the store. Why would the seller be selling them on the streets? Cassie, still convinced it's cigarettes, says that he could be selling them to kids.)

*Kendra:* It's that green stuff. You stick it into white paper and then they light it up and smoke.

*Kendra, Renee, Jeremy:* That's blunt! Some people use brown paper or white paper. It's the same thing.

*Tonisha:* Crack dealers be callin' people up to the corner.

*Junior:* The guy is trying to sell crack or cocaine to them, so they run away.

*Kendra:* It almost killed someone in my family.

*Anitra:* Usually people be sellin' little packages of crack or cocaine.

*Ellen:* Ritalin. It could be Ritalin. My little sister takes Ritalin because she's hyper.

(I try to point out that Ritalin is a prescription drug for people with attention deficit hyperactivity disorder, not an illegal drug that's sold on the streets, but Ellen insists.)

No people take to get high, like crack or cocaine. I know. And they take too much and it can kill.

*Renee:* There could be a pocket knife in the package.

*Lena:* It could be crack. Someone in my family does crack. They try not to show me, but he left it on the floor. It was brown little pieces of grass and a ball.

*Tonisha:* My m—someone in my family, She promised me one thing, that she wouldn't do it again. She thought I was stupid or something. She promised. But she got all broke doin' it. I was scared because she was all hyped up. But I'm not stupid. I heard her talking to my uncle. I knew what she was doin.' But I made her promise she wouldn't do it again. Now they don't do it no more.

*Kendra:* Someone in my family, we put her in a group home. We put her in a hospital. Then she got pregnant and was doing crack and now she is off crack, but she's pregnant.

Obviously, this class had a lot of information about and personal experiences with drugs. Not only did their knowledge exceed the bounds of the

Madison Metropolitan School District (MMSD) curriculum, but it also showed my ignorance in some areas. I checked with the school nurse about the uses of Ritalin. She told me that Ellen's information was accurate. Ritalin is indeed a drug that is being sold on the black market. It is taken by adults as an upper, an amphetamine-type drug, to lose weight and stay awake. Also, it is taken by crack users to smooth the descent from a crack-induced high. So much for teacher's knowledge. I quizzed my friends to find out what a "blunt" is and was told that it is a Jamaican-style reefer. The district's "Here's Looking at You, 2000" curriculum may need an updating.

A resource I found more useful was *The House That Crack Built* by Clark Taylor (1992). I prefaced reading the book aloud by asking the kids to describe a house that crack built:

> "All broken down," they said. "Old, broken windows, people going in and out selling crack." Then I showed them the picture on the first page, an illustration of a mansion with a swimming pool. "This is the house that crack built." Renee, who often seems lost in class, raising her hand and then saying, "I forgot," or "What was that again?" spoke up. "It's a rich house, 'cause they got rich from selling all that crack." (Taylor, 1992, p. 121)

Since the interest in this book was intense, I decided to use it for my reading group with Renee, Henry, Tonisha, and Dana, all of whom had tested at a Preprimer (kindergarten) level at the beginning of second grade. I knew that the book would be considered at least a year above their levels, but I thought it would be a motivating change from the kindergarten primers. I sat down with Renee and Henry, while the instructional assistant read with Tonisha and Dana. They took turns reading, using their fingers to mark the words. Asking for help only occasionally, they read through the book confidently, reciting the last page in unison:

> *And these are the Tears we cry in our sleep*
> *that fall for the Baby with nothing to eat,*
> *born of the Girl who's killing her brain,*
> *smoking the Crack that numbs the pain,*
> *bought from the Boy feeling the heat,*
> *chased by the Cop working his beat*
> *who battles the Gang, fleet and elite,*
> *that rules the Street of a town in pain*
> *that cries for the Drug known as cocaine,*

*made from the Plants that people can't eat,*
*raised by the Farmers who work in the heat*
*and fear the Soldiers who guard the Man*
*who lives in the House that crack built.*

# UNIT ON AFRICAN AMERICANS' STRUGGLE FOR CIVIL RIGHTS

## Including the Voices and Experiences of the Students' Families Can Enhance the Relevance of and Add a Multitude of Perspectives to a Topic.

This year, as in previous years, I used Martin Luther King, Jr.'s birthday as a springboard to explore the many facets of African Americans' struggle for freedom in the United States. Along with background biographies of Martin Luther King, Jr., and Harriet Tubman, the class read biographies of other African Americans. We engaged in many activities that helped bring those stories to life, including role-playing famous people, reenacting the Underground Railroad, watching segments of *Eyes on the Prize*, and writing fictitious slave autobiographies.

The assignment to write a story "as if you were a slave" resulted in some of the best writing to date. Two of the biracial girls, Lena and Kendra (both second graders), reached new levels of sophistication in their writing. Lena had started the school year as a solid reader, but a rather limited writer.

Over the Summer (August 29)

*I saw a blue-jay it was pritty! I like flowers. There are all kinds of flowers. I think flowers, birds are pritty. Me and my little sister like flowers.*

In the autobiography assignment, Lena made tremendous strides in using descriptive language in narrative to express experience and meaning.

Emily (March 22)

*My name is emily. I am 28 years old. I have dubble twins. Their names are Lanny, Anwon, Lynnda, Cortes. I sew inside the house. I've bin sewing all my life. I have a hussband. His name is Nathan. he is 29 yuears old. He was born in 1846 and I was born in 1845. He worked on the field he howed all the weeds out of the gardan. I am very brave and so is my hussband. I am thinking about running away but oh no the master reads my mined he waches me while I look at the forest like the sky preparing for thounder I dort to the forest and with no ferher or do [no further ado] he shots me. Blood goshing blood coming out of my shoolder. Thinking about turning around but thinking abot the wipings I've got I hide in a bush. I take a leaf off a tree and bandeg my shoolder. I check to see if the slave cacher is nere. I run fast without looking back I run through a swamp, ponds, crecks, rivers, soon I come to the ohio river I look all aroune. I find a boat. I quick get in. I quick get acerost the river. I reach Caneda. I am free free free!*

This assignment may have been particularly meaningful to Lena because of her yearlong identity struggles:

(September 20—Lena was unhappy, whiny, disobedient. [The student teacher] got a chance to talk with her, and it turns out that the girls who jump-rope will not accept her. Lena is biracial, but acts White. The girls who jump-rope are all conceptually Black. I think that Lena is having some profound identity problems. I think that at home [with a White mom and White stepdad] she lives in a White culture, yet is constantly aware that she is not White.)

Lena displayed an interest in the Black history unit and a culminating sense of pride and awareness when the unit culminated: "You know what I feel lucky about? That I'm half Black!"

Kendra experimented with the use of dialogue (including dialect) and humor in her first-person slave narrative.

*Shanada*

*By Kendra*

*I be workin all night in the kichin. One higt I had two set's of twin's in the master's soup. I was tring to get the sening (seasoning). I pulled all 4 baby's up fast and went to my cabin. My master toke his wipe (whip) and wipt me and my baby's 82 times. We scremed loud we woke up my boy frind. Who was 16 just like me. My master said "you make her have baby's in my soup? Ha, ha, ha. I atae (ought to) wipe (whip) you to." "No you wont." my boy frind sied. Anoter slave came runin and sayin "It's the free time. We is free. We is free. We is free. It is the free time" "We is free, a free slave. We is free slave!!!!!!!!!!!!!!!!!!!!!!!" we shouted with glory. that is the end of my life.*

I decided to try to help create a closer link between our studies and the students' families by asking students to interview a parent or grandparent about the civil rights movement. I wrote out interview questions: "What do you remember about the Civil Rights Movement? How did you learn about it (personal experience, TV, school, and so on)? How old were you at this time? What do you remember about the leaders? How has the Civil Rights Movement changed our lives? What still needs to be changed to achieve justice and equality?" When I shared my plans with another teacher, I was warned that I might get negative, even racist reactions. I decided to take the risk. I hoped that our classroom activities were bringing the students closer to an understanding of the struggles endured and the bravery shown by African Americans living in the United States during the Civil Rights Movement; what could bridge the achievement gap better than learning about the students' own families' involvement in and feelings about the movement?

> January 30: The added perspective that we have gained from parent and grandparent interviews and presentations has given depth that the unit lacked in the past. Stories have come out from Black and non-Black families alike that have amazed me. Caleb's mom's experience [as a Catholic growing up in Tennessee] with the Ku Klux Klan burning a cross on her family's front yard and killing their dogs was particularly fascinating to the class. I think that we too often think of the African Americans being the sole victims of racism.

> From Sarah's interview with her mom: "Once I was called a nigger lover. My best friend was Afro-American. Sometimes I was sad, but my parents helped me feel strong and brave."

> Grandparents of two of the White kids and one aunt were active in the movement.

> Samantha's mom said, "I remember my oldest sister going to Alabama to help Black people register to vote, and my father being very upset about it."

> Cassie's grandma came in and talked about how she and several others from their church collected petitions to get an NAACP chapter started in a city in Oklahoma.

> How did the relatives interviewed learn about the Civil Rights Movement?

> Family, school, TV, personal experience, books, other people, church?

> One African American parent answered this way,

> "I was there. I remember the marches in Chicago."

Another African American parent who *was there* volunteered to speak to the class about his experience hearing Martin Luther King, Jr., speak. He told the class that he was so impressed with the power of Dr. King's speeches that he went to hear Dr. King whenever possible. This parent impressed the class by reciting from memory several parts of Dr. King's speeches. Henry, who usually tries to find any excuse to avoid working on a writing assignment, sat down enthusiastically to work on that week's class news.

### Aaron's Speech

*I don't believe my eyes. Somebody met Dr. King. Aaron (Dana's dad) went to see Dr. King. Aaron was 20 years old when he saw Dr. King. Aaron did Dr. King's speech. It was good and his speech was, "I have a Dream."*

This year has been the first year that I felt the kids are realizing that, although the Civil Rights Movement was an exciting and powerful agent of change, it did not eradicate racism and inequity. The last question of the interview, *"What still needs to be changed to achieve justice and equality?"* gave parents an opportunity to communicate their feelings about this issue to their children and to their classmates.

*"Mainly I say racism. It's still racism going on,"* responded one African American parent.

*"Maybe if we could rid the world of so much prejudice that still exists today,"* said another.

*"That we use hearts and not our attitudes to live together,"* was another response typical of Black and non-Black family members.

*"Equal pay for equal jobs,"* was mentioned more than once.

*"There is still a lot of prejudice and oppression and poverty. We need to continue to educate fairly and provide equal opportunity for all,"* summed up one parent.

Many of the interviews were done with parents, who ranged in age from 7 years old to 20 years old at the time of the Civil Rights Movement. It was interesting that, even though they were young, they still remembered it having an impact on them. The intergenerational personal histories, in some cases from grandparents, helped make this unit come alive for the classroom.

## AIDS AWARENESS UNIT

### The Realities of the Children's Lives Will Connect With a Relevant Topic. A Class Project That Includes an Element of Activism Will Cement a Classroom Community.

I wasn't sure if I should do a unit on AIDS this year because 15 of my students had been in my class last year when I taught an extensive unit on the subject. However, at parent-teacher conferences, a girl whose sister had been in my class last year asked to learn about AIDS. Also, the topic was coming up frequently.

September 29: Yesterday I (again) saw the kind of focused attention a topic of relevance can bring. (Another teacher) came into the classroom to give me the $10 he had pledged for the AIDS walk. One of the kids said, "Why are you giving Kate money?" He explained, and Renee asked, "What's AIDS?" Several students responded, both from my class last year and new students. Some kids talked about activities we did last year during our unit on AIDS. Lots of hands were up; people were interrupting with questions and comments. I was aware that everyone was participating, including the African American students whom I have had so much trouble getting involved. There was a clear difference between this discussion and our discussion of the wetlands, when I often have three or four children answering all the questions.

I asked the class why they were so interested in AIDS. Jana raised her hand, and then said, "It's so interesting, why? I really don't know why. It just is really interesting." Anitra said, "It's because all the teenagers talk about it." I had a sense that AIDS was part of the street talk and street reality for the kids who live in the projects; Anitra's comment confirmed my suppositions. Kendra answered, "Well, some of us have relatives with AIDS. And there's this house by my house that's for people with AIDS—you know, so they can live there and people can take care of them and help them." Tonisha could relate to this comment (she lives by Mendota Mental Health Center). "Oh, it's like the house for the crazy people! Except they're different. I mean, they're the same, but they're different. People don't die from being crazy, but they die from having AIDS." Tonisha spoke animatedly, excited by her new insight.

November 3: We had a mundane protective behaviors lesson on Monday, which ended up being very intense, as do most things in this class. This is a routine brainstorm in which kids list things that are unsafe. Second on the list (after "hitting on others in the family") was "not wearing a condom." "Why?" I asked. "Because of teenage pregnancy and AIDS." After continuing a list of about 50 unsafe behaviors, ranging from "Riding no-handed" to "Sexual harassment," I started a column on "How You Can Be Safe." "Wear a condom when you have sex, unless you want babies," was first on the list.

I decided to do a curriculum web on AIDS to learn what the students know about AIDS and what they want to learn. My housemate arranged to film the AIDS web for a video project she was doing for a graduate school class. I had just announced to the class that it was AIDS Awareness Week and I was about to write the word "AIDS" on a large sheet of paper when Kendra and her mom appeared at the door. Both looked distraught. "Sorry Kendra's late," apologized her mom. "My cousin is dying of AIDS; in fact she will probably die tonight. The whole family's upset. Kendra wants to see her cousin, but I don't want her to. She looks like a skeleton; it would be too scary for her." Kendra joined the group with her head lowered and her chin cupped in her hands; she was not her usual animated self. Slowly, she started joining in the discussion. "My cousin is dying of AIDS," she contributed. "She wants to die at home. She's so far into the AIDS process that she doesn't want to go to the hospital. She just sits there. She doesn't move. We're going to see her today." The next day, Kendra wrote a story about her cousin.

> Hi my name is [Kendra], My sackint casin Wande died of AIDS. "a. acqured." "I. Immune." D. Deficieney" "S.Syndrome." she had AIDS for 9 years. she got it from drugs. I miss her. the end.

Last year our class had made red ribbons and sold them to raise money for AIDS. I had tried not to repeat the project this year because I didn't think I could duplicate the excitement and pride created by that project. I thought that it might be disappointing to the kids from last year's class if we had negative responses to our efforts and/or failed to raise as much money. However, after we did the web, one student suggested, "Let's sell red ribbons again and get money for people with AIDS!" "Yeah!" chimed in several others. Henry's half-jesting comment that our class should keep part of the money was quickly hooted down. "No, we can't do that. We're raising money for people with AIDS!" "Well, let's take a vote," I suggested. Every hand went up.

Someone suggested that we give the money to the moms in the Madison AIDS Support Network (MASN), instead of to the children in the support group: "The moms are the ones with AIDS."

"But, listen," said Adam. "Let's say we get one hundred dollars again. If the medication costs two hundred for one bottle, then we are only buying half, only half for one person. But one hundred dollars for the kids' group to spend will mean a lot more!" Discussion and debate followed, with the proposal of giving half the money to the kids and half to the moms gaining support.

On Friday (video camera rolling again), I asked for volunteers to count the money we had collected that week. I was worried that we would have only $30 to $40. Kids had diligently checked off lists of Hawthorne staff members so that no one, from the student teachers to the principal to the custodian, was not solicited. However, unlike last year, this year only a few parents had been in to buy ribbons. When someone ran up to Caleb's mom, she pointed out that she was wearing her ribbon from last year. "I was ready for you guys!" she said. Tonisha volunteered to count the dollar bills, and Jeremy opted to add up the change. Tonisha checked and double-checked her calculations.

"Sixty-six dollars! WHOA!" she announced. Jeremy carefully made piles of coins and added a can half full of pennies.

"I got nineteen dollars and twelve cents," he said, adding his figures to Tonisha's on the board.

I gathered the group together to view the results. Tonisha shared her figures.

"What did you count?" someone asked Jeremy.

"Oh," responded Jeremy, "You know, pennies, quarters, nickels, dimes, and them big old things. There were two of those." Kids shared strategies for adding the two numbers together: Sarah wrote "85" and Adam added ".12." Tonisha added the dollar signs. I asked them to figure out how much more we needed to make $100. When they settled on $15, they jumped up and cheered; we were close to surpassing the $96.91 the class had made last year.

December 6: I think back to September when I apprehended two kids stealing. They had devised a rather elaborate plan for sneaking Emily's necklaces off the art teacher's desk, meeting in the bathroom, and hiding them under their clothes until they could stash them safely away in their backpacks upstairs. Who would have thought that I would have no second thoughts about trusting Tonisha, Jeremy, and various helpers to count out $85.00? Yet, as I worked with other kids around the room, only intermittently checking on the progress of the money counting project, it never occurred to me to worry about the security of so much cash.

## CONCLUSION: CULTURALLY RELEVANT TEACHING WORKS FOR ALL KIDS

December 10: Today, as I watched the kids writing quietly at their tables and desks, constructing fictional stories about AIDS, I thought about my worries early in the semester:

I need to get a grip on these internal tensions for the class to function . . . How will I cut down or eliminate such incidents (the playground fight) as happened last week? . . .

They all have histories (already, by second grade) of school failure. They have been pegged as discipline problems by their former teachers and their moms. They have started school with "attitudes," meaning not only attitudes of disobedience and lack of respect for "authority," but attitudes of street-wise toughness. They have picked up the walk and talk of their rebellious teenage siblings or neighbors . . .

I wonder about the academic split in this class. All the high achievers (except for two biracial girls) are White and all those achieving below grade level are African American. I have six kids reading at a preprimer level. They are all African American or biracial. I have seven kids, five White and two biracial, reading from a fourth- to eighth-grade level. I'm most concerned about the first six. Not reading at all at second grade is unusual . . .

Will the integration of topics of high interest to my African American kids improve their reading and writing skills? . . .

The papers (research on wetlands animals) aren't great, but they'll do for a first research attempt. I feel guilty that all the casualties are African American. If I were a better teacher, this wouldn't happen.

As I watch them write, I realize how much has changed. Renee, Henry, and Tonisha have all made gains in reading, from one level (Renee) to a whole year's growth in 3 months (Tonisha). Renee is contributing meaningfully to discussions. She is beginning to write:

*you ca gent HIV fom playeing the prcn wo gant the HIV.*

*you ca gent HIV fom plas gams yet the prcn wo gant the HIV.*

*or you ca gent HIV fom reed wo the prcn wo gant the HIV.*

Henry has softened up. He shows a very vulnerable side under his toughness. He, too, is writing and even volunteering to share his stories with the class. This story he requested to read aloud to the class twice:

*I do not have AIDS. I know somebody that has AIDS. Around my house is a boy 10 years old. He told me that he got AIDS. I think I will get AIDS when I grow up because I might forget to use safe protection for having sex.* [edited for spelling]

Kids have questions about Henry's story. They wondered why he thought he would get AIDS and if other African American boys, like Henry, envision contracting AIDS as a likely part of their future.

Tonisha is still intense, but involved, enthusiastic, less frequently oppositional. She was totally absorbed in the AIDS unit. At first she balked at the writing assignment, doing a lot of erasing and starting over several times. "Can it be a true story about someone in my family?" she asked. "Sure," I said, "Kendra wrote about her cousin and Emily is writing about her uncle." Tonisha sat down to write and didn't stop until she finished this story:

AIDS

*My gamaemom [grandma] died ove AIDS Be cas she was going wethe some one wa [who] had AIDS and he's stell allve. I hat ham becos he cod [killed] my gamaemom. his name os Owie Navr come back Owie be Cos my whole fimey [family] hates you in clating [including] me Owie I whs [wish] you wan [wouldn't] did that cod [killed] my gamaemom I hat him vare vare much I happy [hope] you no neve come back and he never will come back!!!!!!!!!!!!!!!!!!!!!!*

After school, Tonisha wanted her mom to know that she had filled up a whole page and a half (her longest story so far this year). Her mom said, "She's reading and writing a lot better, I've noticed that!" I asked her if she minded if I included this story in a book of kids' stories about AIDS. "No, I just was worried that other kids might treat Tonisha different if they knew that her grandma died of AIDS. It's okay with me; I was just worried about Tonisha." I was able to assure her with confidence that such discrimination would not happen in *this* class.

The students from last year who had started off the year in crisis, either from family stress or because the classroom dynamics had changed with the addition of the new kids, have filled up the holes left vacant by the kids who had moved. Kendra is definitely now a leader, both socially and academically. Jeremy, once pegged as a troublemaker with a borderline IQ, has (with the help of medication for ADHD [attention deficit hyperactivity disorder]) become a math whiz and a confident contributor to group discussions. The class feels like a unit, a positive community. Ironically, a new child, whom the principal purposely assigned to my class ("She'll be a good influence on your kids. She's *blonde*. And I think she's a good student.") has been posing major problems, both for me and the others. Lena and Kendra rushed in from recess today, very upset. "Ellen discriminates!" they said, in one voice. "She said she wouldn't play with us because we are half Black!"

Ellen is coming without the benefit of our monthlong exploration of the effects of name-calling and stereotyping. She is also coming into a closely knit classroom community, with internal rules of operation that she is yet unaware of. Ellen, too, coming from a school history of frequent moves and a family damaged by domestic abuse, has problems of her own to figure out. It will take her time to realize that stellar academic performances alone will not give her a place of prominence in this community.

I have focused in this study on my African American and biracial students' growth in reading, writing, and participation. However, I believe that the other students (White, Asian American, and Mexican American) benefit as much from this curriculum as do their classmates. Curriculum that deals with the real world and enables the children to be active participants and agents of change, brings out the best in all kids.

During the AIDS unit, Caleb came in with a big smile on his face. "I have an announcement to make!" He opened an envelope containing a big wad of bills. "I made $51.05 from selling red ribbons at my moms' bowling place. It was kind of scary, going up to perfect strangers, but I did it! I even got five dollars for a ribbon . . . well, they gave me a five and I gave them four ones for change." Caleb took out a crumpled sheet of paper. "Here's the math work. We now have $136.17 in all!"

At writing time, I suggested that everybody write a story about AIDS. Several kids asked if their story could be part fact, part fiction. "Sure," I said, wondering what they had in mind. When I saw Cassie's title, "The Ghost with AIDS," I was skeptical. "Well, I like ghost stories," she said defensively. This was her story.

*The Gost whth AIDS*

*Once upon a time there was a gril hwo got AIDS from drugs. Her name was Sue. She was 8 when she diad. Her gost comes out evry niht. Some times she comes out in the day time and talks to kids about AIDS. She says . . .*

*"You ca'nt get AIDS from kissing, hugging, being frands, going to the same bath room, You can only get AIDS from un prtakted sexs, durgs, your mom having AIDS, tocing some bodys blod."*

*She will stop coming out when AIDS gos away.*

Blia wrote a fictional story:

*A Wnaman wow get AIDS*

*Oens ther was a wamon who get AIDS. Her name was Mai. She had a fian name Pa. Pa was nice to her. Now Mai is 20 yis old too. Pa tok her to the soiy [store] and biat her some madsn [medicine] to eat. And Pa tok Mia to her houe to sepp [sleep] fro awhiyl. She died win she was 40. Pa war role sad.*

Adam wrote a science fiction story about how AIDS started:

*The fikshinl beegening of AIDS*

*Long ago ther was a planit cold [called] Bla and ther wer lats of aleens on it thae had onlee one problem thar was a dozez [disease] cold Araim. One tim a aleen got a spas sip and left the planit then the saps ship ran uot of gas and krashd on rth [earth] but wut the aleeen didn't know is that he had Araim and wen he got ot of the spasship he spred Araim to the wrld. PS the hemins [humans] named Araim AIDS.*

Finally, several students decided that a letter to the government was in order. Here is Emily's:

*Dear Prasadont Clonton,*

*Plesae loer pricis for the matason for AIDS. Pepole with AIDS want to live loggor. Evin thwo I Don't have HIV or AIDS I want siintists to find a cure for AIDS. I want to help people with AIDS. My class is hlping peple with AIDS by seling red robons. We ernd $136.17. Thars a lot of way's to help pepol with HIV or AIDS so plese loer the price of the matason for AIDS Ples?*

*Sonsirly [Emily]*

## THE CONSCIENCE OF A NATION

Kozol's book *Amazing Grace* examines the effects of "ghettoizing" the castoffs of society. The South Bronx, whose residents are almost all either African American or Puerto Rican, has a very high percentage of people who are or have been affected by poverty, homelessness, drug abuse, and AIDS. "One quarter of the women of Mott Haven who are tested in obstetric wards are positive for HIV" (Kozol, 1995, p. 4). Kozol's book is a tribute to the people who survive—or don't survive—against these tremendous odds. However, in giving his book the subtitle *The Lives of Children and the*

*Conscience of a Nation,* Kozol is focusing on the people who live elsewhere in New York and in the United States, people who passively accept the plight of the inhabitants of the South Bronx and of others similarly ostracized from "the good life." He questions the consciences of people who can live comfortably in their affluence, while children lack basic human rights, like hospital care, clean air, safe housing, food, and protection from violence:

> The search for explanations of the sadness heard in many of the voices of the people I have met is not answered by the factual questions one might ask about "environment" or "health care" or "the public schools." The questions that need asking seem to go beyond these concrete matters. One wants to know instead how people hold up under this terrible ordeal, how many more do not, how human beings devalue other people's lives, how numbness and destructiveness are universalized, how human pity is at length extinguished and the shunning of the vulnerable can come in time to be perceived as natural behavior. (Kozol, 1995, pp. 185–186)

A culturally relevant curriculum provides a forum in which the minority children in our society can actively participate in their schooling and can learn and develop their strengths and talents. But a culturally relevant curriculum is equally important for the White students. First, many of them, too, are outside of the American Dream; they are females, they come from alcoholic or abusive families; they have gay or lesbian parents; they are disabled or poor. (As I run through my class list, I cannot think of a single child who does not fit into at least one of these categories.) But even those children who may grow up to "make it" in the mainstream of U.S. society need to learn that they are part of a larger community that they, too, are responsible for. Projects like learning about and raising money for people with AIDS teach children respect, compassion, and activism. When my students gave their $153.67 to the MASN representative, the woman (who is HIV-positive) told them that what they did was commendable. However, she asserted that even more important was that they "Keep doing things like this. Keep caring about people and working to help them, so that you will continue to do so as an adult, so that you will work to change the world. Far too few adults do what you did."

"How does a nation deal with those it has cursed?" asks Kozol (Kozol, 1995, p. 186). Education can offer no more than a partial answer, but in a nation in which, says Reverend Overall, " . . . social blindness is accepted as a normal state of mind . . ." (Kozol, 1995, p. 188), culturally relevant teaching can begin to help children create a vision for the future—a vision of a caring, healthy, and just society.

## REFLECTIONS

It's almost May. My students are far from perfect. The principal says they are the noisiest class in the hallways. I got a report that Henry had stolen a Popsicle from the lunchroom last week. Renee still scores a Preprimer 1, Level 5 on the Running Records Inventory. Although Tonisha has progressed almost to a fourth-grade level in reading, she still has days when she needs to sit on my lap in order to calm down enough to listen to a guest speaker.

But when I think back on how this year started, I realize that our individual and collective progress has been significant. The students' reading levels, as measured by the district's Running Records Inventory, increased during the academic year by an average of about two years. Although the gains of the African American and biracial students ranged widely (from Renee's increase of one level to Tonisha's increase of 3.5 years), the average improvement for that group also was about two years. At the end of the year, the average reading level in the class was 5.1, with the African American and biracial students at 3.8, still significantly above grade level. All third-grade students—except four students classified as learning disabled (LD) or English as a second language (ESL), who were not tested—*scored above the state standard* on the state third-grade reading test.

The gains in writing are more difficult to quantify. The average score in the class on the second-grade district writing sample was 6, which is considered at grade level and is an average score in the district. However, the many pieces of writing I collected throughout the school year clearly show that there was a significant gain in all aspects of writing skills, including mechanics, sentence construction, writing to a topic, organization, and using voice.

Looking through student portfolio records, I realize that behavioral progress could be measured by the decreasing number of pink slips (office referrals) during the second semester. Student progress in motivation, participation, and community building is much better illustrated, however, by my journal entries and narratives and by the children's stories. The students' final self-evaluations revealed that behavioral and academic progress are integrally connected with learning about culturally relevant issues. When asked to write about what they had learned, what they felt proud about, and what they need to work on, two second graders and one third grader responded:

> I now [know] a lot nouw. I love Being in 2nd grad. I learned a lot about Aids. Now I can read about Aids. I need to work harder on my homework. (Tonisha)

> I have learned a lot about the reprdtson system, making frainds, Jews and notsys. Now I can writ better than when I started. I need to work harer on math. I'm really prod

*about my reading and writing. Sometimes I forget to put . , ! ? [punctuation] in my storys. (Cassie)*

*I have learned a lot about newspapers, A.I.D.S., math, books, things on the news. Now I can write, read, do math do my homework well. I need to word harder on not getting my name on the brod. I am really proud about read[ing], math. [I need to] raise my hand when I want to say sometime. (Anitra)*

Also, through this year's process of self-reflection, data collection, and observation, I have learned a lot about culturally relevant teaching; above all, I've gained confidence in its power. Using culturally relevant curricula is, in essence, controversial:

> Subject matter in these classrooms is regularly tied to the lives and experiences of the children. The teachers challenge the students to bring the community into the classroom. The teachers are not afraid to tackle controversy and/or issues that may seem too adult for their students . . . (Ladson-Billings, 1994, p. 78)

Along with other Hawthorne teachers, I currently find myself embroiled in a conflict between teaching staff and school and district administration about our decision to display a photographic exhibit of gay and lesbian families called "Love Makes a Family." After an emotionally draining three weeks (garnering support from staff and parents, communicating with the press and the teachers' union, battling an evasive administration, and answering to a small but vocal minority of angry, hostile, and often hateful parents), I remember my feelings at the beginning of the photo exhibit project.

> April 12: When (another teacher) brought up the possibility of having the photo exhibit of gay and lesbian families here, I heartily agreed, but at the same time something inside me balked at the idea. I felt some fear, maybe, but mostly I just felt tired. I didn't want to have to go through all the controversy that we had encountered last spring when we did the filming for "Don't Look the Other Way" (a documentary about teaching issues of homophobia in elementary schools). I just wanted to finish off the year on an easier note—endangered animals, maybe, or cooperative games. I had done racism, name-calling, alcohol and other drugs, AIDS, the Civil Rights Movement, the human body, and birth and reproduction. I wanted a rest from teaching potentially controversial subjects . . .
>
> And then I remembered my conversation with Caleb's moms. I had asked them if they were planning to participate at the protest that night (at an evangelical church sponsoring an inflammatory, anti-gay minister). They both said that they supported the people who were picketing the church, but that

they were too tired to go themselves. "I've gone to so many marches, so many rallies," said Jane. "There isn't a day in my life when I'm not confronted with homophobia. I'm just tired of it. I'll let the younger people do it for me. More power to them!"

I'm not any younger, and I'm also tired, but I can't look the other way.

The administration's conflicting messages and muddled tactics, along with full coverage by the press (Hawthorne School was in the front-page headlines for a week and on television news and radio talk shows), created even more of a controversy out of the photo exhibit than I had originally anticipated.

However, the reactions to culturally relevant curricula from administrators and parents are not always so predictable. I had not expected that Sarah's mom's decision to use a placenta for her presentation on birth would have the effect of raising administrative eyebrows. The principal admonished Kendra for running in the hall (Kendra was on her way to the bathroom because she had felt sick to her stomach after touching the placenta) and then paid a rare visit to the classroom. "What was wrong with Kendra? . . . Did you inform parents about this? . . . What is Kendra's mom's reaction going to be?" I explained about our unit. I reminded the principal about the frequent newsletters we send home. I reassured her that, in fact, Kendra's mom would be thrilled to hear about the activity, especially because Kendra's sister was going to have a baby soon, an event that Kendra was fully informed about and was participating in, even to the point of planning to be present at the birth. I tried to explain the wonder and fascination experienced by students and teachers alike. But, like the unit about the placenta, a culturally relevant curriculum has to be experienced to be fully understood. And culturally relevant teaching also is organic. It grows from the unique combination of students, teachers, families, and events in the particular classroom and community. There are no formulas, no right or wrong answers. There are only constant questions, constant challenges, constant surprises. I never start out a year knowing exactly what I will teach, nor do I have the security of knowing that what I attempt will succeed. Yet, in Sylvia Ashton-Warner's words:

> I've got to do what I believe. And I believe in all I do. It's this price one continually pays for stepping out of line. I'm feeling too old to pay it. But I must do what I believe in or nothing at all. (Ashton-Warner, 1963, p. 198)

Sitting here in the crowded, stuffy computer room of the UW–Madison Memorial Library, on my seventh hour of typing and revising, I find myself remembering the words and melody of a poem that we read over and over this year, a poem that a visiting poet-in-residence spontaneously put to music.

> *Hold fast to dreams*
> *For if dreams die,*
> *Life is a broken winged bird*
> *That cannot fly.*

—Langston Hughes ("Dreams," 1932)

## EPILOGUE

It has been more than 10 years since I wrote this account of my action research. When I first thought about how the process changed my life, I thought that not much has changed. I am still teaching second and third grade at the same school. I still teach culturally relevant curriculum, trying to inspire my students to learn through topics and activities that are central to their lives and interests.

However, teaching the way I believe best helps students learn has become more and more difficult. Curriculum is dictated to us through increasingly confined and difficult standards, standards that, unfortunately, due to my students' cultures, funds of knowledge, and academic preparation, are increasingly irrelevant to them and hard to meet. Furthermore, curriculum more often comes in boxed kits with "teacher-proof" scripts. All of our science curriculum is now supposed to be delivered through that means. And my students are even more diverse and less part of the mainstream Euro-American culture. For the last five years I have had clusters of up to 90 percent English language learners, some with histories of education in their first language, but more with little or none. Seventy-five to 85 percent of my students are at or below the poverty level. Many of their parents do not speak English. Most do not read or write in English. Yet, in spite of all these differences, standardized testing has taken up more and more of the curriculum. Because of the No Child Left Behind Act, third graders now have to take a standardized, high-stakes test, the Wisconsin Knowledge and Concepts Exam. We are told to start "test prep" in September and continue throughout October. Then in November, we spend a large chunk of our academic time on testing.

So, somehow, I must find the time to teach the way I have described here. And I do find the time, but it is squeezed in between the testing and the mandated curriculum.

Writing about action research inspired me to pursue writing about education. I used a section of the chapter (the one on AIDS) to write a story for the education journal *Rethinking Schools*. Since then I have had eight other articles published. The topics have ranged from teaching about child labor, homelessness, and the Civil Rights Movement to doing a direct action project for hurricane victims in Nicaragua. I have also written about high-stakes testing and about the value of animals in the classroom. Most of my stories have been related to using culturally relevant curriculum.

After completing my master's degree in curriculum and instruction (in multicultural education), I again went back to the university to study teaching English as a second language. In my classes and readings, I learned that teaching culturally relevant curriculum is even more important for the success in school of English language learners. Not surprisingly, bringing the students' cultures and background knowledge into the classroom can bridge the language and culture gaps that impede learning. Also, my studies reinforced my practice of exploring social justice issues and then incorporating social action into the classroom. "Critical pedagogy" makes the curriculum more meaningful to all students, but it especially speaks to students on the periphery of the mainstream culture.

Some of the topics I deal with have changed along with the experiences and the histories of my students my classroom. We still explore homelessness and the Civil Rights Movement, but now we spend several months studying the cultures and family histories of the students in my classroom. Social action projects range from the local (appearing at the school board meeting to lobby for the right to have animals in the classroom) to those on a national scope (writing to the president about threats to arctic animals because of global warming). Many of the ideas and impetus for our curriculum come from the students.

I am nearing retirement age. I know that I will miss teaching. But I will not miss all the time spent preparing for and administering tests. I hope that the pendulum will swing away from rigid standards, boxed programs, and high-stakes testing to teaching students relevant, motivating, and action-oriented curricula. I hope the day will come again when teachers are supported not only for their students' gains in test scores, but also for the way they help connect student learning to their families, their communities, and the world.

## REFERENCES

Ashton-Warner, S. (1963). *Teacher*. New York: Simon & Schuster.
Comprehensive Health Education Foundation. (2000). *Here's looking at you, 2000*. Retrieved January 25, 2007, from http://www.chef.org/prevention/looking.php

Greenfield, E. (1991). *Night on Neighborhood Street.* New York: Dial Books.

Grimes, N. (1994). *Meet Danitra Brown.* New York: Lothrop, Lee and Shepard Books.

Hughes, L. (1932). *The dream keeper and other poems.* New York: Alfred A. Knopf.

Kozol, J. (1995). *Amazing grace: The lives of children and the conscience of a nation.* New York: Random House.

Ladson-Billings, G. (1991). Like lightning in a bottle: Attempting to capture the pedagogical excellence of successful teachers of Black students. *International Journal of Qualitative Studies in Education, 3*(4), 334–344.

Ladson-Billings, G. (1994). Blurring the borders: Voices of African liberator pedagogy in the United States. *Boston University Journal of Education, 172*(2), 72–94.

Ladson-Billings, G. (1997). *The dreamkeepers: Successful teachers of African American children.* San Francisco: Jossey-Bass Publishers.

O'Brien, T. (1990). *The things they carried.* New York: Broadway Books.

Scieszka, J. (1989). *The true story of the three little pigs.* New York: Scholastic.

Taylor, C. (1992). *The house that crack built.* San Francisco: Chronicle Books.

# 10

---

# *Conclusions on Using a Constructivist Approach in a Heterogeneous Classroom*

Van E. Valaskey

## EDITORS' INTRODUCTION

Valaskey's project provides a unique account of one high school's efforts to de-track its Biology classes. Working in tandem with the special education department, Valaskey and his colleagues use assessment data, interviews, questionnaires, and student work to justify their efforts in providing equitable experiences for all students regardless of age, sex, cultural or ethnic background, or interest and motivation in science. By analyzing attendance rates, examining responses to attitudinal surveys, and interviewing all actors within the project, Valaskey recounts the successes he encountered, while also identifying areas for future study.

\* \* \* \*

## INTRODUCTION

Teachers who, like me, have been in the classroom for more than 30 years and have seen teaching fads come and go are very selective about what new pedagogy and teaching tools they put into practice. Teachers who keep current by reading professional journals and attending professional conventions often pick up good ideas to use in their classrooms. Often these new ideas look good on paper but then don't work well in the classroom. So, as the years of teaching go by, veteran teachers often become leery of new pedagogical practices that come across their paths. Will this one be just another fad or will it endure the scrutiny of those in the trenches?

I was one of those veteran teachers; I taught biology and other sciences for 32 years at an urban public high school attended by approximately 2,000 students. During that time, the high school's minority population more than doubled. Many of these students had high needs because they came from dysfunctional families and poverty. As the school's population continued to change in composition, many perceptive and experienced teachers at this school were finding that they needed to change their teaching methods. Traditional modes of teaching were not engaging many disadvantaged and minority students in the classroom experience. I saw numerous frustrated teachers wondering why they could not get many of their students excited about their curriculum.

In the early 1970s, the school district created special classes to serve students with special needs. Some of those classes still exist today. Ability grouping seemed like the perfect solution, and teachers became experts at imparting knowledge to homogeneously grouped students right at the students' level of understanding.

Why would a biology staff at the public high school described above want to change the practice of homogeneous grouping? All those homogeneously grouped classes were started with the best of intentions and seemed to be working over the years. However, as the minority population continued to increase, it became painfully obvious that the lower-level classes contained a disproportionate number of minorities who were also often tagged as special education students. Apparently, this trend was occurring at many high schools. Black students nationwide are twice as likely as White students to be assigned to special education (Richardson, 1994).

The biology staff felt the need for a new approach to address the school's changing population. Most of the staff attended workshops and several attended summer school sessions on multicultural education. They also studied the new science standards and read professional journals about new constructivist pedagogy that could be used to address the needs of all students. As a result, the biology staff and special education staff made the decision to abandon two lower-level biology classes as well as some special education science classes. Over the years, the staff had come to believe that the changes they would be undertaking were necessary for the benefit of all students.

The decision to group students heterogeneously in Biology I classrooms left us wondering if we would be able to manage all the students in an inclusive environment. To address this concern, more effort was made to give all students opportunities to work together and experience biology in ways meaningful to them and their peers. Teachers used a constructivist approach by giving up some control of the learning process as they spent less time feeding students information and more time interacting with students while guiding them in their quest for knowledge. Students gained scientific knowledge by using the tools and processes of science in their design of laboratory protocols to solve problems while interacting with their peers. Teachers had to adjust to guiding students, because they were accustomed to dispensing scientific knowledge by simply presenting textbook facts obtained by others and offering "cookbook" labs that contained problems already solved by others. Academically talented students also played a part by serving as role models for their peers during the learning process. Would these academically strong students accept the challenge and benefit from it, or would they feel burdened and in the process eventually lose interest in science? Our biology staff embarked on a journey that we hoped would result in lasting and meaningful change for the benefit of all our students.

The following study reflects the experiences of biology staff, special education staff, and students working together on "inclusion" in a Biology I classroom. Because I expected my students to use a format that required showing how they worked with scientific processes, I decided to conduct this study using a similar format to present my findings on inclusion in heterogeneously grouped classrooms. Therefore, this action research paper includes the following processes: question, problem, hypothesis, rationale, materials, procedure, observations, analysis, conclusion, and extension.

## THE QUESTION AND PROBLEM

**How can the science department and the special education department group a wide variety of students heterogeneously in an inclusive regular education biology classroom and make the experience successful for all students and staff?**

Our high school had homogeneously grouped special education science classes and lower-level biology sections with disproportionately high numbers of Black students in them. The lower-level classes were made up of combinations of students who had poor reading scores, discipline problems, poor grades, and/or attendance problems. These special education classes and lower-level classes were formed with good intentions; however, federal studies have found that students of color achieve better in "regular" classes if they receive extra support (Richardson, 1994). These special classes were provided for students with learning disabilities, deficiencies in math and science, and other problems that normally would prevent them from experiencing success in the traditionally taught "regular science" classroom. Students often were absent from the special science classes, and the frequent absences kept students from having a successful science experience. One researcher notes that "creating special science classes frequently leads to a lowering of standards, because teachers of these classes often employ prescriptive teaching and remedial approaches that result in lower achievement" (Heshusius, 1988). All students deserve access to an equal education, and the biology staff realized that access to equal education was never going to happen unless significant changes were made.

## HYPOTHESIS

If the biology and special education staffs embrace change by heterogeneously grouping students and by implementing inclusive strategies and other practices consistent with the objectives set forth in the National Science Education Standards, this will result in a successful experience for students and staff as measured by increases in student attendance and grade point averages among lower-achieving students, and increased positive attitudes as reflected by surveys administered to all biology students, the biology staff, and the special education staff.

## RATIONALE

The biology staff at the high school wanted to test the above hypothesis because we believed that all students, regardless of age, sex, cultural or ethnic background, disability, or interest and motivation in science, should be accountable for meeting higher learning and social standards. The staff was not satisfied with the school's homogeneously grouped lower-level life science classes, which, they thought, lowered standards for students and were comprised of students with poor attitudes toward science and school. The lowered standards also existed in the Project 9 biology classes that were designed for students with low reading skills; however, these students generally had better attitudes about school than did the life science students. Many of the special education students were either in the Life Science class or in a particular science class taught by a special education instructor. The life science, Project 9, and special education science classes contained few students who could serve as role models of motivated students interested in science.

The National Science Education Standards assume the inclusion of all students in challenging learning environments. Excellence in science education embodies the ideal that all students can achieve understanding of science if they are given the opportunity (National Research Council, 1996). The biology staff embraced a constructivist teaching approach, which leads to the type of learning environment that the National Science Teachers Association (NSTA) suggested would benefit all biology students (National Science Teachers Association, 1996).

Most of the biology staff had extensive professional development experience with multicultural science education, in which "cooperative learning" activities were created and the importance of these activities in getting all students involved in the science classroom was emphasized. "Tomorrow's classroom will be a more social place, since teachers will recognize the social component of learning. Collaboration and discourse will be constant components of lessons, as teachers assume the role of leading students in a community of learners" (National Science Teachers Association, 1996). The biology staff also considered Howard Gardner's theory of multiple intelligences in designing curriculum (Gardner, 1993). Traditional teaching strategies and assessment depend either on how well a student uses logic and mathematical intelligence to analyze language and mathematics or on how well an individual can memorize facts. Therefore, students who have mastered analytical skills and who can memorize well get good grades. Grades and test scores may reward only a fraction of the students who should be rewarded. "The more we teach and assess students based on a broader set of abilities, the more racially, ethnically, and socioeconomically diverse our achievers will be" (Sternberg, 1997, p. 22). At times, assessment of multiple intelligences was frustrating to some students and parents because those students who demonstrate logical/mathematical intelligence generally get good grades when traditional school evaluation methods that emphasize test scores are used. The evaluation of new skills as part of overall intelligence means that such students will not always get the top scores in class. One summer workshop placed an emphasis on the "three P's" (problem posing, problem solving, and peer persuasion) of science. The implementation of the three P's can occur when cooperative groups of students propose a problem and construct their own labs to solve a problem. They are generally persuading their peers when decisions are made about what steps to take in problem solving and with the presentation of data. In addition to learning about the topics described above, which were covered in multicultural science summer workshops, some of the biology staff had read about or taken workshops on implementing the learning cycle. "Research supports the learning cycle theory as an effective way to help students enjoy science, understand content, and apply scientific processes and concepts to authentic situations" (Colburn & Clough, 1997, p. 32). Some staff members had also studied brain-based learning. Practices suggested in brain-based learning provide a framework for learning and teaching that moves us away from the methods and models that have dominated education for more than a century. Students are no longer the passive recipients of knowledge, but acquire it actively through collaborative effort by solving problems that have meaning to them. The staff believed that they could take pieces from all these practices and assemble them into a pedagogy that was congruent with the National Science Education Standards (National Research Council, 1996).

A constructivist approach formed the backbone for implementing the National Science Education Standards (National Science Teachers Association, 1996). Fundamental to this approach is a shift from teacher-directed instruction, typically using books and worksheets, to student-centered instruction, where students learn by exploring, predicting, researching, and investigating concepts. The biology staff would help students to see that learning science is something that students do themselves, not something that is done to them by their teachers. The purpose of testing the hypothesis was to evaluate if using this approach in biology would result in better attendance, attitudes, and success for all students.

## SOURCES

- The school district database for attendance
- The school district database search for grades
- The school district database search for Wisconsin Student Assessment System (WSAS) science scores
- The school district database search for WSAS reading scores
- Surveys to measure students' and teachers' attitudes
- Middle school teachers' recommendations for student placement into lower-level life science classes
- Special education teachers' recommendations for student placement into life science classes

## PROCEDURES

1. In the spring semester before the inclusion model is implemented, meet with a facilitator from the school district's staff development

department to lead the biology staff in discussion and planning for curriculum change.

2. Invite the building principal and a representative member from the special education department to the first meeting. (The biology staff felt a need for support from the administration and input from the special education staff to proceed. The principal provided us with staff development funds for the extra hours when meetings occurred beyond the school day.)

3. Set up ground rules at the first meeting and establish a calendar for future planning.

4. Develop a philosophy statement (Appendix A) that the biology and special education staffs can agree on, and use this statement to guide all future changes.

5. Meet with the special education staff and develop a plan for their regular involvement in planning and for their presence in biology classes.

6. In the spring semester before the implementation of the inclusion model and during the fall semester when the inclusion model was implemented, use extended afternoon meetings once per month for long-range curriculum planning and use weekly morning meetings for updates and assigning of tasks to biology team members.

7. In the spring semester before the inclusion model is implemented, administer a survey (see Appendix B) to students in the current lower-level life science classes.

8. In the fall semester when the inclusion model is implemented, obtain WSAS scores in reading and science for students taking Biology I.

9. Obtain input from the special education staff about students they normally would select for a lower-level life science class.

10. Get recommendations from middle school teachers about the previous year's students whom they would have recommended for lower-level life science courses.

11. Use the information from steps 8, 9, and 10 to identify students in Biology I who would have been in either a Project 9 class or a lower-level life science class. Students with very poor reading scores and good attendance who demonstrated a desire to learn were selected from Biology I students (I will always refer to this group as the heterogeneously grouped Project 9) to compare to the previous year's Project 9 class (I will always refer to this group as the

homogeneously grouped Project 9). Middle school and special education teachers' recommendations along with poor WSAS science scores were used to select from Biology I students (I will always refer to this group as the heterogeneously grouped life science) to compare to the previous year's lower-level life science Class (I will always refer to this group as the homogeneously grouped life science).

12. At the end of the fall semester, gather the previous year's first semester data from the lower-level, homogeneously grouped life science classes to compare attendance and grade point average (GPA) data from this year's heterogeneously grouped life science students in Biology I.

13. Gather previous year's first semester GPA data from the homogeneously grouped Project 9 class to compare to GPA data from this year's heterogeneously grouped Project 9 students in Biology I.

14. Compare the attitudes of the homogeneously grouped life science students toward conventional labs (see Appendix B) to how it might have changed the following year with heterogeneously grouped life science students doing constructivist labs in Biology I.

15. Administer a survey on student attitudes toward project activities as learning experiences (see Appendix C).

16. Have students who had an "A" average in biology at the end of the semester identify themselves on the survey to get insights into the attitudes of these students toward constructivist labs and cooperative learning.

17. Conduct a survey of the special education staff and the biology staff to determine the level of support for the curriculum changes and the staff members' perceptions of the impact of this philosophy on students (see Appendix D).

18. Revisit the philosophy statements developed in step 4 to see if the special education and Biology I staffs still feel that they apply.

19. Analyze the impact of curriculum changes (independent variable) on the attendance, attitudes, and success of inclusion of all students (dependent variable) in Biology I.

## OBSERVATIONS

The first-semester data for the heterogeneously grouped life science students in Biology I were compared to actual data from the previous year's first-semester, homogeneously grouped life science classes. Table 1 displays the results.

Attendance data from the school district's database for the previous year of the homogeneously grouped life science classes shows students absent 9.5 percent of the time (see Table 1.). The heterogeneously grouped life science students in Biology I were absent 5.8 percent of the time. The grade point average of the heterogeneously grouped life science students in Biology I was 1.74, which was slightly higher than the 1.71 grade point achieved by the homogeneously grouped life science students. That is significant, since students in the homogeneously grouped life science classes were given passing grades if they showed up on a somewhat regular basis, regardless of their classroom performance. Approximately 45 percent of the heterogeneously grouped students in Biology I who were used for the comparison were from a minority population, which was similar to the minority makeup of the homogeneously grouped life science classes.

The heterogeneously grouped life science students in Biology I had a 16 percent failure rate, as compared to the 19 percent failure rate for the homogeneously grouped life science classes. The homogeneously grouped and heterogeneously grouped Project 9 students attended class regularly and demonstrated a desire to learn; however, their WSAS reading scores were very low compared to their peers. Table 2 displays the first-semester GPA data for the heterogeneously grouped Project 9 students in Biology I compared to the first-semester GPA data from the homogeneously grouped Project 9 classes.

One of the heterogeneously grouped Project 9 students failed Biology I. However, the GPA of all heterogeneously grouped Project 9 students in Biology I was 2.06, which was slightly higher than the 1.94 GPA of all students in the homogeneously grouped Project 9 classes.

A large part of the Biology I class experience involved constructivist labs. The special education staff administered a survey to the Biology I students (see Appendix B) to find out how they felt about some of the constructivist lab activities done in cooperative groups as compared to conventional labs done in groups where roles were not assigned. Table 3 displays the results.

Biology I "A" students were asked to identify themselves. Table 4 displays the results for these students.

All students preferred the constructivist labs, in which each student had a cooperative and interdependent role, to the conventional labs. When students participated in constructivist labs, they worked in cooperative groups to define problems and they designed lab protocols to solve those problems. Students working in cooperative groups strongly supported the

**Table 1**  Data on Biology I students who would have likely been in lower-level life science classes versus actual data on lower-level life science students from the previous year

| Number of Students | Ethnicity | WSAS* Average Science Score (out of 7) | 1st Semester Average GPA in Life Science (out of 4.0) | 1st Semester Average GPA in Biology | 1st Semester Absences in Life Science | 1st Semester Average Biology I Absences |
|---|---|---|---|---|---|---|
| 17 | White | 5.82 | 1.69 | 1.64 | 8.20 | 5.59 |
| 7 | African Am. | 4.14 | 1.59 | 1.57 | 3.52 | 0.86 |
| 4 | Asian | 4.00 | 2.49 | 2.50 | 4.53 | 2.25 |
| 1 | Native Am. | 4.00 | 1.33 | 2.00 | 1.17 | 0.00 |
| 2 | Hispanic | 5.50 | 0.84 | 1.50 | 9.67 | 7.50 |
| **Overall Avg:** | | **5.1** | **1.71** | **1.74** | **6.54** | **4.03** |

*WSAS = Wisconsin Student Assessment Proficiency exam

**Table 2**    Data on Biology I students who would have likely been in a Project 9 class versus actual data on Project 9 students from the previous year

| Number of Students | Ethnicity | WSAS* Reading Score Average (out of 7) | 1st Semester GPA Average in Project 9 (out of 4.0) | 1st Semester GPA Average in Biology I |
|---|---|---|---|---|
| 8 | White | 3.75 | 2.18 | 2.25 |
| 4 | African Am. | 3.00 | 1.29 | 1.50 |
| 3 | Asian | 2.33 | 2.39 | 2.33 |
| 1 | Native Am. | 4.00 | 1.33 | 2.00 |
| **Overall Avg:** | | **3.31** | **1.94** | **2.06** |

*WSAS = Wisconsin Student Assessment Proficiency exam

**Table 3**    All Biology I students surveyed on constructivist lab activity

| Survey Question | % Agree | ◄——► | | | Disagree |
|---|---|---|---|---|---|
| I prefer constructivist labs over conventional labs. | 34 | 20 | 23 | 11 | 12 |
| I prefer working in lab groups versus individually. | 63 | 19 | 9 | 5 | 4 |
| I like groups made up of students with various skill levels. | 45 | 16 | 23 | 11 | 5 |
| Everyone is learning when peers help peers. | 49 | 19 | 19 | 7 | 6 |
| Students get to know each other better in constructivist lab groups. | 55 | 27 | 11 | 5 | 2 |
| Students should evaluate other students. | 59 | 14 | 11 | 8 | 8 |
| Group work results in less classroom conflict. | 42 | 20 | 25 | 5 | 8 |
| I use cooperative skills during constructivist lab activities. | 70 | 20 | 7 | 2 | 1 |
| Everyone in my group carries out their role. | 47 | 23 | 18 | 5 | 7 |

opportunity for evaluating the effort of each group member and they believed that group work resulted in less conflict. While students preferred constructivist labs to conventional labs, the "A" students seemed to prefer them more. All students in the biology classes in general felt they used cooperative skills during constructivist lab activities; however, "A" students seemed to use them less.

Students made a variety of comments on their surveys. A distillation of some of the more important statements includes: students would like to have some input on the selection of groups; they said it was a good way to meet and get to know new people; peer evaluation seemed to be one of the

**Table 4**    Students with "A" grades in Biology I were identified

| Survey Question | % Agree | ←→ | | | Disagree |
|---|---|---|---|---|---|
| I prefer constructivist labs over conventional labs. | 15 | 57 | 21 | 7 | 0 |
| I prefer working in lab groups versus individually. | 36 | 29 | 21 | 14 | 0 |
| I like groups made up of students with various skill levels. | 22 | 7 | 57 | 14 | 0 |
| Everyone is learning when peers help peers. | 36 | 14 | 29 | 14 | 7 |
| Students get to know each other better in constructivist lab groups. | 29 | 50 | 14 | 7 | 0 |
| Students should evaluate other students. | 72 | 14 | 7 | 0 | 7 |
| Group work results in less classroom conflict. | 65 | 14 | 14 | 7 | 0 |
| I use cooperative skills during constructivist lab activities. | 28 | 22 | 29 | 21 | 0 |
| Everyone in my group carries out their role. | 36 | 32 | 21 | 4 | 7 |

more popular choices; group activities can work well, but group members did not always listen; and students enjoyed working in groups as long as everyone worked.

In addition to constructivist activities, the Biology I students completed more projects than biology students did in previous years. These projects were often done in cooperative groups. Interdependence was created within the groups, because all group members were assigned different roles. Students were encouraged to be creative with their projects. Groups created models, produced videos, performed skits, and wrote songs and poems, to name just a few of the activities.

To obtain feedback on project activities, the Biology I staff decided to have Biology I students complete a survey (see Appendix C) that looked at a specific project completed during the unit on cell structure and function. Table 5 displays the results.

One response on the project survey that stood out above all others was that students felt they used cooperative skills with project activities. Students also seemed to feel comfortable with guidance they got from their teachers and thought that there were adequate resources to complete projects and that they could not have earned a higher grade if they had done the projects individually.

The survey in Appendix D was administered to the special education and biology staffs after they had worked for two semesters on curriculum changes. Table 6 displays the results.

One of the six biology teachers felt strongly that not all students learn well in a heterogeneously grouped environment, which lowered the

**Table 5**    Biology I students were surveyed on a project activity

| Survey Question | % Agree | ←→ | | | Disagree |
|---|---|---|---|---|---|
| I enjoyed doing this activity. | 36 | 35 | 21 | 6 | 2 |
| I learned a lot during this activity. | 47 | 22 | 23 | 6 | 2 |
| I learned a lot from other groups on the subjects they presented. | 31 | 35 | 25 | 8 | 1 |
| I used cooperative skills during this activity. | 70 | 17 | 10 | 2 | 1 |
| I could find the information I needed to complete the project. | 58 | 25 | 13 | 3 | 1 |
| My teacher provided enough guidance. | 62 | 19 | 15 | 2 | 2 |
| Everyone in our group contributed to the success of the project. | 40 | 25 | 19 | 13 | 5 |
| There was enough time to complete the activity. | 40 | 23 | 24 | 8 | 5 |
| I could not have gotten a higher grade doing the project myself. | 47 | 15 | 19 | 5 | 14 |

average for this statement to 2.67. All the other biology teachers felt that students learn well in a heterogeneously grouped environment.

At the end of the first semester, the biology and special education staffs revisited the philosophy statements (see Appendix A). All staff members felt that the philosophy statements were still appropriate. The three statements that everyone believed were the most appropriate were:

1. All students, regardless of educational or ethnic background, have the ability to learn and be successful in an integrated Biology I classroom.

2. Biology should be an active, hands-on process that includes the three P's of problem posing, problem solving, and peer persuasion.

3. All students need to learn the skills of working together successfully in group settings.

The three statements that were the least appropriate include:

1. If teachers plan and work together, Biology I will be a quality experience for all.

2. Students learn in diverse ways, therefore need diverse assessment strategies to measure diverse learning styles.

**Table 6**    Biology I and Special Education staff feelings on Biology I program

| | Average for Survey Question Agree (5) to Disagree (1) | |
| --- | --- | --- |
| | Bio | SpEd |
| I feel that heterogeneous grouping is a good idea. | 5.00 | 4.75 |
| I feel that students of all ability levels should learn to work together. | 5.00 | 5.00 |
| Students learn the subject matter better if they are guided into finding the information themselves rather than the teacher presenting to them. | 3.67 | 4.50 |
| Students working in cooperative groups tend to get more out of labs than if they work individually or in pairs. | 3.67 | 4.25 |
| Learning is going on by all heterogeneously grouped members | 2.67 | 4.00 |
| Students tend to prefer constructivist labs over conventional labs. | 3.00 | 3.75 |
| Students should have the experience of evaluating peers. | 4.00 | 4.50 |
| Student groups should be made up of students with various ability levels. | 4.83 | 4.75 |
| Placing special education students in a regular classroom is a good idea. | 5.00 | 5.00 |
| Placing special education instructors in the classroom to team with a regular education teacher is a good thing to do. | 4.83 | 4.75 |
| I believe we are headed in the right direction with our Biology I program. | 4.83 | 4.75 |

3. Parents need to serve as partners in the education of their children, and therefore need to be involved in the assessment of their children.

In addition to responding to the statements in Appendix A, the biology and special education staff members made these paraphrased comments:

1. It is important to take responsibility for the learning of all students.

2. Ensuring participation by all group members is a challenge.

3. Roles need to be clearly defined for each cooperative group member.

4. Students claim they have to work too hard with constructivist labs.

5. Some ninth graders are not ready for self-evaluation and peer review.

6. Some students with involved learning and behavior problems may interfere with the learning of their peers.

7. Some special education students do not like the stigma of being seen with their special education teacher in an inclusive classroom setting.

8. Staff time is needed to communicate and plan.

In general, the observations that the students and the biology and special education staffs made about the program were very positive.

## ANALYSIS

Our principal handed out a survey designed to get input from the entire high school staff on what issues needed attention in next year's school improvement plan. The number one issue the staff identified was attendance. Every teacher knows that students will not be successful if the students are absent on a regular basis.

One of the major problems with the homogeneously grouped life science classes was poor attendance. The attendance for the first semester of the homogeneously grouped life science class was actually much better than for the second semester, but data collected was only for the first semester. There were days during last year's second semester when more than half of the students in the homogeneously grouped life science classes were absent. This seldom happened with the heterogeneously grouped life science students in Biology I. In fact, the data collected showed that the heterogeneously grouped life science students in Biology I were in biology classes almost twice as often as the average attendance for their other classes at school. There were too few students in the homogeneously grouped life science classes who could serve as positive role models for other students, and this may have been responsible for the many negative behavior issues in those classes.

A possible reason that the heterogeneously grouped life science students in Biology I attended classes regularly is because they felt psychologically safe and felt included in the classroom. Our data showed that all students, especially "A" students, felt that group work resulted in less conflict. Group activities in which roles were assigned made students feel as though they were a part of the classroom action. Students said they got to know classmates better, and used cooperative skills, when they worked in groups on constructivist labs and projects. Our data indicated that students believed that everyone was learning when peers helped peers. It makes sense that the general population of students would feel more positive about peer tutoring than "A" students; however, even the majority of "A" students agreed with the benefits of peer tutoring for all students. The biology staff believed that thinking is clarified and learning is reinforced in "A" students if they take the time to explain material to a peer. "A" students often need to work on interpersonal relationships. They may gain as much or more from this part of the experience than do the students who get lower grades.

Another possible reason for improved attendance was the peer pressure that took place in cooperative groups. Students felt pressure to attend when they were placed in cooperative groups, because of the interdependence created by group roles. There were some days when I had ill students in my class tell me they would not even be in school if it were not for the work they needed to share with their group so that the group could complete a lab or project. When students had more ownership in a laboratory exercise or project and experienced the pressures brought about by group dynamics, attendance generally improved.

Success as measured by overall grades was an area everyone was concerned about when the Project 9 students, who were previously homogeneously grouped, and special education students were included in Biology I. Remember that the Project 9 classes were made up of students who were not only failing biology after 6 weeks, but were also identified with poor reading scores. After the curriculum changes in Biology I, only 6 percent of students with poor reading scores failed. More than 80 percent of the heterogeneously grouped Project 9 and life science students earned a B or C grade in Biology I, and only 15 percent failed. This happened in spite of the higher standards they had to meet.

All special needs students benefited in Biology I, because the special education teachers worked not only with special education students but also with any students who needed extra help. The teachers would be at the laboratory stations offering assistance to whoever needed it. The teachers also offered reading help on exams to all students who had reading problems. Forty special education students took Biology I. Those with the most need were placed in classes where a special education teacher was often present. No more than four special education students were generally put into any one class. Most of the special education students were learning-disabled, and only five of these students did not pass biology.

Our data also showed that most students liked peer evaluation. The staff was less comfortable than the students with peer evaluation, perhaps because they were used to having control of evaluation for most of their teaching years. Robert McGarvy, of *Entrepreneur* magazine, has written that "multirater feedback is rapidly replacing the traditional boss-to-employee performance review. Multirater feedback gives employees information from peers and subordinates as well as the boss. The best systems include ratings by at least three coworkers and three subordinates. That preserves raters' anonymity and gives the employee considerable information" (McGarvy, 1998, p. 15). Students should be exposed to peer evaluation before entering the workplace, where such evaluation is a more common practice.

The biology staff members had different approaches to evaluation. All used some form of peer evaluation, but some did not use it as much as others. Those teachers who used peer evaluation at least once per week felt more comfortable with this practice, and their students seemed to appreciate the opportunity to use peer evaluation. Half the staff used student self-evaluation on a regular basis. They believed it was a good way to get students to reflect on their past work in order to improve on future work. I used an end-of-semester portfolio in which a rubric was used for self-evaluation, peer evaluation, and parent evaluation of the students. This explains why most staff members did not give alternative assessment and parent assessment as high a priority as the other staff philosophy statements when revisiting the staff philosophy at the end of the year. It is difficult for some teachers to share control of the grading process.

Two of the surveys (see Appendixes B and C) showed that all students felt positively about constructivist labs and projects. The number one complaint about constructivist labs was that they were too difficult; however, "A" students generally appreciated that challenge. Some students would rather have others do their thinking for them, and constructivist labs forced them to think fully about the problems with which they were working.

Some comments made by students and staff suggest areas that the biology team should include as topics for future discussion. These include:

1. When groups are chosen, students would like to have some input into the selection of people who are placed in their groups. To facilitate success for all students, teachers need to walk the fine line between listening to their students and maintaining some control over group composition. In a survey, the students did say that all ability levels should be represented in the groups.

2. Some students would like to see more equalization of the work required of each group member to complete a particular task. An effort should be made to make roles as equal and fair as possible. What also has to be taken into consideration is that some students have the ability to handle more complex tasks, and more should be expected from these students for successful completion of a group activity; however, equal effort should be anticipated of everyone.

## CONCLUSION

This research project set out to look at the hypothesis: "If the biology and special education staffs embrace change by heterogeneously grouping students and by implementing inclusive strategies and other practices consistent with the objectives set forth in the National Science Education Standards, it will result in a successful experience for students and staff as measured by increases in student attendance and grade point averages among lower-achieving students and increase positive attitudes on surveys administered to all biology students, the biology staff, and the special education staff." The majority of our research supports this hypothesis. The data clearly showed higher attendance rates for the heterogeneously grouped life science students in Biology I than for students who were previously in homogeneously grouped life science classes. While the grades for the heterogeneously grouped life science and Project 9 students in Biology I were not significantly higher than the grades of the homogeneously grouped life science and Project 9 students, many of the special education and biology teachers were still pleased that the grades were not lower, given the new tougher expectations. Guidance counselors normally would have steered students with poor grades in middle school away from Biology I, because it was considered a difficult course for freshmen. Certainly, the attitudinal surveys indicated that the majority of students, special education instructors, and biology instructors favored the curriculum changes.

Parents and students gave lots of feedback in addition to the data collected in this study. The majority of this feedback was positive, and the data certainly supports that feedback. The biology and special education staff members also commented positively on a regular basis.

## EXTENSION

This study had some potential for experimental error. One source of error in a scientific study is the existence of an independent variable that has the potential to be inconsistent. In this study, one such potential inconsistency concerned the fact that the homogeneously grouped students who took lower-level life science and special education classes one year could only be compared to similar students who were heterogeneously grouped in Biology I the following year. There was no way that the same students could be used both years. Another potential inconsistency concerned the fact that the attendance data collected was based on the daily scan sheets completed by the teachers. There may have been days when scan sheets were not turned in, but an assumption had to be made that the overall attendance data was reasonably accurate.

I continue to have a number of questions to which I did not get answers:

1. How many heterogeneously grouped Project 9 or lower-level life science classes in Biology I were not included in the data because they either dropped out of school or were dropped from class before the end of the semester?

2. How would the number in (1) above compare to the number that started out in the homogeneously grouped life science classes and dropped before the end of the semester? The teacher who taught the homogeneously grouped life science classes for many years felt that the dropout rate in these classes was normally substantially higher.

3. What was the primary reason that the heterogeneously grouped life science students dropped Biology I this year and the homogeneously grouped life science classes last year? Was it because of family and personal problems, the curriculum, or something else?

4. What kinds of information do parents receive from their sons or daughters regarding curriculum changes? Students involved with group work might place the blame on others if the group was not successful. The biology staff shared stories about how parents often complained that the group was dragging down their child's grade. However, students commented in the surveys that they could not have done as well individually as they did in these cooperative group activities.

5. Do the Project 9 and heterogeneously grouped life science students in Biology I have other classes as difficult as Biology I? The GPA for the heterogeneously grouped students in Biology I was slightly higher than the same students' overall GPAs. In other years, biology grades tended to bring down grade point averages.

6. Will the changes made in the biology curriculum have an impact on the number of minority students found in the advanced science classes? Currently, while there seems to be an equal representation of males and females in advanced science classes, the number of minorities taking these classes is not representative of the school's minority population.

The study could have revealed a more accurate picture on attendance if we had compared attendance sheets at the beginning of the semester to attendance sheets at the end of the semester, to find out how many of the heterogeneously grouped Project 9 and life science students dropped Biology I. The grade point averages and attendance data might have been inflated because the students having the greatest problems were no longer in the class. However, the sample size used in the study was probably large enough to give some accurate results in spite of only using data from the end of the semester.

From the data collected in this action research, there is evidence to show that with the pedagogy presented, inclusion can successfully take place in our schools. Using a constructivist approach rather than primarily teacher-directed activities is important in any classroom, but it is essential in an inclusive classroom. Grouping together students of different abilities and interests is an important part of the inclusive-classroom environment; however, simply putting students together in groups to complete activities would be disastrous. Teachers need to have their students practice good cooperative learning skills if grouping is going to be successful. Teachers also need to create roles for each student so that all students can be engaged within their groups. Students need to practice skillful reflection and self-evaluation of these activities. Teachers must use a variety of assessment instruments, and students need to be involved in evaluating the effort of their peers. Ensuring that peer evaluations have credibility requires skillful guidance by teachers.

## EPILOGUE

I was happy with the results of the changes we made in our biology classrooms. The data we collected shows that there was an increase in attendance and in grade point averages of minorities and special education students, which suggest that the changes made were very beneficial to these populations. While grade point averages and attendance improved overall, the students also learned how to solve problems and developed skills to work cooperatively. The entire Biology I population had a more enjoyable classroom experience in this environment. This model was held up within the high school and within the district as evidence that inclusive classrooms can work. Teachers throughout the school district came to our classrooms to learn more about our model because they also were attempting to embed inclusive teaching practices in their classrooms.

During my last semester of teaching before retiring, Dr. Sharon Derry, an educational psychologist at the University of Wisconsin–Madison, came into my classroom for an entire topical unit of study to create a videotape of successful practices used in constructivist teaching. She conducted several large, theory-based instructional technology research and development projects in several different schools focusing on individual and collaborative problem solving. I recall how amazed the video crew chief was at the amount of collaboration that took place in my classroom among students of diverse abilities. The second summer after I retired from teaching high school students, I presented a summer workshop at UW–Madison to science teachers who were interested in the constructivist approach to science teaching. Many of the attendees found this workshop useful, because many of them were under pressure from their school districts to create inclusive classrooms.

Recently, I went back to my former high school to talk to members of the biology team who had worked with me to make the significant curriculum changes used in our inclusive classrooms. They said that the model we developed is still working, but that it is being threatened by change. Before starting to use inclusive classrooms, the administration offered support by paying our biology staff beyond the school day to sit down with a coordinator from the central office to set goals and prepare a philosophy on which we could all agree. Partial support from the administration came in the form of keeping class sizes to 24 or fewer students, for classrooms in which special needs students were included. The special education department assigned several special education instructors to the biology staff to help modify curriculum and evaluations, as well as to provide some classroom support for activities and projects. They also assigned no more than four special education students to a class. This did not mean that there were not other students in the classroom who required special attention, but the special education students were to be divided among 20-plus sections of biology, with no more than four to a class. The biology staff met a couple of times a week before school and once a month for several hours after school to strategize and share ideas for working with students in their diverse classrooms. Members of the special education staff met with the biology teachers to give their insights on the pedagogy being discussed. There was a concerted effort to make inclusion work.

A number of changes have occurred since the early years of implementing the inclusion model that, I believe, are threatening its success. Several of the biology team members who took the lead for making changes in our biology curriculum have retired, and the newer teachers do not appear to have the same level of commitment to this model. The current staff does not hold regular team meetings to continue this work; team meetings are necessary if new staff members are going to be properly grounded in the model. Members of the staff are no longer compensated for participation in planning sessions that take place outside of required hours. Some teachers have established a reputation for doing a good job of dealing with needy students, and so the special education department is no longer equally distributing its students among all the Biology I sections. Now there may be twice as many special education students in some classrooms and fewer in others. This can be a real problem for student-group dynamics. The special education department, which has had staff cuts, offers less help. Now parents of regular education students complain more often about their children not receiving enough attention in classes with high numbers of special education students. Class sizes are also increasing. Two new head principals and many changes in the administration have resulted in lack of awareness of the history of the model by current school administrators. As a result, some biology teachers have many special education students in their classes, and those classes often exceed the old limit of 24. Class size is crucial to the success of the model.

I still believe that the biology department's model for inclusion is a very effective model that promotes a fair and equitable education for all students—more than what one might see in a traditional classroom. As budget and staff cuts erode quality education, the overall effectiveness of any kind of teaching will be diminished. For "no child to be left behind," good educational practice has to be properly funded and supported.

## APPENDICES

**Appendix A:** Philosophy Statements Created by the Biology I Staff

**Appendix B:** Student Attitudes on Constructivist Labs Versus Conventional Labs

**Appendix C:** A Project Activity as a Learning Experience

**Appendix D:** Survey of Biology I and Special Education Staffs on Curriculum Change

## APPENDIX A: PHILOSOPHY STATEMENTS CREATED BY THE BIOLOGY I STAFF

1. Biology should be an active, hands-on process that includes the three P's of problem posing, problem solving, and peer persuasion. This will allow students to experience the true nature of what science is and how it can be used to solve everyday problems.

2. All students, regardless of educational or ethnic background, have the ability to learn and be successful in an integrated Biology I classroom.

3. All students, regardless of educational or ethnic background, should be challenged through high expectations in an integrated biology classroom.

4. Biology will be more relevant if it is taught with an interdisciplinary approach that allows students of varying interests to participate more enthusiastically, and make connections to relevant use of science in the larger world.

5. All students need to learn the skills of working together successfully in group settings.

6. All students can make a significant contribution to an integrated Biology I class through their talents and interests.

7. Students should be taught to understand and use science, not memorize it.

8. If teachers plan and work together, Biology I will be a quality experience for all.

9. Students should reflect on past experiences and use this information to improve future performance.

10. Students need a clear definition of levels of achievement in order for all students to be successful.

11. Students learn in diverse ways; therefore, diverse assessment strategies are needed to measure diverse learning styles.

12. Parents need to serve as partners in the education of their children, and therefore need to be involved in the assessment of their children.

13. Since science uses technology of all types at a very high level, the most current technology available should be used whenever possible.

14. Students need to put their own work in perspective through self-evaluation and peer review.

## APPENDIX B: STUDENT ATTITUDES ON CONSTRUCTIVIST LABS VERSUS CONVENTIONAL LABS

Directions: Laboratory experiences are of two basic types. The conventional labs give you a hypothesis and you follow procedural step by step instructions to completion, while the constructivist labs ask you to come up with the hypothesis and you create the procedure. Circle the number that you feel best represents your attitude on the statements. Then comment on why you responded the way you did, and if your score was less than 5, then state what you believe it would take to make your rating a 5.

|  | Agree |  |  |  | Disagree |
|---|---|---|---|---|---|
| 1.  I prefer constructivist labs over conventional labs. | 5 | 4 | 3 | 2 | 1 |
| Required comments:<br>What would it take to make this a "5"? |  |  |  |  |  |
| 2.  I prefer working in lab groups rather than doing a lab required individually. | 5 | 4 | 3 | 2 | 1 |
| Required comments:<br>What would it take to make this a "5"? |  |  |  |  |  |
| 3.  I like groups made up of students with various skill levels. | 5 | 4 | 3 | 2 | 1 |
| Required comments:<br>What would it take to make this a "5"? |  |  |  |  |  |
| 4.  Everyone is learning, even when one student is explaining and others are listening. | 5 | 4 | 3 | 2 | 1 |
| Required comments:<br>What would it take to make this a "5"? |  |  |  |  |  |
| 5.  When we work in groups, students get to know each other and feel comfortable with one another. | 5 | 4 | 3 | 2 | 1 |
| Required comments:<br>What would it take to make this a "5"? |  |  |  |  |  |
| 6.  Students should be asked to evaluate other students as part of their grade for a lab activity. | 5 | 4 | 3 | 2 | 1 |
| Required comments:<br>What would it take to make this a "5"? |  |  |  |  |  |
| 7.  When we work in groups, there is less conflict within the classroom. | 5 | 4 | 3 | 2 | 1 |
| Required comments:<br>What would it take to make this a "5"? |  |  |  |  |  |
| 8.  I used cooperative skills during this activity, such as facilitating, evaluating peers, recording, consensus building, etc. | 5 | 4 | 3 | 2 | 1 |
| Required comments:<br>What would it take to make this a "5"? |  |  |  |  |  |
| 9.  Everyone in my group carried out their role and participated in the required activity. | 5 | 4 | 3 | 2 | 1 |
| Required comments:<br>What would it take to make this a "5"? |  |  |  |  |  |
| 10.  I enjoyed doing this activity. | 5 | 4 | 3 | 2 | 1 |
| Required comments:<br>What would it take to make this a "5"? |  |  |  |  |  |

## APPENDIX C: A PROJECT ACTIVITY
## AS A LEARNING EXPERIENCE

Directions: Circle the number that you feel best represents your attitude on the statements. Respond to each statement based on your experience with the unit on cell structure and function, where your project was the creation of a cell model. Then comment on why you responded the way you did, and if your score was less than 5, then state what you believe it would take to make your rating a 5.

| | Agree | | | | Disagree |
|---|---|---|---|---|---|
| 1. I enjoyed doing this activity. | 5 | 4 | 3 | 2 | 1 |
| Required comments: What would it take to make this a "5"? | | | | | |
| 2. I learned a lot during this activity. | 5 | 4 | 3 | 2 | 1 |
| Required comments: What would it take to make this a "5"? | | | | | |
| 3. I learned my group's subject matter doing this activity and I learned the subject matter presented by other groups. | 5 | 4 | 3 | 2 | 1 |
| Required comments: What would it take to make this a "5"? | | | | | |
| 4. I used cooperative skills during this activity, such as facilitating, evaluating peers, research, art work, consensus building, etc. | 5 | 4 | 3 | 2 | 1 |
| Required comments: What would it take to make this a "5"? | | | | | |
| 5. I could find the information I needed to complete the project. | 5 | 4 | 3 | 2 | 1 |
| Required comments: What would it take to make this a "5"? | | | | | |
| 6. My teacher provided our group with enough guidance during the activity. | 5 | 4 | 3 | 2 | 1 |
| Required comments: What would it take to make this a "5"? | | | | | |
| 7. Everyone in my group contributed to the success of the project. | 5 | 4 | 3 | 2 | 1 |
| Required comments: What would it take to make this a "5"? | | | | | |

|  | Agree |  |  |  | Disagree |
|---|---|---|---|---|---|
| 8. There was enough time to complete the activity. | 5 | 4 | 3 | 2 | 1 |
| Required comments:<br>What would it take to make this a "5"? | | | | | |
| 9. If I had completed this project myself, I would not have received a higher score than I got for the group project score. | 5 | 4 | 3 | 2 | 1 |
| Required comments:<br>What would it take to make this a "5"? | | | | | |
| 10. I like learning through projects and constructivist activities better than with traditional lectures and worksheets. | 5 | 4 | 3 | 2 | 1 |
| Required comments:<br>What would it take to make this a "5"? | | | | | |

## APPENDIX D: SURVEY OF BIOLOGY I AND SPECIAL EDUCATION STAFFS ON CURRICULUM CHANGE

| My current assignment is: Regular Ed. |
|---|
| Special Ed. _____        LD CD ED<br>                           (circle one) |
| Directions: Please complete the following questions. They are intended to gather data concerning cognitive, attitudinal, and affective issues related to the biology curriculum.<br><br>Part I. Beliefs Related to Student Success In Biology—The following beliefs last year were considered essential to curriculum change. Please indicate how you feel now by placing either a 5, 4, 3, 2, or 1 in the square provided and also indicate how important you feel the statement is to the success of the biology curriculum by ranking each statement either a 5, 4, 3, 2, or 1 in the square provided. |

*(Continued)*

(Continued)

| High Agreement | | | Low Agreement | | High Rank | | | Low Rank | |
|---|---|---|---|---|---|---|---|---|---|
| 5 | 4 | 3 | 2 | 1 | 5 | 4 | 3 | 2 | 1 |

| Agreement | Rank | |
|:---:|:---:|---|
| ☐ | ☐ | 1. All students, regardless of educational or ethnic background, have the ability to learn and be successful in an integrated Biology I classroom. |
| ☐ | ☐ | 2. All students, regardless of educational or ethnic background, should be challenged through high expectations in an integrated Biology I classroom. |
| ☐ | ☐ | 3. Students need a clear definition of levels of achievement in order for all students to be successful. |
| ☐ | ☐ | 4. All students can make a significant contribution to an integrated Biology I class through their talents and interests. |
| ☐ | ☐ | 5. Biology should be an active, hands-on process that includes the three P's of problem posing, problem solving, and peer persuasion. This will allow students to experience the true nature of what science is and how it can be used to solve everyday problems. |
| ☐ | ☐ | 6. Biology will be more relevant if it is taught with an interdisciplinary approach that allows students of varying interests to participate more enthusiastically, and make connections to relevant use of science in the larger world. |
| ☐ | ☐ | 7. All students need to learn the skills of working together successfully in group settings. |
| ☐ | ☐ | 8. Since science uses technology of all types at a very high level, the most current technology available should be used whenever possible. |
| ☐ | ☐ | 9. Students learn in diverse ways; therefore, diverse assessment strategies are needed to measure diverse learning styles. |
| ☐ | ☐ | 10. Students should reflect on past experiences and use this information to improve future performances. |
| ☐ | ☐ | 11. Parents need to serve as partners in the education of their children, and therefore need to be involved in the assessment of their children. |
| ☐ | ☐ | 12. Students need to put their own work in perspective through self-evaluation and peer review. |
| ☐ | ☐ | 13. Students should be taught to understand and use science, not memorize it. |
| ☐ | ☐ | 14. If teachers plan and work together, Biology I will be a quality experience for all. |

Part II. This is similar to the questionnaire given to our students.—Circle the number that you feel best represents your attitude on the question asked. You may comment on why you responded the way you did in the space provided after each question and at the bottom of the last page.

|  | Agree |  |  |  | Disagree |
|---|---|---|---|---|---|
| 1. I feel that heterogeneous grouping is a good idea. | 5 | 4 | 3 | 2 | 1 |
| 2. I feel that students of all ability levels should learn to work together. | 5 | 4 | 3 | 2 | 1 |
| 3. Students learn the subject matter better if they are guided into finding the information themselves rather than the teacher presenting to them. | 5 | 4 | 3 | 2 | 1 |
| 4. Students working in cooperative groups tend to get more out of labs than if they work individually or in pairs. | 5 | 4 | 3 | 2 | 1 |
| 5. Learning is going on by all heterogeneously grouped members. | 5 | 4 | 3 | 2 | 1 |
| 6. Students tend to prefer constructivist labs over conventional labs. | 5 | 4 | 3 | 2 | 1 |
| 7. Students should have the experience of evaluating peers in the classroom. | 5 | 4 | 3 | 2 | 1 |
| 8. Student groups should be made up of students with various ability levels. | 5 | 4 | 3 | 2 | 1 |
| 9. Placing special education students in a regular classroom is a good idea. | 5 | 4 | 3 | 2 | 1 |
| 10. Placing special education instructors in the classroom to team with a regular education teacher is a good thing to do. | 5 | 4 | 3 | 2 | 1 |

Part III: Bottom Line—Are we headed in the right direction with our Biology I program?

| | COMMENTS: |
|---|---|
| _____I strongly believe we are<br>_____I believe we are<br>_____I am not certain<br>_____I don't believe we are<br>_____I strongly believe we are not | |

# REFERENCES

Colburn, A., & Clough, M. P. (1997). Implementing the learning cycle: A gradual transition to a new teaching approach. *The Science Teacher, 64*(5), 30–33.

Gardner, H. (1993). *Frames of mind: The theory of multiple intelligences* (10th ed.). New York: Basic Books.

Gardner, H. (1993). *Multiple intelligences: The theory in practice.* New York: Basic Books.

Heshusius, L. (1988). The arts, science, and the study of exceptionality. *Exceptional Children, 55*(1), 60–65.

McGarvy, R. (1998). Multirater feedback. *Bottom Line Personal,* October 1, p. 15.

National Research Council. (1996). *National science education standards.* Washington, DC: National Academy Press.

National Science Teachers Association. (1996). *NSTA pathways to the science standards: Guidelines for moving the vision into practice.* Arlington, VA: National Science Teachers Association.

Nummela-Caine, R., & Caine, G. (1994). *Making connections: Teaching and the human brain.* Menlo Park, CA: Addison-Wesley.

Richardson, L. (1994). Minority students languish in special education system. *The New York Times,* April 6. The New York Times Current Events Edition Index, 1994, fiche 31:43A.

Sternberg, R. J. (1997). What does it mean to be smart? *Educational Leadership, 54*(6), 20–24.

# 11

## *Using African American Students' Preference for Working in Self-Selected Partnerships to Promote Math Achievement*

Julie Melton

## EDITORS' INTRODUCTION

Researching in the area of mathematics, Melton focuses on her fourth graders' struggles in accessing the content and their desire to work in partnerships. Although they appease her students, these partnerships cause greater frustration for Melton, and spur her to further analyze classroom interactions. Employing a "fishbone" diagram, Melton is better able to determine the source of difficulties that continue to arise. Using the insights gained by employing this tool, Melton looks at her data (videotapes, observations and field notes, student work, and her teacher research journal) through a different lens in order to more appropriately address the issues with which the classroom community is struggling.

\* \* \* \*

When I began my action research, I had been teaching at Lincoln Elementary School for almost six years. Lincoln is a third- through fifth-grade school paired with Midvale Elementary School. Students from the two attendance areas attend Midvale for kindergarten through second grade and then attend Lincoln for third grade through fifth grade. The two schools' diverse student populations reflect the strikingly different neighborhoods in which the schools are located. Households in the Lincoln neighborhood are predominantly low-income, while households in the Midvale neighborhood are middle-income. Lincoln and Midvale are the most racially diverse in the Madison Metropolitan School District, with each containing almost equal numbers of minority and nonminority students. Of the 340 students at Lincoln, 35 percent are Black, 8 percent are Hispanic, 7 percent are Hmong, 49 percent are White, and 1 percent are Native American. The total number of students who enter and leave during an academic year is equal to 29 percent of the enrollment; this is considered high for the district.

I became interested in classroom action research as a way to examine my own teaching, with the goal of improving the achievement of those of my African American students who were more than a year below grade level in math. I was teaching fourth grade at the time. The racial composition and achievement level of the students in my class was typical of the school as a whole. About half the students lived in each of our attendance areas. Half were minority students. The students who were having the most difficulty learning math in my class were African American. The students who were most advanced were White. Some students from both racial groups were making average progress. Most of my African American students who had previously attended schools in other school districts viewed themselves as successful in tasks that required memorization, but not in problem-solving tasks. These were the students whom I wasn't reaching, my target students. They used but did not understand algorithms, preferring rows of problems on worksheets to discussions about problem-solving strategies. These students had no number sense and no other strategies for solving problems. They were not able to do math with understanding. I had learned from my professional development that understanding was the foundation of mathematics education. Students who understand what they know are able to use that understanding to solve problems and learn new ideas (Fennema & Carpenter, 1993). Some of my students did not have experience constructing meaning in math.

They were not used to talking about numbers and relationships between numbers. In order to construct knowledge, these students would have to be active participants in their learning. My teaching had to be based on student thinking, not just on a text or grade level.

I believed that helping my students construct knowledge would prepare them for higher-level math classes and algebra. This was in alignment with the philosophy of our school district, which was moving away from elementary math based on computation skills to instruction based on supporting students' growth of understanding.

One of the interesting observations I have made in recent years is that most of my African American students like to work with partners in math. Working together could be viewed as peer coaching between two active learners, or as one person learning while the other watched passively. My study of multicultural teaching influenced my view that this preference might be due to a stronger emphasis on community between African American students than between White students, who were more comfortable with an individual approach to learning. Whether working together was a cultural preference or simply an expression of friendship, I wondered if I would be more successful organizing my teaching in math around this learning style. So my two-part question became:

**How can I apply my African American students' preference for working in small, self-selected partnerships to help them become active learners and problem solvers in math? How can I evaluate the effectiveness of these partnerships in promoting individual student achievement?**

## BACKGROUND

When I began meeting with the teachers and facilitators in my action research group, I was perplexed by the lack of progress I was seeing in some African American students' problem-solving abilities. It was important to me that students do more than memorize facts and algorithms. My goal was to help students develop understanding of operations and numbers. The questions I posed to them and the activities I used to change how they thought about numbers frustrated these students, who had reached fourth grade without developing basic number sense. First of all, they didn't see anything wrong with the way they understood math as solving computation problems with standard algorithms. Second, they were embarrassed when I asked them to use concrete models to represent their understanding, even though this was a general expectation in my classroom. Many of my students struggled with place value. They didn't know how to break numbers apart. Given a story problem to solve, they didn't know where to start. They tried to use algorithms that they understood incompletely. Even though these gaps in math understanding indicated a need to go back to a more basic level, I felt pressure to prepare all my students for standardized tests and fifth grade. There had to be a way to move struggling students forward while respecting their diverse needs.

I was unsure about my ability to measure whether or how my teaching of problem solving was effective in getting kids to think and be active problem solvers. Many students seemed to want to get the right answer without having to think about it. They were motivated to learn to duplicate a process or algorithm instead of understanding the process and inventing their own algorithms, which was faster. I knew that some students lacked the fundamental number knowledge that they needed to do what I was expecting, based on my understanding of math learning. However, I was unsure of how to assess how well students were moving from one level of understanding to another. There was no curriculum for what I was trying to do. On the advice of a district consultant, our school had moved away from using a text. Teachers were expected to formulate their own curriculum based on their students' needs. I had to decide on my own when the class was ready to go on to the next concept and, at the same time, keep in mind the progress of each student. There was no scope and no sequence. I was uncomfortable about the lack of a plan for showing parents and students that specific goals had been met.

Another factor in my decision making was the students themselves, including their life experiences, background knowledge, and ideas. The students were my teaching partners. The students in my target group were resistant to changing how they thought about math, but they were motivated by the opportunity to work with a partner of their choosing. Observing their continued preference for partner work, I wondered if by honoring this preference I could create a situation in which they would be drawn into the activities that would help build their understanding. I briefly considered whether simply switching to a direct, prescriptive approach with less emphasis on constructing knowledge would create more equal opportunities for all my students to be successful.

My own sense of success as a teacher was tied to my students' success. If a system of students working with partners in math could help me meet the needs of the diverse learners in my classroom, I could feel more positive about my teaching. It was worth a try.

## THE BEGINNING: COLLECTING DATA

The challenge for me was to support the preferred learning style of my African American students and make it beneficial to their learning. In the fall, interest in working with partners was not limited only to African American students. Nor did all those students prefer to work with partners. While I encouraged students to work with partners and in cooperative groups in a variety of contexts, I was less confident about math. I wasn't sure that allowing students to work together on math problems would result in more learning for students who were struggling. For these students, I suspected, the effects of partner work would be neutral or negative if I did not intervene.

After a few sessions with the action research team, I began data collection by noting the positive and negative effects of students working with their preferred partner or partners. On the plus side, students looked forward to math. They were motivated to finish assignments. Three boys who were working together literally dove into their work. What these boys accomplished during the problem-solving work time was perhaps less positive. The more opinionated and confident of the three argued with the other two about strategies. Usually the less dominant boys gave in to him, even when he was wrong. When they worked without him, they were more open to learning, constructing their own understanding and explaining it.

Two of the girls who worked together seemed to confuse each other. One tried to show the other how to directly model a multiplication problem, but the first girl thought the model was unnecessary. She had a somewhat better understanding based on her knowledge of facts, but she was confused about applying the facts to problem-solving situations. Over the first few weeks of my action research, whenever I gave these girls challenging problems they would wait for help from me, find someone from whom they could copy ideas, or struggle with computations they thought would help, regardless of whether the algorithms or numbers they used fit the facts of the problems.

Two other girls were initially more successful. They both had good knowledge of facts and communicated their strategies, even if it took a great deal of time. When the tasks were easy, they used counting materials to model the numbers in the problems, drew diagrams of their work, and wrote appropriate number sentences. With more complex problems, one girl became frustrated and gave up. Her partner worked ahead without her. Another set of partners, one an advanced math student, the other not, talked a lot about their work and explained it to me very well. When they worked apart, it was apparent that only one of them could solve problems independently.

Partners working together in math class had many of the same issues as individuals working independently: some finished early, some needed much more time, and some were hesitant to begin. Although I was concerned about many issues, the students were solidly in favor of continuing the practice of working together.

## FIRST REFLECTIONS

After my early observations, I wrote and reflected. I knew that there were problems with partner math. How could I define what was and wasn't working?

First I made notes of when and how partnerships worked in other areas of instruction. They worked well in story writing. Sometimes this was parallel work, during which the students just sat together and occasionally shared what they had written. Another story writing approach was collaborative in nature, with one person recording the other person's ideas and the two students taking turns writing and thinking. Unless students were required to work independently, they almost always completed worksheets with a friend. Students also read the weekly newsmagazine together and helped each other with the questions on the back page. Partners or small groups of students working together usually did social studies research projects. This was most successful when each student was assigned a role; otherwise, one person did the work while the other observed.

I was noticing that these forms of collaboration provided students with a measure of security and empowerment. They also reduced isolation and competition in the classroom, which was a benefit to the classroom community as a whole. What seemed to be lacking was a structure to ensure that one partner wasn't passively observing while the other partner did all the work. I just didn't know what form the structure would take.

## THE INITIAL SURVEY

I wanted to find out if my observations that the students preferred working with partners could be substantiated. At a class meeting, I told the students about my research and asked them to help me collect data. They responded eagerly to the following three questions:

1. Do you like working with a partner? Why?

2. What subject do you like to work on with a partner?

3. Do you think you have learned something from working with a partner? What have you learned?

As I expected, the responses confirmed that my students liked working with partners in math. Only one person said she didn't want to work with anyone else. Two students said that they best liked working with partners in science. Another liked working with a partner best in writing. Comments about what they had learned from their math partners included: "learned how to use cubes," "it's easier," and "learned how to do division a different way."

I now had two types of data: observational notes that I had gathered while teaching, and survey results. I also kept a reflection journal. This was where I periodically reflected on and analyzed my teaching and my data. I felt confident that I was making progress. One of our action research facilitators told us, "Data can be information that is your friend." Although that statement seemed self-evident, applying it to action research helped me better understand the power of data from my own practice. I had forgotten just how much information I could gather from analyzing my actions and observing my students' actions. I observed and reflected every day, but there never seemed to be time to really think about the changes that I needed to make based on those observations. Instead it seemed that the observation of a problem led to a plan made in haste instead of a lasting solution. The idea of collecting more data and taking the time to relate the data to effective teaching was very appealing. Teachers in my school who had completed action research projects agreed.

My next step was to make a list of opportunities to collect more information about my class and target students, including videotaping students as they worked, interviewing students to find out what they were thinking, and doing individual assessments of my target students to find out if they understood the concepts they had worked on in partnership groups.

## DEEP TROUBLE

While I continued relying on partners to enrich each other's math experience, my observations led to concern about the progress students were making in math. Looking back, I see that the students' difficulties had a variety of causes. These included the students' learning styles, the fact that I did not give specific directions about how they should accomplish partner work, my erroneous assumptions about students' prior knowledge, and my lack of effective interventions for students who were just beginning to develop number sense.

As I observed the whole group sharing problem-solving strategies, I noticed that when a student in my target group explained her or his strategy, she or he was very involved and confident. When other students explained their strategies, some of my target group students didn't even listen or try to follow along. In summary, the target group students weren't learning new strategies from their classmates during either partnership work or whole-group sharing. Participation increased when students were required to record strategies as their classmates shared them and to explain what they understood about those strategies. Yet some students were still disengaged from the process.

In December, my informal assessments showed that partner work was not aiding students' acquisition of number sense. Six of the students, when working on their own, weren't consistently able to add two-digit numbers correctly. It didn't matter that they had learned the standard algorithm. They were unconcerned about the columns of 1s and 10s. They didn't connect the use of concrete objects that represented the groups of 10 with the use of columns of numbers that provide an abstract representation of numbers of 10s and 1s. This showed me that some big gaps in understanding base-10 concepts still remained. It also indicated to me that my students had been "doing math" without actively thinking about it.

My best plans for listening in on partner work and recording conversations were thwarted by the realities of having to instruct, help, and answer questions as well as give positive feedback. I found myself running around the room so that I could encourage everyone and then getting caught up helping one or another group for a longer time.

## PULLING BACK

I eliminated partner work for the rest of December. Students worked independently or as one group. I put more focus on individual learners.

I remained committed to my action research question. It seemed apparent that my enthusiasm for the question had led me to neglect the need to develop a well-structured framework for answering it. I knew that I needed such a framework; I just hadn't progressed far enough in my own thinking or found the time to put it together.

## MORE REFLECTION

It was time again to reflect. In the past, journal writing about my students helped me to clarify my thoughts and led to much-needed insights. So I began with more journaling. I also wanted to try out the problem analysis strategies we had learned in our action research seminar.

Writing led me to realize that my target group still wasn't defined. Although my action research group leader's advice was to target only a couple of students, I thought all my African American students could be my group. Then I decided to include all students of color, and then I decided to include all my students. But I realized that this would be unworkable. I couldn't collect data on everyone and still stay focused on my research question.

In addition to the problem of my lack of clarity about the target group composition, I noticed that I had been directing an inordinate amount of my time and energy toward one particular student. This student was undermining the whole notion of partner activity and risk taking in a nurturing environment by intimidating his partners and other students in the class during math. With the help of materials from a special education teacher who worked with emotionally disturbed students, I planned to look at his behavior, then set up a course for effective intervention. In the meantime, we were all distracted by his behavior.

I wanted to be ready with a new plan to present to the action research group in January. I was feeling inadequate. The students who needed to learn the most were not learning from my methods. They weren't making progress equal to that of some of their peers.

## TIME TO THINK

During winter break, I was able to see the problem more clearly through the use of a problem analysis tool called the "fishbone." The fishbone is a graphic organizer for seeing cause-and-effect relationships. I used a fishbone diagram to define the parameters of the problem, which was essentially that my African American students were not learning enough math. The fishbone framework helped me organize all the information I had about the conditions in my math class that contributed to the problems my students and I were having. These conditions, causes, and effects fit into four categories, which became the "bones" of the fish. I now had a framework for cataloging all issues that needed attention, including problems with partner math. The fishbone also helped me focus on the items I could change. It became a document to guide my data collection. See p. 240 for the fishbone diagram.

The process of creating the fishbone diagram helped me identify a critical factor that I had ignored, which was that I had only vaguely defined my academic and behavioral expectations for partners. Students needed

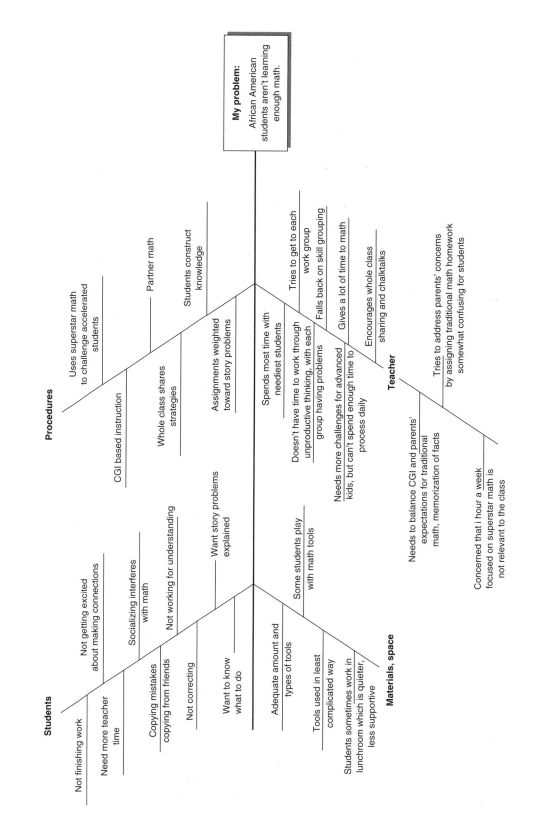

**My problem:**
African American students aren't learning enough math.

**Procedures**

- Uses superstar math to challenge accelerated students
- Partner math
- CGI based instruction
- Whole class shares strategies
- Students construct knowledge
- Assignments weighted toward story problems

**Teacher**

- Spends most time with neediest students
- Tries to get to each work group
- Doesn't have time to work through unproductive thinking, with each group having problems
- Falls back on skill grouping
- Gives a lot of time to math
- Encourages whole class sharing and chalktalks
- Needs more challenges for advanced kids, but can't spend enough time to process daily
- Needs to balance CGI and parents' expectations for traditional math, memorization of facts
- Tries to address parents' concerns by assigning traditional math homework somewhat confusing for students
- Concerned that i hour a week focused on superstar math is not relevant to the class

**Students**

- Not finishing work
- Not getting excited about making connections
- Need more teacher time
- Socializing interferes with math
- Copying mistakes copying from friends
- Not working for understanding
- Not correcting
- Want story problems explained
- Want to know what to do

**Materials, space**

- Some students play with math tools
- Adequate amount and types of tools
- Tools used in least complicated way
- Students sometimes work in lunchroom which is quieter, less supportive

240

defined criteria for success. I needed to be explicit in my expectations. After more reflection, I was able to list all the behaviors and goals that seemed intuitive to me but not to the students. The list was lengthy:

- Stay with the group.
- Use an "indoor" voice.
- Discuss the problem.
- Determine what is being asked.
- Take turns giving ideas.
- Take turns explaining the strategy.
- Instead of telling me you don't get it or the problem is too hard, say, "Does this mean?" or "Could we do this?"
- Make an estimate of the answer (using number sense).
- Take risks.
- Use time for math instead of socializing.
- Practice explaining the strategies and understandings.
- Record (on one piece of paper, if possible) how the problem was solved.
- Ask yourself, "Does this answer make sense?"

How could I share these ideas with my students in a way that was understandable and motivating to them? What next step would invite them into the process and build ownership in defining successful partner work?

Another issue that the fishbone diagram helped identify was that the students in my target group did not seem to learn by listening to or observing others. I recalled and later confirmed the fact that three of my students absolutely ignored math sharing when other kids were explaining strategies. They even ignored me, unless I was working with them one on one. This was a danger sign that called for an immediate response. I decided to do more direct teaching and to tutor the target students during our Drop Everything and Read (DEAR) time. While this independent reading time was very important, it was the only time available; doing math during recess time, before school, or after school was considered a punishment, not a help.

## TALKING TO MYSELF: MORE REFLECTION

Our action research group met during the first week in January. As we shared what we had done since the last meeting, I put into words some of my insights. Partners and student-formed groups were not supporting the learning that I expected in math. I had decided that it was necessary to combine partner work with other teaching strategies: whole-group instruction, math fact memorization, math sharing, individual tutoring, and afterschool math club participation. I shared my plan to give students a clearer explanation of how to work together.

The discussion in the research group prompted me to think more about how students see themselves. Maybe some of them didn't perceive themselves as active learners. Perhaps they needed more encouragement to define themselves as learners rather than as vessels to be filled with knowledge (facts and procedures) or simply as doers. I wanted to communicate to them that doing wasn't learning if they weren't thinking about making sense of what they were doing. One of the research group members reminded me that the copying that some students interpreted as doing and learning was likely undermining their confidence as well as their understanding.

I began to wonder about the role of the feedback I was giving students when I complimented them on their work together. Was I validating the behaviors I wanted to see? Or was I rewarding finishing over thinking? Was I rewarding the product instead of the process?

I thought more about the process of learning in math. What was math thinking? Why were some students more successful than others? Could I justify going forward in a curriculum-driven track when I knew that some children didn't have basic understanding? I kept thinking about grade-level expectations.

One of the underlying issues for my students was self-respect. Many of my African American students seemed to feel threatened by a system of learning math that wasn't giving them a chance to show what they knew. They asked me, "Can we do multiplication facts?" or said, "Let's do 'Around the World'" (a competition to see who can say a math fact first). Usually I didn't want to spend time on this game, even though students often requested it. Now I was realizing that some students had been waiting all year to be able to show that they had memorized their "times" tables at a previous school. My constant prodding to think and problem-solve with understanding was frustrating them and possibly eroding their self-concept. They wanted the facts, just the facts. One boy borrowed flash cards from his third-grade teacher so that he could use them in class. I bought a set for the class. Another student frequently asked for "regular" math problems. They were saying, in effect, "Enough of that 'Show me' and 'How did you get this answer?' and 'What does this problem mean?'" My target students were really sick of it.

I began to wonder if an underlying issue was my emphasis on solving word problems. Was there something wrong with my problems? Was my instruction culturally biased toward brainteasers and mental gymnastics because I was successful at doing them? Did my problems require kids to have middle-class vocabulary to talk about math and the ability to navigate across cultures as they struggled with basic math concepts? If my instruction was disconnected with my students' lives, what could I do about it?

## BEGINNING AGAIN

I didn't implement my plan for January until the end of the month. I was prepared to videotape partner work during math class, decide which students were going to work together, define partnership work in a class meeting with class participation, and evaluate partners and their learning. The plan would be implemented for one week.

This time, I picked the partners. I matched each target student with someone who was a successful math problem solver, but not so different in skill level that they would both be frustrated. At a class meeting, I shared my ideas for how partners should work together and asked students for their suggestions. They said that partners should listen to each other, give praise, and share ideas. Then we role-played how successful partners should respond when they found out who their partners would be. We also role-played what not to do. My students liked it when we used humor to illustrate permissible behavior. The students bought into the plan for implementing our rubric for successful partner work in math. They wanted their plan to succeed. No one wanted to be left out for behaving inappropriately.

We reviewed partnership expectations before getting to work. I gave each pair of students a form for recording problem-solving strategies, and I directed partners to choose roles. One student was to record the problem-solving process with numbers. The other was to record the process in words (narrative). It was up to each pair to decide whether the recording would be done on one page or on separate pages. That mattered, because if partners used separate pages, they could work on their tasks simultaneously, while if they used one page, they had to take turns.

During the last week in January, we implemented our new plan. We called it Partner Week. The first day was great. Students were very conscientious and goal oriented. They focused on their assignments without delay. They chose roles. I heard students reading the problems to each other and discussing them. I could tell from the finished work that the students understood the problems.

The rest of the week was about the same. For 40 to 50 minutes of each math period, students worked busily with their partners. Each day began with a reminder about the criteria for success. I roamed around the room during math, making notes of student thinking and partner behavior.

## PARTNER WEEK: WHAT I LEARNED

Partner Week was a powerful experience. I learned as much as the class did, although I was learning about process while they were learning about math problems. I began to appreciate the importance of two factors in addition to careful planning and structure. They were the physical space and the emergence of a more cohesive math community.

### Location

In response to an item on my fishbone diagram, I observed more carefully the work setting for my fourth graders. Work location was important to the children. Students were comfortable spreading out into any part of the room when I allowed them to do so. Sometimes I permitted students to read in the hallway or work on group projects in the cafeteria next to our room. But during math I expected everyone to stay in the classroom, where I could see what they were doing and provide help if needed. My room was fairly open, with desks taking up less than half the space. There were three large tables with chairs for group work. Some smaller tables were available for displays or small work spaces. I wanted the partner groups to have enough room so that they wouldn't be in each other's way, and so I assigned each group to a particular spot, which we called "offices" or "workstations."

I noticed that toward the end of the week some of the partner groups were getting close enough to other groups to make "nonmath" communication too easy. I learned something else about partners as well. When four students were in close proximity, the interactions tended to become social. The optimal number of students in a space was two. Assigned places in the room enhanced concentration.

A less obvious reason why partners needed to have private space was related to peer pressure. When friends were too near to each other, they seemed to feel obliged to send the message that the other person, their partner, was not really a member of the friendship group. When students focused on their partners instead of on their friends, they were amazingly on-task, polite, and cheerful.

### Constructing the Community

At the beginning of the week, I focused discussion more on how well partners worked together than on solutions to the math problems. My goals were for partners to work cooperatively and creatively and to engage in problem solving with understanding. My students were thrilled and very proud when, after a problem-solving session, I went around the room praising each pair for the behavior and thinking that I observed. One anecdote shows how important this was to the group.

After the first work period, we discussed whether we had done well at meeting our goals, and I shared my observations of how each group worked. Two students who were unable to do the partner assignment due to a schedule conflict returned to the room in time for the discussion. When I had nothing to say about how well the two students had worked together, the rest of the students pointed out my omission. They hadn't noticed that these students were not in the room for math, and they didn't want them excluded from what was regarded as a celebration of our success as a learning community. I quickly explained the situation and then commented about the quality of their peers' work at other times. This seemed to satisfy the concern.

The generous amount of praise and feedback was reassuring to students who weren't confident about their math ability. Private praise worked, too. I didn't always have time for public recognition of accomplishments because students often worked on problem solving until the bell rang. They didn't want to stop doing math.

I was able to videotape one math period. Children were very willing to talk to the camera. Most of their comments were very positive. Two new girls who didn't want to work with partners made honest comments about their reluctance to participate in the study.

## Evaluation

Looking back, I know that what students learned about working together had lasting positive effects. Partner Week was a success for several reasons: I was well prepared with a structure; students had a clear definition of success with limited choices; they felt a sense of ownership in the plan; everyone was working in an atmosphere of security because they didn't have to defend their choice of partner or work location; and finally, there were intrinsic rewards, as well as recognition and praise, for following the directions for successful partner work.

Did learning take place? Yes and no. The target students participated fully. They seemed to gain confidence as a result of our shared expectations and of the more clearly defined learning environment. They were more successful solving problems and explaining their thinking. I don't think any large gains occurred, but a pattern of success was established. We didn't have as much time as I had expected for whole-class discussions of student work.

## FEBRUARY

My action research goal for February was to analyze my observations from Partner Week. I also wanted to find time to give target students individual math instruction, adapt another math topic to partner math, videotape more partner interactions, survey students about their attitudes toward math, and find math puzzles for partner work.

I didn't accomplish all these goals. Action research has to fit in with your routine, and this list of additional activities was too much for mine. I did change some math partners. I wrote math problems and curriculum around the topic of energy conservation to complement our electricity unit. Two of the assignments were more open-ended, with opportunities for students to illustrate their ideas, graph information, and do more writing. Some students were more successful with these assignments than with the previous ones.

My group of target students changed when two African American boys transferred to another school and two African American girls transferred to our class. The girls came with little number sense and felt quite intimidated by our math class. They were reluctant to work with anyone except me. To ease their discomfort, I planned to expand partner work to include playing math games or practicing multiplication facts with flash cards because I thought that these activities would be less threatening.

During a class meeting, I conducted an informal survey. My question was, "What do you think would help you be more successful in math?" The person with the strongest opinion was one of my target students, who told me that she liked math class in Chicago better because there they did more problems with just numbers. Our policy at the time was to give homework in a different subject each night. The math homework was usually based on the day's lesson or was an extension of the science or social studies topic.

Math homework assignments became a way to build on my target students' strengths. After I gave one student multiplication worksheets for homework, everyone else wanted them too. Simple computations using a standard algorithm were a relief to my target students. Even though it didn't fit my criteria for good teaching, the benefits for some students were obvious. Students completed their homework. Most students in my target group were successful. They had something they could show their parents.

I began to make time for students to do more multiplication algorithms on the chalkboard during class. Because not all the target students had memorized their facts, I also started sending home fact practice sheets for a sequential review of multiplication facts. Because they knew most of the answers, students could finish them fast. I wasn't giving up on problem solving and constructing knowledge—I was just doing a better job of building on the strengths of my target students, developing their confidence, and reducing the stress of learning in a way that was unfamiliar to them.

## MORE THAN PARTNER MATH

Some of my target students continued to need one-on-one instruction. They were uncomfortable asking questions in a group or admitting that they couldn't understand some math talk. There wasn't time for enough individual instruction during math, and so I took time for it during our 30 minutes of independent reading each day and during an afterschool math club that I created.

The afterschool club met for 6 weeks in our classroom in the half hour before our school's regular afterschool program started. The eight girls who attended the club were very motivated. They enjoyed having a snack and discussing math in the smaller group. In this less threatening environment, the girls took more risks and asked questions. The activities included problems similar to those we did in math class, challenges that extended the problems, and some introduction of upcoming content in preparation for class work. On the days that the classroom computer was functioning, I split the group into two smaller groups. One group worked with me while the other played computer math games. I gave the boys from the target group, who were not in the afterschool club, differentiated assignments and continued to tutor them during part of the independent reading time.

My target students' families were supportive of my efforts. It was easy to get permission for students to stay after school, as long as the students were willing to participate. Parent attendance at conferences was good, too. I nurtured the home/school connections with home visits or conferences scheduled at parents' convenience, even when the only time we could meet was at the dinner hour, in the student's home. To keep parents informed about math, I often printed an example of student problem-solving strategies on the back of my weekly newsletters. When one of my target students was having a particularly difficult time understanding double-digit multiplication, I went to her house to show her mother how I was teaching her to think about decomposing the numbers in a multiplication problem. Her mother looked on as the student and I went through a problem together. She nodded and smiled. "Oh, now I know what you are doing. I saw a problem like that on the back of your newsletter." I am not sure whether working through a few math problems at the kitchen table gave this mother enough support for her to help her daughter with math, but we had a good time.

## WHAT DID I LEARN FROM MY ACTION RESEARCH?

Since Lincoln Elementary School opened in 1985, the school's staff has been concerned about the gap in achievement between students of color and students from Euro-American backgrounds. Our school was created following a court-ordered desegregation order, to address the inherent inequity of separate and unequal schools for different groups of students. In 1995, when I participated in action research, the staff formed a self-study group to learn more about school reform and schools that were successful in closing the gap. As part of this study, we met with Fred Newmann, from the University of Wisconsin Center for Educational Research. Dr. Newmann headed a five-year, federally funded study that examined the relationship between school restructuring and student achievement. As I listened to Dr. Newmann explain some of his findings, I made these connections to my action research and what I learned from it.

1. *Cosmetic reform doesn't necessarily lead to attention to intellectual quality.* In other words, my innovation—a structure for partner math—by itself is not guaranteed to result in quality thinking. I communicated to my students that I was inviting them to be partners in the pursuit of quality thinking instead of just working to please me or to be able to say they finished an assignment.

2. *Student participation may be mistaken for thinking.* This leads me to wonder whether participating in Partner Math fosters thinking or just the *appearance* of thinking. I have more to learn about how to help students build understanding in mathematics.

3. *The school staff as community is very important to the learning process.* Colleagues in my research group enriched my classroom action research. The group and its facilitators became a teacher community. I am encouraged to work with other teachers at Lincoln in support of developing our professional community. We have already begun talking about the need to work together to create a predictable and consistent learning environment for our students. For me to be successful and for my students to be successful, I need to look outside the door of my room and spend some energy building the professional community.

4. *Successful schools have high expectations across the board. The goal is to challenge students to do higher-order thinking. Always measure your success against that criterion.* During my action research project, I learned how to explain my expectations to students so that they would share them. I also evaluated how I praised progress, to make

sure that I wasn't giving students confusing messages. Now when I praise students' work in math, I look for evidence of thinking that leads to understanding. I remind them that they are all very capable. To remind students of our goals, I give math problem set worksheets special names like "Bright Minds" or "Turned on Math."

## MORE QUESTIONS

Is Partner Math a valid instructional tool? Yes. It was a useful instructional tool after I clearly defined my expectations for this form of classroom collaboration. Applying students' preference for working in partner groups helped me reach my goal, to help my African American students become active learners and problem solvers in math. Partner Math and flexible classroom organization benefited my target students as well as the other students in my class. Working together in a structured setting promoted teamwork that supported active learning. Students whose confidence was challenged by the unfamiliar expectation that they be able to explain math understanding orally and in writing gained confidence and found security in working together. Taking risks in learning became less threatening. We built a more solid math learning community than I have seen with previous classes.

I have different questions now, based on my reflection and writing. The major new question is, "How is my math instruction culturally biased by my own experience of learning math, and what should I do about it? How can I make it more culturally relevant for my students?" I am beginning to discuss this question with colleagues. I have already found several interesting articles on the subject, such as those in the *Journal of Negro Education*, published by Howard University. *Teaching Children Mathematics*, a professional journal published by the National Council of Teachers of Mathematics, is also a great resource. Another equally important question I have is, "How can I create a learning environment where it is safe for students to work with math manipulatives long enough to really develop their understanding of math concepts?"

## EPILOGUE

Equity in education is my passion. It is what keeps me going professionally. Years ago I heard the criticism that White teachers merely collect a paycheck and go home, whether their students are successful or not. Even though I have never felt that this is true, I am haunted by the fact that I am guaranteed a measure of comfort in life because of my work, but my students are not. It seems to me that how students view themselves in relation to mathematics is critical for educational equity. Math understanding and proficiency are prerequisites to higher educational opportunities. I have noticed that elementary students' lack of achievement in math contributes to diminished self-esteem as learners.

Looking back a decade to the time when I conducted this classroom action research project, I believe that, to some extent, the activities surrounding the study promoted classroom equity. My students learned that issues of inclusion and fairness could be discussed safely in a learning community. They knew that their opinions were important and their ideas valued because they saw them put into practice when we developed our model for partner work. I hope that this shared responsibility for the learning environment was, for them, a model for making the kinds of changes that could lead to greater equity.

The staff at Lincoln School cared deeply about equity. Five Lincoln teachers conducted classroom action research studies during the school year. I don't remember that we ever shared the specific details of our findings. In that sense, my study by itself didn't promote equity on a school-wide level. Equity was something we talked about in terms of learning styles, discipline, and multicultural activities. Most teachers didn't work together on a daily basis. Equity wasn't a topic at our grade-level team meetings. Our learning coordinator, principal, and members of the community facilitated serious professional discussions about equity. I was proud to be part of a staff that recognized the challenge of educational inequalities for different ethnic and racial groups. My classroom action research topic fit perfectly with the professional environment at Lincoln.

In the years since I conducted this study, most of my professional focus has been in the area of effective math instruction. The year following the study, I helped select a new math series for our school. Then I began team teaching with another multiage classroom teacher so that I could teach two classes of math each day. I joined a number of professional organizations, attended workshops and conventions, and sought out professional resources. Four years ago, I participated in a yearlong, grant-funded project to promote diversity in math education. As part of the project, I taught in a pilot summer school program for students of color who were failing math and then participated in a yearlong math education seminar with the university advisor and a cohort of classroom teachers and math resource teachers. The next three summers, I led staff development in math instruction at my school for teams of teachers. For the last three years, I have held a math coaching position at my school. I run afterschool math programs, match students with mentors, give presentations to the staff, coach teachers and interns, write lessons, provide teaching resources, and work with students. These activities have led me to a much deeper understanding of how children learn mathematics than I had 10 years ago.

The results of inequality are increasingly obvious to me: years of consistently low test scores for certain groups and high test scores for others, students who can't or won't finish high school, dreams unattainable and unmet. Maybe part of the problem is that the educational establishment, including universities and government institutions, fails to take seriously the need to change. Change might begin with a better definition of equity in math as it relates to the readiness of teachers to teach math. For me, equity in math education means first of all that all students are taught by teachers who are fully prepared to teach the subject to all students. It is unfair to expect students to be able to compensate for poor teaching and for the inaccurate conceptual understanding they formulated in the early elementary years.

For me, equity is impossible without accountability. Teacher training institutions have to be accountable for better training of teachers. School districts need to be accountable for ongoing professional development embedded in schools. In order to be accountable to all students, we need to have a deep understanding of the subjects we are teaching. Equity in math instruction will occur when all students are taught to fully understand math, rather than simply learning empty rules and algorithms that they can't explain. Students who are not proficient must receive extra instruction based on their level of readiness, especially in the early grades. They must be taught in such a way that they learn the big ideas that make math exciting and fun. But until math education is as valued as reading instruction, many—if not most—elementary teachers will not get the support they need to be prepared to teach all students successfully.

The issue of equity is multidimensional. There isn't one easy strategy to achieve it because the problem of inequity is so complex. In my research study, I attempted to demonstrate the power of inclusion. I believe that students deserve the opportunity to learn together as opposed to learning in separate spaces with different curricula and different outcomes. Racism contributes to inequities in the math classroom. Students come to school with vastly different levels of readiness, which are closely correlated to income levels—which, sadly, in our community are closely correlated to race. African American students in my urban school enter the primary grades brimming with confidence and motivation to learn math. For too many, this excitement evaporates as they fall further behind their nonminority peers. Students who don't receive effective interventions that could lead to higher achievement begin to show signs of apathy and failure by the time they are in fourth or fifth grade. In an ideal situation, part of every math period in the elementary grades would include differentiated small-group instruction provided by the most highly trained professional in the room, the teacher. Otherwise these bright, competent students will continue to think of themselves as "not good in math."

Equity in the classroom won't be realized until every student is engaged in learning. Every teacher has to be committed to make the changes that will create a culturally relevant and welcoming environment that is intellectually the best for teaching each subject. This is a tremendous task for elementary teachers who must master several subjects. We need to fully understand, accept, and honor the different cultural competencies of our students. When we accept the norms that each culture brings to the table, we will teach differently.

A teacher's understanding of equity should include understanding how gender equity adds complexity to teaching with cultural competency. Our elementary school is now more diverse than ever. Yet the majority of students sent to the office are African American males. I believe that success in school is an important factor in reducing the number of incidences of behavior problems. Lack of school success leads to frustration that increases time out of class. This may be truer for boys than girls. Maybe we need a close examination of the relationship between low math achievement and negative classroom behavior. Teachers who want to promote equity have to keep students engaged in learning.

Disengagement leads to lack of learning, which leads to avoiding the subject of math. Girls and boys of all cultures practice math-avoidance behaviors that teachers need to recognize and overcome by engaging the students in active questioning, teaching students the language of math and ways to explain their thinking, and encouraging the use of models that students can use to build their conceptual understanding.

This year I began cofacilitating a mentoring program for minority students. The mentors are undergraduate minority students from the University of Wisconsin Math Department who have participated in two semesters of math courses. Each mentor is matched with students with similar backgrounds. Recently I had a conversation about equity and learning with a mentor who works with three African American fifth-grade girls. She shared some of her school experience with me. She told me that whenever a teacher stopped by her desk to ask if she understood, or if she needed any help, she would say "No." Then the teacher would walk away. A feeling of relief would come over her because she was able to stay under the radar, away from attention. As I listened to her describe this teacher-avoidance behavior, a light of recognition went on in my head. Although she did not consider herself to be a very advanced math student in elementary and middle school, she felt the need to avoid teachers more than the need to understand what she was learning. She told me that she would have answered differently if the teacher had asked her to explain her thinking or given her more time. Fortunately, she could go to family members to find out what she needed to know. But many unsuccessful students don't have that option.

Equity means knowing every child as a person and being prepared to do whatever is necessary to reach him or her. Equity means never just walking away.

## REFERENCES

Fennema, E., & Carpenter, T. (1993). *Cognitively guided instruction readings.* Unpublished paper, Wisconsin Center for Education Research.

Newmann, F. M., & Wehlage, G. G. (1995). *Successful school restructuring: A report to the public and educators by the Center of Organization and Restructuring of Schools.* Washington, DC: American Federation of Teachers.

# 12

---

# *Crossing Bridges of Culture, Color, and Language*

## Denise M. Hanson

## EDITORS' INTRODUCTION

Through her work as a teacher researcher, Hanson explores the status of Latino students in her high school Spanish classroom. Concerned that her native Spanish speakers are disconnected from the school community and perceived as deficient, Hanson attempts to draw on these students' strengths. By "employing" native speakers as teaching assistants in her Spanish classes, Hanson examines the traditional roles that students typically play in schools and suggests ways to validate the knowledge of marginalized student populations. A powerful example of teaching for educational change, Hanson's study implores educators to reexamine the assumptions and biased practices prevalent in our schools.

\* \* \* \* \*

*"Knowing another language is always important in the world. It will always help you in other things. And I believe that it has been a beautiful experience. Besides that, I have met people in this class who are very nice . . . I met new friends . . . and now, well, I am happy, I see them in the halls and they greet me. I see that they are happy with the things that I taught them. You know I can tell that they like it that I*

*have been here teaching them . . . and this is why I feel content about the work that I have done."*

—Glenda, reflecting on her experience
of being a teacher assistant in Spanish 1A

# INTRODUCTION

In this chapter, I will describe an innovative action research project using Spanish classes to help change the status of Latino students in the high school where I teach. The aim of this project is to provide native English speakers with Spanish-speaking models so that the native English speakers can improve their Spanish and their understanding of Latino culture. I believe this project is crucially important, for two reasons. The first is the alienation of many Latino students from our public schools, which is directly linked to poor grades and high dropout rates for such students. The second is that many English-speaking students graduate from high school without experiencing what it is like to communicate in another language with people from another culture. My action research project centered around empowering young Latino students as leaders, in part to ensure their ongoing investment in their own education.

# THE SETTING

I work as a high school Spanish teacher in the Madison Metropolitan School District (MMSD). I currently teach three sections of beginning-level Spanish at West High School. I also work at the University of Wisconsin–Madison, where my duties vary from semester to semester, and include teaching instructional methods to undergraduates seeking certification in foreign language education and placing, advising, and supervising these students during their practicums and student-teaching semesters, as well as keeping in communication with their cooperating teachers in the field.

The city of Madison is considered by many to be upper-middle-class. It is regularly mentioned in publications such as *Money* magazine as a desirable place for the upscale family to live, and it has been called a "latte town" (implying upper-middle-class values and tastes) in books such as *Bobos in Paradise* (Brooks, 2000). Despite this reputation, Madison has the same type of economically and racially segregated educational settings as many other large urban areas. The ethnic and racial composition of each school's student body in the district varies widely. Some schools in the district are more than 70 percent White, with fewer than 20 percent of the students classified as low-income (Madison Metropolitan School District, Ethnicity, 2007). Other schools have as few as 25 percent White students. In some schools, more than 80 percent of the student body is classified as low-income (Madison Metropolitan School District, Income, 2007). Achievement levels also vary.

The academic achievement gaps between racial, ethnic, and socioeconomic groups grow wider with each year that students attend school in the MMSD. Student scores on standardized reading tests provide a good example. The number of Latino students scoring as either "proficient" or "advanced" drops from 63 percent in fourth grade to 54 percent in tenth grade. (Wisconsin Department of Public Instruction, 2007.) Also, in both the fourth and tenth grades, many more White students received proficient and advanced scores than their peers.

Although the MMSD makes great efforts to ensure quality instruction for all students, anecdotal evidence indicates that many low-income and Latino students in the district are on the receiving end of what Haberman (1991) calls the pedagogy of poverty, a cycle in which many poor students and students of color are tracked into less challenging classes and too often fall far behind. At the same time, White, middle-class English speakers receive the intellectually challenging education commonly found in an upper-middle-class university town.

Madison as a whole has fairly high rates of high school graduation, ranging in recent years from 85 percent to 90 percent. West High School, with approximately 2,200 students currently enrolled, is no exception. It is a somewhat diverse school in terms of students' ethnic and socioeconomic backgrounds. In 2002–2003, the school's student population was 9.2 percent Asian, 16.2 percent African American, 7.4 percent Hispanic, and 66.5 percent White. During the 2001–2002 school year, the graduation rate for Hispanic students at West High was 64 percent—the lowest of all ethnic groups at West. During the previous year (2000–2001) the Hispanic graduation rate was 55.17 percent. Although West High School boasts an extremely high population of National Honor Society students, it also has shockingly high numbers of students of color who do not graduate.

## LATINOS IN THE LITERATURE

Many researchers (for example, Baker, 2002; Zanger, 1994) have noted that English language learners (ELLs) are hampered both in their efforts to learn English and in their overall school achievement when they feel that their home cultures are not valued in the school. This problem is alleviated or eliminated by teaching their native languages in the school. My action research project challenged the traditional White roles by giving status to the Latino teaching assistants (TAs). Latino students are empowered by teaching their language and culture. Furthermore, teaching a foreign language that is already spoken at the school encourages the interaction of languages and cultures. This gives both Spanish learners and English learners the social contact and exposure to each other's languages, as well as the understanding of the need to speak the target language, that are a crucial part of any language learning experience (Wong-Fillmore, 1991). Having Spanish-speaking TAs, who are also peers of the students in the class, prevents English speakers from learning a fossilized, stagnant Spanish. Keeping a language alive and vibrant is a two-way street, helping both English speakers and Spanish speakers.

It has also been established that many students from Latino cultural backgrounds are disengaging from school learning, because of stereotypes that they are not capable of academic success or, in situations in which they attend schools with some degree of integration, because they are culturally and socially marginalized within the school itself (Zanger, 1994). Latino test scores in the early years are relatively similar to those of their White, English-speaking peers. However, with every year that Latino students continue in school, the achievement gap widens, until by the time they take the standard battery of tenth-grade tests, they are far behind their more economically privileged classmates. This seems to reflect a general tendency on the part of the Latino student to become disengaged, and to value their culture negatively. In fact, Walsh (1991) has documented a process by which many ELLs develop an increasingly negative view of their native language and culture as they learn English. This devaluation of self and culture is not conducive to academic success. Ma (2002) and Hakuta and August (1998) point out that one of the most crucial factors in supporting the academic progress and self-esteem of English language learners is for native English speakers in the school to become more literate in their first language and to share the language learning process with their classmates.

## ORIGIN OF MY RESEARCH QUESTION

West High School has many international students. Students from roughly 40 countries are represented in the English as a second language (ESL) program; the majority of these students are Spanish speakers. There are more than 175 ELLs in the West High ESL department, representing roughly 20 languages. Spanish is the first language spoken by more than half of these students.

It has always concerned me that the ESL students in general, but particularly the Latino students, are disconnected from the rest of the school. My perception is that ESL students connect with each other, especially with other speakers of their native languages, and often they form close relationships with the ESL teachers and staff. However, they tend to remain enclosed in a small community within the school and do not easily form friendships with English speakers. One Spanish-speaking student who later became one of my TAs told me that he felt frustrated because all the other groups were included in school activities such as soccer and fine arts, while the Latino students—who, he felt, could excel in these areas—were not encouraged to take part. Like my TA, I am deeply concerned about the invisibility of these students in the larger school community. I see these students as a great educational resource that I know could be tapped into.

Currently, there are few or no native Spanish speakers taking Spanish IV or V at West High school and very few at levels I, II, or III. It is obvious that native English speakers take English language classes (literature, composition, theatre, language, and usage). We know that Latinos who engage in academic learning of their native language develop increased self-esteem, establish a positive identity with their ethnic group, and consequently gain an incentive to remain in school and succeed academically (Peale, 1991; Sheets, 1996; Trueba, Rodriguez, Zou, & Cintrón, 1993). Why then are native Spanish speakers underrepresented in high school Spanish classes?

Over the years, I have worked to open my classroom to these students and encourage them to take my classes. Unfortunately, my attempts to move native Spanish speakers into my classroom often backfired when the other students made comments to native Spanish speakers like "What are *you* doing in this class? You already *know* Spanish," or worse, "You *should* know Spanish." According to María Kellor, a retired MMSD Spanish teacher:

> *At an age when peer approval is especially important, this could be psychologically devastating. Not only is this experience in the Spanish classroom harmful to the Spanish speaker's desire to learn his own language, it also has a tremendous impact on his self-concept. His chance to excel turns into a catastrophe; his "special talent" turns into a problem.*
>
> —Kellor, master's thesis, p. 29

Kellor's research provides evidence that supports the value of Spanish classes for native Spanish speakers. Furthermore, she applauds Spanish teachers who include Latinos in Spanish classes, if the teachers individualize education for the students by finding personally relevant literature and differentiating pedagogy in and out of class (Kellor, 1994). Though the native Spanish-speaking "recruits" I brought to my Spanish classes may have heard the types of damaging statements noted above, I have always tried to differentiate teaching and learning, with the ultimate goal of empowering my students. By this I mean that I have always individualized the educational goals and programming for my students as I—and they—see fit. This is not something specific only to native Spanish speakers; it is something that I believe in and do for other students as well.

Before my current project began, I catered specifically to the needs of native Spanish speakers by individualizing my plans and expectations, giving them more appropriate literature, and most important, asking them to take leadership roles in order to help other students with oral practice. The benefits their presence brought to the class were plentiful in the years before I placed Latinos in teaching assistantships, but have multiplied since the implementation of this project. The learning occurred on many of the same levels as it does now: through recognition of each native speaker's distinct accent, through their cultural sharing, and through the inclusive community environment that I constantly try to establish. The contributions these students made to my classes in the past inspired my current project, in which I specifically target Latinos as a resource.

The benefits these students would bring to any Spanish class were clear to me. What was not clear was how to deal with the concerns I had about the native Spanish speakers' own frequent literacy deficiencies. I knew that these would come to the surface, and that I would need to address them. Many of these students have recently escaped from war-torn or economically ravaged areas of the Americas, where education took a backseat to food, shelter, and safety. The lack of a strong background in Spanish language literacy haunts them as they struggle with written exams, papers, and the like. It is important to note that until recently, foreign language classes nationwide have heavily emphasized writing skills, with grades being based mostly on traditional paper-and-pencil test scores. When tests are returned in this type of class, other students' eyes strain expecting to see the brightly colored "A" on the native speaker's paper, but to the non-Latino students' astonishment, the native speakers often receive less than stellar scores. The native Spanish speakers are then immediately—and mercilessly—devalued by their peers from the United States. And the taunting continues: "How could you get that grade when you *are* Spanish?"

This brings us to the unfortunate fact that the average U.S. teenager often does not know or acknowledge the difference between Spain and the Spanish language. Instead, he or she assumes that all Spanish speakers are Spanish, rather than Mexican, Nicaraguan, Chilean, Peruvian, Venezuelan, or any of the other nationalities (21 in all) whose national language is Spanish. Due to the complexities of teaching Spanish to both native and nonnative Spanish speakers, I felt that individualizing the educational program for the native speakers was the only path of integrity I could take. Offering differentiated instruction to the native Spanish speakers in my Spanish classes required extra work and attention, but helped keep the students' self-esteem intact— a goal that I consider to be of supreme importance. However, my intentions, albeit worthy, were not always matched by a level of success I deemed sufficient, and many of these students were still left feeling separate from the other students and from the school as a whole.

I learned early in my teaching career that the native Spanish speaker was, quite simply, out of place in the average Spanish classroom—and my own classroom was no exception. Something was not right. It was clear that these students provided a wealth of knowledge to my classes that could not be found elsewhere. I also knew the native Spanish speakers were learning extremely valuable information about their first language. It was obvious that both the native Spanish speakers and the native English speakers were gaining cultural and linguistic knowledge due specifically to the integration of foreign students into our classroom community. Yet, I also feared that the negative impact of incorporating the native Spanish-speaking students into Spanish classes that were specifically geared toward native English speakers might outweigh the benefit.

It was for these reasons that I determined to do something new to meet the needs of both the native English-speaking and native Spanish-speaking students. Some scholars (Merino, Trueba, & Samaniego, 1993; Peale, 1991; Ramírez, 1992) have called for special provisions to be made for second language speakers in foreign language classes. I was determined to find a model that would work in our high school without making major changes in the school's curriculum. Although many MMSD teachers and administrators agree theoretically with the need for Spanish classes for Spanish speakers, the current economic crisis makes it difficult to implement this type of curricular change.

## FINDING A UNIQUE SOLUTION

With all this in mind, a solution occurred to me that, I thought, could maintain the positive aspects (both for the Spanish learner and for the native Spanish speaker) of having native Spanish-speaking students in the classroom while simultaneously protecting the native Spanish speakers' self-esteem. I decided to incorporate native Spanish speakers into my classes under the empowering title of "teacher assistant." It seemed to me a very appropriate role for many reasons: (1) the native English-speaking students would benefit from authentic oral practice in Spanish; (2) the native Spanish speakers would naturally become more literate in written Spanish; (3) the native English-speaking students would become more familiar with the geography, history, and culture of the teaching assistants' countries of origin; and (4) the native Spanish speakers, given an opportunity to become a part of a classroom community within the school but outside the ESL department, would thrive in their own literacy in Spanish and in English but also as individuals in a country away from their homes. These TAs, like other TAs at West High School, receive credit (without a grade) for the class—another potential benefit for many Latino students because they are at high risk of dropping out.

**What is the impact of including native Spanish-speaking ELL students as teacher assistants into my beginning-level Spanish classes?** I hypothesized the following: (1) that this experience would help ELL students to feel part of the wider school community; (2) that these students would experience more success in school because of this leadership role; and (3) that the English-speaking students in the classroom would benefit (both in terms of their Spanish language skills, as well as gaining a clearer sense of belonging in today's global society) from the connection with the native Spanish speakers.

Instead of Spanish class being a mere exercise in learning grammar and vocabulary that has no immediate use for most youth today, students are able to put their skills to use immediately in interacting with classmates. The TAs, who are also English language learners, gain self-confidence and feel supported in their language learning process, because their school values and supports linguistic and cultural diversity. This allows them to become a resource to the school community, rather than being seen as having a deficit that needs to be remedied. My research question evolved into a question of whether self-contained foreign and second language programs work together to produce significant benefits for both English language and foreign language learners.

## DEVELOPING THE PROGRAM

As I look back at my years of teaching, it is clear that the achievement gap has long consumed my thoughts and burdened my heart. My attempt to find a solution builds on the thoughts of scholars such as Paulo Freire, Gloria Ladson-Billings, Jose Martí, and Lidia Turner Martí. The works of this group of scholars have given me a sort of runway, from which I could take off and continue my quest to make a difference for the students whose lives I touch. From the very moment I began teaching, I saw all too clearly the ways in which many students ended up being excluded from the academic successes that were easily attained by others. English language learners carry multiple burdens, and I turned to scholars whose work and practice were rooted in ways that practitioners could alleviate some of those burdens.

These scholars all call for a model of social justice, as well as student- and community-centered teaching. As these scholars themselves have done, I have rooted my project in community involvement, a desire to work toward the needs of all my students, the need for cultural relevancy, and, above all, the concept of teaching with *love*.

## Recruitment and How I Employed Teaching Assistants

With this research and theory supporting my style and belief systems, I buckled comfortably into the pilot seat, and the school year took off. My "passengers" were the 28 students in each of my classes. Because my project was not fully formed, I initially had two English-speaking TAs, as opposed to native Spanish speakers. Meanwhile I was looking for other solutions (i.e., native Spanish speakers). An educational assistant in the ESL department who liked my idea helped me find ESL students who were in study halls during the hours I had class. By late September, I had signed on two native Spanish-speaking students per class, for a total of six students representing five different Spanish-speaking countries. Four were boys and two were girls. Two were from Argentina, one from Mexico, one from Perú, one from Ecuador, and one from Spain.

These TAs participated in the classes in multiple ways. The following are a few examples of the important and growing role they played in our classroom. I immediately gave each individual TA the floor and offered the students in each class the opportunity to ask the TAs anything they wanted to know, as long as they did it in Spanish. This provided the students the opportunity to hear the distinct accents of each TA and to get to know biographical information about them: where they were born, their age, their family size, and their first and last names.

Each TA had small jobs, such as keeping track of participation or taking attendance. The objective was for each TA to get to know who was who. In October, I asked each TA to recall a typical school day schedule for a high school student in his or her respective country. The TAs either typed this up or wrote it by hand. I made copies of each TA's hypothetical schedule, and we used them in class as we were studying the theme of schools, schedules, and subjects. This theme of class schedules was also connected with time-telling, which allowed students to ask one another as well as the TAs more specific questions about their current schedules, and other topics. By mid-October I began to give the TAs mini-plans telling them what

I wanted them to do during class. I gave them each a copy of the seating chart, which had each person's name and seating location. Each day I gave the TAs two or three questions I wanted them to work on with the students in the class. They were to go around the room one by one to ask these questions, as well as to ask each student to ask *them* each question. I told the TAs that whenever I was not teaching a new concept in front of the class, they were to move through the room with their charts, working from their lesson plans. They began to engage all the students in the classroom.

They became the "flight attendants" of the class while I remained the "pilot." By using these student teaching assistants, I had great help in achieving my goals of keeping my students extremely engaged and interested by pushing them to use authentic language in context—imparting knowledge as our Spanish voyage continued. Each student had more of a chance to be engaged in Spanish more of the time. Achievement in these activities was defined simply, by the mere act of answering and asking the questions, by reading a children's book aloud, or by simply speaking in Spanish with the TA. I placed value on involvement, connection, and growth, along with the acquisition of knowledge and skills. The native Spanish speakers started to find their places within the Spanish class. They knew they played a very important role in our classroom community. They taught skills in a way I could not have. While they were circulating, communicating, connecting, and sharing about themselves and their cultures, a community was emerging, and all students had the opportunity to work individually on their oral communication skills. The TAs were able to teach in a nonthreatening way that did not involve formal assessment or grades. This interpersonal way of learning a language is similar to what occurs in first language acquisition and in second language acquisition in natural settings. Students were provided with a sense of what they could accomplish each day, and they were learning that what they could do was communicate in Spanish. The beauty of this was that they did not have to be put on the spot in front of the whole class to do so. Everyone else was engaged in whatever the task was: oral, reading, or written work in pairs; individual reading or writing; or vocabulary study. In my view, more was being accomplished within the same amount of time. I was able to work with more individuals or pairs during the course of any given activity.

## DATA COLLECTION AND METHODS

### Teaching Assistant Surveys

I gave a questionnaire to each of my six teaching assistants in October. They had a class period to complete the survey while the other students were working on a written assessment. All questions were written in both Spanish and English, and I told the TAs that they could answer in either or both languages. The questions requested information including current address; phone number; family members' names; the name of the TA's counselor; the TAs' full class schedules; and whether they had any classes outside the ESL department. I also asked why they decided to become teaching assistants; what, if anything, they were learning in class and how they were learning; what they enjoyed most and least about the class; and what their goals were for personal and academic improvement, including how I might be able to help them achieve those goals. Finally, they had the opportunity to comment on any other issue.

## Teaching Assistant Interviews

I interviewed each teaching assistant during March and April. All interviews were private (one-on-one with me). I explained that the purpose of the interviews was to gain insight into how they felt this method of Spanish study was working in our classes, what its strengths and weaknesses were, and how the system could be improved for future students. All interviews were taped and transcribed. For the purpose of this chapter, each TA was given a pseudonym.

## Surveys With English-Speaking Students

I surveyed the native English-speaking students early in March. I told the students that they could respond to questions in either Spanish or English. All questions were provided in both languages. I asked the following questions:

1. When the teaching assistant talks to me, I feel _____.

2. Do you enjoy having the opportunity to speak with the native speaker when she or he comes around to ask questions?

3. What is the most valuable/interesting part about having a native speaker in the classroom, and why?

4. Question four was a check-off list of all the activities the TAs do during the class period. Students were asked to check off each one they felt was useful.

5. What was it like to read books aloud to the teaching assistant?

6. How would you change the system if you were the teacher?

7. What other comments do you have?

**Outside Observer Reflections**

I asked two West High School administrators, the ESL Department chair, and one ESL staff member to come into my classrooms to observe. I asked them to respond to an open-ended question: "What is the effect of the inclusion of native Spanish-speaking ESL students as teacher assistants into my beginning-level Spanish classes?" I urged them to tell me any impressions they might have had during the brief time they spent in my classroom. I also asked them if they saw any benefits or pitfalls of this system and what they were. Finally, I asked them what effect, if any, this program might have on the school as a whole.

## INTERPRETATION OF FINDINGS

I grouped my results into three categories: (1) the TA perspective; (2) the Spanish student perspective; and (3) the administrative and ESL staff perspective.

### The TA Perspective

While I was transcribing and coding the data that reflected the TAs' perspectives, I identified several themes that came up repeatedly. Most of the TAs reported some sort of interest in teaching, or said that they experienced an "aha!" moment when it dawned on them that they could be teachers—perhaps Spanish teachers. Half the TAs reported that their experiences in the cafeteria were different and better after they became TAs. Five of the six TAs brought up something about their new experiences in the hallways—the students in our classes regularly greeted them in the hallways. All TAs reported that since this experience began, they feel much more valued as members of the West High community.

#### *"I Can Teach"*

The teaching assistants reported to me that they began to think of themselves as teachers, and adept ones at that. Evidence of this comes from the TA interviews, in which five out of six mentioned something about either their ability to teach or their consideration of teaching as a future career. I heard comments from TAs similar to the following from Joaquín:

> At first it was like playing, without importance, but once I saw that the students actually wanted to learn my language as I want to

learn theirs, I took it seriously . . . I liked it . . . I know that now I can teach also.

Comments like these indicate that the TAs increasingly recognized themselves as a resource to the class and that they gained self-confidence and self-esteem.

### Cultural Crisscross in the Cafeteria

A couple of the TAs brought up their concern about the social structures of the cafeteria. They noted that the African American students sit in one area, the European American students sit in another, the Asian Americans in another, and the Latinos in another. They reported that, much to their chagrin, there was little cultural crossover and that it was difficult for students from one population to break into another cultural group. They even pointed out that these cultural groups were not only physically separate but also judged the other groups without having spoken with their individual members. The following is Alejandro's interpretation of what being a TA has done for him and his peers in the lunchroom.

> This helps us a lot . . . I know a lot of kids who are afraid of speaking with an American. Because of my being a tutor, people open their eyes and make friendships, friends everywhere, and something that I don't like . . . I feel part of them because I am Latino also, but at the same time I am not part of them. You can see it everywhere. You always see Latinos on one side, Americans on another, Blacks on another, and like that, and you go ask them why and they say the Americans are bad . . . But when you go where the Americans are and converse with them, they want to be your friends. But you have it stuck in there that you don't speak much English . . . but this doesn't have anything to do with it. For example, there was a bunch of kids who approached me and they speak little Spanish. And the others who were seated with me speak little English. And they asked one another questions, and they began to speak in Spanish, and some in English, and they got along mutually.

### Hallway Hellos—A Sense of Belonging

Almost all the TAs reported, with happiness, that they are now being greeted regularly in the hallway by the U.S.-born students, and they no longer feel so isolated. Joaquín states:

Well, there were two girls who were friends, they were Black . . . Well, they thought that I was well, like bad, right? And that I wasn't going to teach them anything, and they just ignored me, and when they approached me they said bad things . . . and I . . . and in the halls they looked at me and they bothered me, and I paid them no attention . . . but little by little, they started to be nice and I taught them and well, they didn't want to ask me questions because they thought I'd be bothered . . . but no, it's normal. I can help them. No problem and now I help them once in a while at lunch. Sometimes they look for me, but they look at me, like with fear, like that I remember what they did to me. But I see them as young . . . because I did things like this too with lots of people—treated them badly because I didn't like their face, but then I didn't know what they had inside . . . And now, the majority of them come to me, they greet me, and I like it because they don't just come to me and say "Hi Joaquín" and nothing else. They say "Come . . ." they are affectionate, they give you their hand or a hug or they joke with you or they pass by you in the hall and they are with their friends and they say "Look, my friend Joaquín, my Spanish teacher." And, that's it . . . I like it.

It is evident that their status as TAs and tutors gave these students a position within the high school that they had not had before.

### Bicultural Friendships—Diversity Valued

Every TA had something to say about feeling more valued by peers. For example, Carmen said, "I experienced changes in this class . . . I met more people. I learned to speak a little more of the language—English. I don't know, I met more friends." Joaquín also notes that:

Now when there is a party or something, the kids, at least, tell me, well, if I am going or if I want to go with them. Sometimes I go, sometimes I can't. With some, I go out to lunch, or go for a walk or I help them with some things, with what I can.

When I asked the TAs if they have new friends due to being in this classroom community, all of them said "Yes." Some went on to say that they had met many new friends. As Glenda said, "Now I feel more a part of West High School." Pablo reported that both cultures will benefit from these shared friendships:

For me, I believe that being a TA for Latino students like Joaquín, Alejandro, and me is a very big and great opportunity because before when I started at this school, I thought that I would never have North American friends (laughs). And now, I think I have more North American friends than Latino friends. I got to meet people and also learn how the students learn about our culture, and we learn from them.

## The Spanish Student Perspective

The data also reveal how the native English-speaking Spanish language students experienced this project. A total of 72 of my 84 students returned the signed permission form, allowing me to survey them about this program and its impact on them. Most of the questions were open-ended, giving students the chance to respond as they wished. All questions were provided in Spanish and in English. I told students that they could respond in either or both languages.

### Question #1

Question #1 asked: "When the Teacher Assistant talks to me, I feel _____." I was looking for a concrete feeling that could be described in one or two words, and so I left only enough room for a one- or two-word response. Thirteen of the 72 students responded that they felt "great," "happy," "special," or "important." Another 22 students replied that they felt "good," "fine," or "comfortable." Five students filled in the blank with "normal," "regular," or "same." Six used the term "helped" to respond to this question. Twelve students reported feeling "pressured," "awkward," or "confused." One student said simply "attentive." Three of the 72 students did not answer this question. The remainder of the students went beyond the one-word answers I was seeking and made comments such as the following: "Classes without TAs miss out on all the fun!" "Happy if I do good and stupid if I screw up!" "I'm talking to someone who knows what she's talking about!"

### Question #2

The second question was the only yes-or-no question I asked. It stated: "I enjoy having the opportunity to speak with a native speaker when he or she comes around student by student to ask us questions." Ninety-four percent of the students surveyed answered yes, 2.7 percent wrote in "sometimes," and fewer than 1 percent (one person) said no. The others did not respond. Many students made comments like the following: "It is interesting and a good learning experience to learn from them because it brings a new perspective to learning the language."

### Question #3

The third question was open-ended and read as follows: "The most valuable/interesting part about having a native speaker in the classroom is . . . why?" I categorized responses to this by looking for key words and themes. Forty-seven of the 72 students surveyed reported that the most valuable part for them was to get a better chance to "learn the language" or "have a better accent." Seventeen other students wrote that the best part was that they got to "learn about customs," "learn about culture," or "learn about other countries."

> They tell you things that are not said in the book, you get to hear and learn to understand the native speakers because learning a language and speaking it are two different things. Also, in my class they shared their ideas and differences in different countries, and talked about how different words can mean different things in different areas. These assistants bring life and reality to what we are learning.

One student answered "confused." Another four students mentioned that the TAs "help" when the teacher is busy and that this leads to more practice more of the time. The students had so much to say that I had a hard time deciding which comments to quote in this chapter!

### Question #4

This question was essentially a checklist, in which I requested that students tell me which activities that TAs had been involved with during the year were useful and which were not useful. It was worded: "It is useful when TAs . . ." A: "Assist with dialogues." B: "Work as a pair with someone in the class." C: "Come around one by one asking specific questions for oral practice." D: "Help on written work." E: "Help Ms. Hanson with grading." F: "Lead a 'workstation.' " G: "Others???"

Most students checked off four or more of the possible responses. The response most frequently checked off, however, was option C. This indicates to me that the students do enjoy the one-on-one attention from their native Spanish-speaking peers, and that the practice is—at the very least—comfortable for them. Students provided many additional comments. One student checked off all but item B, and added that she sees "many" other ways TAs can be useful: "It is good to just hear them having conversations with each other. It immerses you in hearing, learning and seeing all at the same time."

I found this comment very reinforcing because although it hadn't occurred to me to put this possible response on the list, I knew that conversations between TAs often took place before, during, and after class. The fact that English-speaking students hear conversations between native Spanish speakers reinforces the national movement in foreign language education to balance classroom teaching, learning, and assessment time among three essential types of communication: interpersonal, interpretive, and presentational. Historically, foreign and second language teaching nationwide has been stuck in the traditional form of presentational communication, a format in which the teacher does most of the speaking.

### Question #5

In question #5, students were asked: "Describe the experience of reading a children's book aloud to the TAs." One of my favorite comments in this category indicates that learning is reciprocal during this activity: "It's kind of neat because it gives us both opportunities to learn."

The theme of "learning the language," "learning accents," and "learning pronunciation" was the most prevalent; 50 of the 72 students surveyed used one of these phrases in their responses. Another recurring theme was "fun"; 10 students used it in their responses. A third theme was simply that the "TA helps." I found 32 responses stating that the activity of reading aloud to the TA was helpful. There were, however, four individuals who either did not respond or who said that the activity was "bad." One student commented that it is "Nerve-racking yet fun!"

### Question #6

The last open-ended question was: "How would you change the system if you were the teacher?" Twenty-five of the 72 students responded that it should be left as is. Ten students urged me to include more TAs. One wrote: "Make sure every class has at least one TA." Another responded: "I would make it so there were more in the class." Twenty students thought there needed to be more TA interaction with students. One suggested:

> I think a good thing to do would be, each day a TA would tell us a story in Spanish. Not reading it, but just a story off the top of their head . . . then you could give us a worksheet on how well we understood. That would really help in actually beginning to understand Spanish . . .

Nine students left the space blank. Many students made other suggestions and comments; I have since begun to employ some of the suggestions.

*Question #7*

The final question asked for other comments.

## The Administrator and ESL Teacher Perspective

Of the four individuals who visited our classes for the purpose of giving me feedback about this project, three filled out my form. All three mentioned something about the "mutual benefit" or the "benefit for both the American students and the ESL students." One of the ESL staff members who observed made the following comment. Like the TAs, he is foreign and therefore brings a unique perspective:

> The first thing I noticed when observing a native Spanish-speaking student interacting with mainstream students is the connection they have among themselves. It was obvious to me that there is a common factor among American students . . . that helps them to be inserted into the learning process, and that is *curiosity.* They feel curious about this person who is a peer but from a different culture . . . Another good aspect of this relationship is that students are more comfortable with a peer and don't feel that barrier they might have working only with a teacher. The benefits I noticed are not only for American students, but also for the TAs who, through this role, feel more inserted into the school environment and have that feeling of belonging which, for a Hispanic student in an American school, is not easy to find.

The theme of inclusion in the greater school community is prominent in the comments above. The other ESL teacher similarly noted: "I think this is a great way for ESL and regular education students to work together and get to know each other!"

Respect and dignity came up in two of the three response sheets: "I think the students showed the TA great respect; this doesn't happen often for ESL students." This comment, for me, is very profound, and reconfirms just how powerful the use of native Spanish-speaking TAs in Spanish class is, and could be on a larger scale. The following comment by an administrator goes beyond respect into self-esteem: "Use of the ESL student as a vocabulary resource demonstrates a level of respect, which could build self-esteem and peer respect."

Finally, the themes of community and cultural awareness rose to the surface, as seen in the following: "I think this will make the school community more culturally aware; they can see ESL students are 'normal.' "

## RECOMMENDATIONS

The most important recommendation came from Alejandro, who concluded that Latinos need to have more experiences like this one so that they can have a chance to be leaders more often and in more venues in the school:

> But the first thing I'd like is that we the tutors not be just three, nor four, because there are a ton of tutors (in the school) but they are Americans, and it is not because I want to say bad things about them, but our Spanish is better—more pure. It would be good to have a meeting with kids from ESL, we should speak with ESL staff, do it in the auditorium, in the cafeteria, wherever, right? For those that would like to come, one hour, right? First period, and bring them in and talk to them . . . because this is something, it is like the presentations they had for the elections of the presidents. It is important. And also it is important because it is in line with the teaching at the school. Or we could go and talk with the principal. But, I don't know myself . . . if you are in agreement. What I am going to do is talk with the principal . . . and tell him my idea . . . and put up like posters, advertise . . . such-and-such a day there is going to be a meeting for the Latino students . . . come, it will be in the auditorium . . . What I am going to do, too, is speak with the ESL teachers to see if they are in agreement.

It is evident from remarks like this that the TAs are very motivated and would like to see this program continue and expand. Several of them visit me regularly, ask me about plans for next year, and make suggestions for expanding the program. This level of engagement shows that the TAs have gained something valuable from the experience, and that it has been deeply meaningful to them. They would like other Latino classmates to share the experience. Furthermore, many of the native English-speaking students have also mentioned how meaningful the program has been for them and how much they have gained from having the opportunity to talk to and to establish authentic communication with native Spanish speakers.

In summary, members of both groups have reported that this program has been an extremely positive and transformative experience for them. This makes a strong argument for continuing the project and expanding it to other Spanish classes around the nation.

# EPILOGUE

As I reflect on this project and its successes and limitations, I feel certain that I will continue to use this method of teaching in the future. I am convinced that the cultural benefits are significant and should not be ignored. Those benefits, as I suggest in this chapter, go two ways. The TAs are given an "in" to mainstream school culture, and begin to see themselves as part of the larger school community. They also learn to recognize their own language ability as something positive and gain confidence in themselves as knowledgeable, even expert, in their language and their culture. The students who are studying Spanish get to know their Spanish TAs on a personal level—often, the TA might be the first Spanish-speaking student they have any sort of relationship with—and benefit greatly from being able to speak Spanish with someone their age. Their sense of their capability as language learners is also strengthened, as they have the opportunity to practice the language in a more real-life setting.

In the future, I believe that this program could have a powerful impact, not only on the lives of the individuals involved in my classes as students or as TAs, but also on the greater school community. The biggest problem I faced was finding students who were available to be TAs during my different class periods. I believe that I solved this problem by connecting with ESL department members and administrative team members, who fully supported the program and collaborated with me during the summer to set up this program for the 2003–2004 school year.

Other schools could certainly look to this program as a model, especially those schools that have experienced recent and significant increases in the numbers of Spanish-speaking students. This program creates effective bridges of understanding and communication between different groups of students and offers an innovative way to really secure Spanish-speaking students' place in the school community.

# REFERENCES

Baker, J. (2002). Trilingualism. In L. Delpit & J. K. Dowdy (Eds.), *The skin that we speak: Reflections on language and culture in the classroom* (pp. 49–62). New York: The New Press.

Brooks, D. (2000). *Bobos in paradise: The new upper class and how they got there.* New York: Simon & Schuster.

Brooks, C., & Fernández, E. (2001). Japanese distance learning: A Kansas summer program for children. *Learning Languages, 6*(3), 22–25.

Freire, P. (1992). *Pedagogy of the oppressed.* New York: Continuum.

Haberman, M. (1991). The pedagogy of poverty versus good teaching. *Phi Delta Kappan, 73*(4), 290–294.

Hakuta, K., & August, D. (1998). *Educating language minority students.* Washington, DC: National Academy Press.

Kellor, M. (1994, May). *Hispanics in our schools* Unpublished paper.

Ladson-Billings, G. (1994). *The dreamkeepers: Successful teachers of African American children.* San Francisco: Jossey-Bass.

Ma, J. (2002). What works for children: What we know and don't know about bilingual education. Online research report, Harvard Civil Rights Project, Harvard University. Retrieved May 5, 2001, from www.civilrightsproject .harvard.edu/research/bilingual02/bilingual_paper02.pdf

Madison Metropolitan School District. (2007). Ethnicity. Retrieved January 21, 2007, from www.madison.k12.wi.us/topics/stats/2006/byethnicity.htm

Madison Metropolitan School District. (2007). Income. Retrieved January 21, 2007, from http://www.madison.k12.wi.us/topics/stats/2006/byincome.htm

Martí, J. (1999). En qué tiempo puede cambiarse la mente de un nino? In J. Martí (Ed.), *Obras completas: Editora política.* Havana, Cuba: Mesa Redonda.

Merino, B., Trueba, H., & Samaniego, F. (1993). Language and culture in learning: Teaching Spanish to native speakers of Spanish. New York: Falmer Press.

Peale, C. G. (1991). Spanish for Spanish speakers and other native languages in California's schools: A Rationale Statement. *Hispania 74*(2), 446–451.

Ramírez, M. (1992, September 6). Rhyme and reason: In this class, Spanish is an asset, not a hurdle. *The Seattle Times/Seattle Post-Intelligencer,* pp. 14–20.

Sheets, R. (1996). Si queremos, podemos: A bilingual, multicultural, gifted model. *The Journal of the Association of Mexican American Educators,* 29–37.

Trueba, H., Rodriguez, C., Zou, Y., & Cintrón, J. (Eds.). (1993). *Healing multicultural America.* New York: The Falmer Press.

Walsh, C. (1991). *Pedagogy and the struggle for voice: Issues of language, power, and schooling for Puerto Ricans.* New York: Bergin and Garvey.

Wisconsin Department of Public Instruction. (2007). [statistics] Retrieved January 22, 2007, from http://data.dpi.state.wi.us/data/graphshell.asp?Group =Race/Ethnicity&GraphFile=GEDISA&DETAIL=YES&Grade=10&SubjectID =0AS&EligibleOnly=NO&Level=ALL&WOW=WSAS&ORGLEVEL=DI&FU LLKEY=02326903ZZZZ&DN=Madison+Metropolitan&SN=Show+Schools

Wong-Fillmore, L. (1991). Second language learning in children: A model of language learning in a social context. In E. Bailystock (Ed.), *Language processing in bilingual children* (pp. 49–69). Cambridge, UK: Cambridge University Press.

Zanger, V. (1994). Not joined in: The social context of English literacy development for Hispanic youth. In B. Ferdman, R. M. Weber, & A. Ramírez (Eds.), *Literacy across languages and cultures* (pp. 171–198). Albany: SUNY Press.

# PART III

*Conclusion*

# 13

## *Tying It All Together*

### *Implications for Classrooms, Schools, and Districts*

#### Ryan Flessner, Kenneth Zeichner, and Kalani Eggington

## TEACHERS MAKE A DIFFERENCE

While many educators understand that equity within and across schools will be achieved only when attention is given to changing the societal structures and policies that affect our educational institutions, it is also true that individual teachers, schools, and districts can and do make a difference in the lives of students. As Gay (2000) observes, "While systematic, multidirectional attacks on educational inequities are most desirable, individuals do not have to wait for these to happen before taking action on their own. Micro-level changes, such as those that take place within classrooms, are important, too" (Gay, 2000, p. 202). The teachers whose work is highlighted in Chapters 3 through 12—as well as the Madison Metropolitan School District of which they are a part—offer examples of individuals and a school district attempting to develop and implement changes to bring about greater equity in educational opportunities and outcomes for all students.

Teachers across the country enquire into their practices on a regular basis. As Caro-Bruce and Klehr (this volume) note, educators participate in action research for a variety of reasons. They follow Noffke (1997) and Fisher (1996) in suggesting that typical reasons for such work include individual progress, student progress, knowledge production, social change, and personal meaning. The Madison Metropolitan School District's Classroom Action Research Program, from which each of the studies in this book originated, has at its core a set of philosophical assumptions that make it a fine example of the work teachers can do to create change in our educational institutions. This set of assumptions includes the following ideas:

- Teachers are competent, capable individuals.
- Teachers are a unique source of information and have much to add to the research base in education.
- Individuals can, and do, effect change.
- While district initiatives are important and shape the topics of study in the Classroom Action Research Program, teachers are respected as competent change-makers who add to the educational research base by developing unique questions and research projects that address the complex problems inherent in educating our nation's youth.

In this final chapter, we examine educational equity issues by first providing a brief overview of attempts to address inequities in our nation's schools. Next we explore aspects of educational literature that are concerned with equity pedagogy, drawing specific examples of equity pedagogy from the action research studies in this book. We then identify the overarching themes evident across the 10 studies, and synthesize key ideas for teachers, administrators, educational policymakers, and others who may be using this book as a springboard to action in our public schools. We close the chapter with a general discussion about the idea of teachers producing educational knowledge and about the relationship between the research of university researchers and action research literature produced by K–12 practitioners.

## EQUITY AS AN EDUCATIONAL ISSUE

Villegas and Lucas (2002) state:

Relative to White middle-class pupils, poor and minority students consistently attain lower scores on standardized achievement tests of reading, writing, mathematics, and science; are overrepresented in special education programs, in instructional groups designated as low-achieving, and in vocational curricular tracks; and drop out of high school at much higher rates and enroll in postsecondary education in much lower proportions . . . This pattern of inequitable education is unacceptable in a democratic society, especially one as affluent as that of the United States. (p. xi)

The struggle for achieving greater equity in opportunities and outcomes in U.S. public schools is not new. Recently, we marked the 50th anniversary of the *Brown v. Board of Education* decision, which formally eliminated desegregation laws across the country. While this celebrated case represented a significant moment in the movement for school equity, inequalities in schooling persist (e.g., Kozol, 2005). Consequently, educators must continue to advocate for equity. Gittell and McKenna (1998) note that "creating an excellent and equitable public education system has become a priority, but the means for achieving this goal have remained elusive" (Gittell & McKenna, 1998, p. 1). Politicians have proposed charter schools and tax reform to equalize school funding and educational quality as just two of a plethora of means by which equity in schooling might be attained (Vitullo-Martin, 1998). Inequities in school funding have been challenged in state and federal courts since the early 1970s (Gittell, 1998), and fiscal equity remains a contentious issue. While these approaches have drawn much attention to the inequities experienced by poor and minority students in our nation's schools, the gap between the haves and have-nots in our society continues to grow (Darling-Hammond & Post, 2000). As a result, educators and researchers continue to explore alternative routes to achieving equity in educational opportunities and outcomes.

Wide variations in teacher quality have also received growing attention, as evidenced by reports such as "Honor in the Boxcar: Equalizing Teacher Quality" (Education Trust, 2000) and *What Matters Most* (National Commission on Teaching & America's Future, 1996) that show inequities in how fully qualified teachers are distributed to schools serving students from different social classes and ethnic backgrounds. The federal No Child Left Behind law, which mandates that a qualified teacher staff each classroom, has brought to higher visibility the issue of the equitable distribution of qualified teachers.

Research on multicultural education has illuminated institutional issues concerning White privilege and racism (Fecho & Allen, 2002; King, 1991; Michie, 1999). Discussion of these *hot lava* topics (Glazier, 2003), though challenging and discomforting to some people, provides a different perspective on problems within our schools and attempts to address growing nationwide achievement gaps among students from different socioeconomic and ethnic and racial backgrounds.

## EQUITY PEDAGOGY: ORIGINS AND DEFINITIONS

Banks (1993) describes five dimensions of multicultural education: content integration, the knowledge construction process, prejudice reduction, equity pedagogy, and an empowering school culture and social structure. Although it is only one piece of the multicultural education puzzle, equity pedagogy describes the types of classrooms students experience when "[T]eachers use techniques and methods that facilitate the academic achievement of students from diverse racial, ethnic, and social-class groups" (Banks, 1993, p. 6).

While the Civil Rights Movement brought attention to the needs of marginalized populations, Banks warns that many schools continue to promote pedagogical practices that foster a cultural deprivation model. Within such a framework, the role of education is to help "at-risk" students overcome their cultural deficits. Rather than valuing each child as an individual, the diverse cultural backgrounds of the students, the experiences of students from diverse communities, and the funds of knowledge and social practices in those communities (González, Moll, & Amanti, 2005), cultural deprivation theories promote an assimilationist philosophy wherein students must adapt to a view of school success that is based on the traditions and expectations of the dominant culture (Nieto, 2002). In order to ensure greater equity through pedagogy, educators must attend to " . . . aspects of diversity including racial/ethnic origins, language, economic status, and learning challenges associated with exceptionalities" (Banks et al., 2005, pp. 233–234). Educators who attend to these matters help form an equity pedagogy that ensures that the necessary attention is paid to the strengths and needs of all students.

According to Banks et al. (2005), equity pedagogy includes:

1. Building a sociocultural consciousness;

2. Attending to cultural frames of reference and boundary crossing;

3. Practicing culturally responsive/relevant teaching; and

4. Engaging in reciprocal and interactive forms of practice.

As a starting point, these ideas provide teachers with the knowledge and awareness necessary to initiate processes of change within their classrooms. We examine each of these factors below and provide examples from the previous 10 chapters that highlight what these elements look like in practice.

## Building a Sociocultural Consciousness

Because all teachers have gone through what Lortie (1975) calls an *apprenticeship of observation*—16 years of experiencing the work of teachers on a daily basis—it is unrealistic to believe that teacher education programs, as they currently exist, can enable teachers to unlearn many of the perspectives and practices institutionalized by their experience in schools. Thus, in intense situations, teachers are apt to revert to practices, curricula, and learning strategies that "worked" for them. From an equity standpoint, this tendency creates problems for students in today's classroom, especially students who live in a world very different from the classrooms of yesteryear, as well as for students who come from backgrounds different from those of their teachers. Given the apprenticeship of observation as well as the consequences of the profound changes affecting our increasingly globalized society, it is essential that teachers acquire a sociocultural consciousness that enables them to see themselves as cultural beings.

Irvine (2003) notes that "teachers . . . operate from the concept of positionality, that is, they have frames of reference for viewing the world depending on how the world makes sense to them based on personal history" (Irvine, 2003, p. 57). In order to connect with students in ways that promote learning, teachers must be willing to examine their positionalities, address the prevailing assumptions and biases, and begin to view the world, their students, and their classroom experiences through a variety of lenses. In developing a sociocultural consciousness, teachers gain an " . . . awareness that one's worldview is not universal but is profoundly shaped by one's life experiences, as mediated by a variety of factors, chief among them race/ethnicity, social class, and gender" (Villegas & Lucas, 2002, p. 27).

The studies presented in this book provide glimpses into real classrooms and illustrate teachers who are working to attend to their positionalities. The chapter authors are teachers who are developing, or have developed, a sociocultural consciousness. For example, in her work with Davonte, a seven-year-old African American boy, Barbara Williams directly confronted her well-established teaching philosophies, rethought her position as an educator, and established "sacred time" with a young man who otherwise may have experienced the failure that too many African American males face in schools. By valuing Davonte as an individual learner with specific educational needs, Williams viewed the world of schooling through his perspective. She then made changes in her practices directed at creating experiences in which Davonte could enjoy the feelings of successful accomplishment so often reserved for students from middle-class, White backgrounds. Williams's work with Davonte is an example of how equity pedagogy requires teachers to move beyond the mechanical use of curriculum programs and teaching practices to instead engage in dynamic and ongoing interaction with students. Through this process, Davonte's individual needs were more adequately met.

Shannon Richards began her study by examining the effects of her teaching on students labeled as English language learners. By studying her own teacher behaviors, questioning her role in contributing to her students' lack of understanding, and valuing her students' input and feedback, Richards established a critical stance toward her own practice. She used information gained from interviews with all her students—English language learners as well as native English speakers—to develop specific strategies that addressed the disconnect between herself and her students, regardless of race, linguistic background, or ethnicity. Richards's willingness to critique herself, to examine assumptions about learners from other backgrounds, and to take action to improve the children's school experiences provides readers with an example of a teacher working toward teaching for social justice and toward equitable schooling for all students.

Another study that addresses the issue of sociocultural consciousness is that of Van E. Valaskey. Valaskey examined tracking at the high school level, a taken-for-granted, institutionalized practice used in many high schools, and one that starts early in a child's educational experience. Many researchers (e.g., Oakes & Lipton, 1999) have concluded that the practice of tracking students into ability levels creates false conceptions of homogeneity within tracks, labels students as deficient, and limits the opportunities available to students placed within lower academic tracks (generally students who come from low socioeconomic or minority backgrounds). By confronting the assumptions, prejudices, and biases in such practices, Valaskey and his teaching colleagues critiqued tracking policies, revisited conceptions of high-quality teaching, and set out to redesign instruction so that all students could succeed. This willingness to rethink structures deeply ingrained in American schooling exemplifies the kind of action that is needed in order to dismantle the elitist, exclusionary policies that inhibit the potential for all students to experience success in school.

## Attending to Cultural Frames
## of Reference and Boundary Crossing

Aside from frequent differences in racial and socioeconomic backgrounds, students and teachers often differ in their cultural frames of reference. The life experiences of classroom teachers are often substantially different from those of the students with whom they interact. For this reason, it is essential that teachers build on the *funds of knowledge* their students possess. González, Moll, & Amanti (2005) define funds of knowledge as " . . . historically accumulated and culturally developed bodies of knowledge and skills essential for household or individual functioning and well-being" (González, Moll, & Amanti, 2005, p. 72).

Rather than superficially addressing diversity only by celebrating holidays or eating foods from "other" cultures, teachers need to capitalize on the resources provided by students' household practices and the funds of knowledge in students' communities. Paying attention to the interaction of students' family, peer, and school environments is essential if educators are to assist students as they attempt to navigate the sometimes conflicting spheres of influence between home and school (Phelan, Davidson, & Cao, 1991).

Rose (1989) observes:

> Through all my experiences with people struggling to learn, the one thing that strikes me most is the ease with which we misperceive failed performance and the degree to which this misperception both reflects and reinforces the social order. Class and culture erect boundaries that hinder our vision—blind us to the logic of error and the ever present stirring of language—and encourage the designation of otherness, difference, deficiency. (p. 205)

From this perspective, failure is redefined as a mismatch between the in-school and the out-of-school cultures in which students are immersed. To successfully navigate the boundaries between these cultures, students must continually evaluate the conditions in which they find themselves, interpret the key structures, norms, and rules in their various environments, and establish the flexibility necessary to succeed in sometimes competing worlds. Rather than leaving students to fend for themselves, educators can lessen this burden by actively seeking information about individual students and their communities and families, and utilizing this information as they create learning experiences that build in positive ways on the cultural resources that students bring to school.

Nieto (2002) likens this process to the building of a bridge that connects the students' environment with that of the dominant culture by acknowledging these differences. By participating in such work, teachers contribute toward leveling the playing field for all students and can also reveal their commitment to each student and validate the knowledge and resources that each student brings to the school and the classroom.

Denise M. Hanson's study is an example of the work necessary to assist students as they participate in dual worlds. Her work with native Spanish speakers shows how teachers can utilize the traditionally under-appreciated talents of students and thereby place the students in leadership positions. By actively engaging high school students with Spanish-speaking backgrounds as teaching assistants, Hanson created authentic learning environments in which native English speakers could experience the knowledge and resources of those who are often silenced in our English language–dominated schools. In addition, she created opportunities for these frequently marginalized students to interact socially with students from majority backgrounds, who might otherwise see them as less intelligent or academically incapable. Rather than providing patronizing opportunities for students to share their heritage, Hanson's approach provides valuable insights into the ways in which teachers can validate and engage students who might otherwise experience an overwhelming disconnect between their lives inside and outside of school.

A second study that represents the ways in which teachers can assist students in their attempts to meld the worlds of home and school is that of Kate Lyman. Lyman's continued attention to the conversations and interactions of her second and third graders allowed her to incorporate the experiences of all her students as she designed learning opportunities for her class. Lyman drew on her knowledge of students' lives, which she gained through careful observations inside and outside of her classroom. By dealing with issues such as racism, gender bias, homophobia, sexual reproduction, drug use, and AIDS—issues that were prevalent in the discussions and writings of her students—she was able to showcase the knowledge and life experiences of children who traditionally have been lost in the rush to raise scores on standardized achievement tests. While continuing to hold all students to high standards, Lyman created a learning environment that stressed the need for multiple perspectives, mutual respect, and collaboration. In her work, she afforded her students the opportunity to link their home lives with their school lives. In so doing, Lyman came to understand the complexities of her students' lives and used this knowledge to deepen the process of learning as a community experience. Lyman took action to acknowledge the fact that, in order to succeed, students must be allowed to build on their prior understandings, their experiences, and their natural curiosity to examine the world around them. She has recognized that learning emerges from the social, cultural, and political spaces in which it takes place and through the interactions and relationships that occur between learners and teachers.

## Practicing Culturally Responsive/Relevant Teaching

Florio-Ruane & deTar (1995) make the point that "[D]iverse teachers and pupils meet each other on the presumed common ground of public education" (Florio-Ruane & deTar, 1995, p. 28). However, this "presumed common ground" is less than neutral territory. King (1991) writes, " . . . education is not neutral; it can serve various political and cultural interests including social control, socialization, assimilation, domination, or liberation" (King, 1991, p. 140). The history of education in the United States (not to mention the social and political history), shows that many students—and teachers—are ostracized by the formal structures of schooling. In order to address this issue, teachers must understand that culture (their students' and their own) is a lens through which different individuals experience the institution of schooling.

Several researchers (Ballanger, 1998; Compton-Lilly, 2004; Gay, 2000; Ladson-Billings, 1994; Villegas & Lucas, 2002) have written about the need for culturally responsive, or relevant, teaching. Rather than taking a color-blind approach, which claims to see "children" instead of "color" but often ignores the important part that culture plays in navigating school experiences (Paley, 1979), culturally relevant teaching helps educators realize that "equity" and "sameness" are not synonymous in classrooms (Ladson-Billings, 1994).

Geneva Gay (2000) stresses:

> [A] very different pedagogical paradigm is needed to improve the performance of underachieving students from various ethnic groups—one that teaches *to and through* their personal and cultural strengths, their intellectual capabilities, and their prior accomplishments. Culturally responsive teaching is this kind of paradigm . . . If educators continue to be ignorant of, ignore, impugn, and silence the cultural orientations, values, and performance styles of ethnically different students, they will persist in imposing cultural hegemony, personal denigration, educational inequity, and academic underachievement upon them . . . It is incumbent upon teachers, administrators, and evaluators to *deliberately create cultural continuity* in educating ethnically diverse students. (pp. 24–25)

In her work with African American males in Madison high schools, Quynh T. Nguyen explored the factors that allow some Black males to succeed while others fall behind in, become disenchanted with, and even drop out of school. Like other researchers in the field of culturally responsive teaching, Nguyen details the need for teachers who are knowledgeable about the curriculum they teach, have effective classroom management skills, tie curriculum to the lives and experiences of their students, form lasting relationships with students, remain open-minded, provide additional support when necessary, and expect excellence from all students. Her interviews with students labeled "high achievers" and "low achievers" bring to light the similarities in each group's educational needs. Unfortunately, not all students experience classroom teaching that exemplifies these characteristics.

Next, Julie Melton examined classroom practices that inhibit or support the mathematical learning of minority children in her fourth-grade classroom. By examining the confusion and frustration of her African American students, she was able to experiment with alternative strategies in order to help them become more flexible, comfortable, and proficient with learning mathematics content. Rather than expecting all children to learn in similar ways, Melton exemplifies the need for teachers to experiment, and to work outside their comfort zones as they attempt to create learning experiences that attend to the needs of students from a variety of backgrounds. Because Melton took seriously her students' needs, she was able to use their experiences as a basis for learning and help them develop into more critical thinkers in mathematics.

Finally, by examining classroom dynamics and social structures in her classroom, Diane Coccari also practiced culturally responsive teaching. Her efforts to address issues of power and domination in her sixth-grade classroom are examples of what Villegas & Lucas (2002) deem a moral imperative—the necessity for teachers to act as agents of change. Rather than allowing a faction of the classroom's male population to constantly dominate discussions and activities, Coccari purposely created nonthreatening situations in which other students, mostly girls from minority backgrounds, could take risks, experiment with leadership roles, and be validated for their contributions to the classroom community. By dealing with issues of difference and by creating collaborative community experiences for her students, Coccari developed an affirming atmosphere in which all students could participate and succeed academically and socially.

## Engaging in Reciprocal and Interactive Forms of Practice

While attempting to build bridges between students' cultural backgrounds and the practices of schooling, teachers need to reexamine the dominant transmission model of teaching. This view " . . . emphasizes the correct recall of content taught by means of highly structured drills and workbook exercises" (Cummins, as cited in Zeichner, 1996, p. 145). Similarly, Villegas & Lucas (2002) argue that in this model, " . . . knowledge is assumed to be a reality that exists separate from the knower and that has always been 'out there' waiting to be 'discovered' " (Villegas & Lucas, 2002, p. 66).

In contrast, reciprocal and interactive forms of practice draw on students' prior understandings, create opportunities for students and teachers to participate in collaborative inquiry, and validate the experiences, knowledge, and curiosity of each member of the classroom. Moll, Amanti, Neff, & González (2005) suggest that reciprocity in teaching practice entails the creation of enduring social relationships between students and teachers. In this type of arrangement, both students and teachers are aware of their obligations to the learning process.

Jane Hammatt Kavaloski's description of her high school students' service-learning projects provides an example of this type of reciprocal and interactive teaching. Hammatt Kavaloski transmitted knowledge to her students, but she also created an environment in which her students were able to become engaged in an exploration of the life of a key figure in the Civil Rights Movement. Because students were responsible for teaching sixth graders about the life of Malcolm X, they were deeply motivated to learn all they could about this historical figure. Hammatt Kavaloski provided resources and classroom structures that facilitated this learning process, but she also remained aware of her position as a learner, not only about Malcolm X, but also about her students, their talents, and their willingness to achieve academically. By taking this position as a learner, Hammatt Kavaloski could better identify with her students. Many scholars believe such identification to be a key aspect of equity pedagogy (e.g., Ladson-Billings, 1994; Nieto, 2002). This stance of the teacher as a learner provides the teacher with continued exchanges upon which to build relationships, and it models the types of connections Hammatt Kavaloski wanted her students to form with the sixth graders they would mentor. In this example, a multidimensional, interactive pedagogy existed that engaged learners of various levels in a common experience that promoted inquiry, community building, and accountability to others. This type of learning opportunity differs substantially from the traditional transmission model of teaching experienced in the majority of classrooms.

Another example of reciprocal and interactive practice is the work of Erik J. Shager and his students. Shager, who was concerned about the school district's dropout rate, challenged his students to conduct a research project on this issue. The students' backgrounds made them well suited to this type of educational task. Each of Shager's students had experienced some sort of disappointment or failure within Madison's traditional high schools and had sought a different type of learning environment by enrolling in one of the district's alternative programs. Shager used these personal experiences of his students as resources to create opportunities for them to share their expertise, gain further information, and explore their findings. What evolved was an in-depth, complex inquiry into the reasons students feel disconnected from the educational system, become disenchanted with and rebel against that system, and eventually drop out of school. Shager's work powerfully explores the importance of redesigning learning experiences within our classrooms, and it shows how individual teachers can make a difference in the lives of their students by attending to the resources that they bring to school and enabling students to investigate an issue of great personal significance to them.

Taking the reciprocal and interactive model one step further, we can examine the impact of these equity pedagogy studies from the students' perspective. So far we have focused on the changes that educators have undertaken to enable greater equity. But if we truly believe that learning is a reciprocal and interactive process, we must also conclude that this form of teaching empowers students to better address the inequalities in their own worlds.

For example, Hammatt Kavaloski's alternative high school students learned lessons in their service-learning projects—about preparing for teaching, diligence, responsibility, and creativity—that they could apply in their own lives in settings where they are subjected to prejudicial actions and behavior. A more subtle lesson they may have learned is that some people resist learning (as was the case with several of the sixth-grade middle school students they were teaching). In a real sense, these experiences helped the high school students prepare for some of the harsh realities that exist in society and that competent and experienced learners such as themselves need to address.

Likewise, Valaskey's study examined and addressed the injustices of tracking and exposed students who would have otherwise been confined within their own "assigned" ability levels to heterogeneous social groupings. Such exposure prepares students to better work with, and relate to, people who do not share the same abilities, attitudes, and experiences. Successful interaction with people who are different is a hallmark of contemporary pluralistic societies.

Coccari recognized that a dominating group of White boys existed within her classroom community. She could have solved this problem temporarily by exerting her own dominant authority. Instead, she chose an approach that resulted in all students being able to see that social problems can be resolved by sharing power, elevating other people, and building a sense of community trust. Obviously this lesson has the potential to assist these students in becoming more socially adept.

These studies and the others highlighted in this book demonstrate the power that action research can have in supporting equity pedagogy. In addition, each study provided students with mechanisms for addressing equity issues in their own lives. With this knowledge, these students were able to take the lessons they learned and apply them to areas of their lives in which equity might not be such a priority. By engaging in reciprocal and interactive forms of practice, educators and their students all benefited.

## LOOKING ACROSS THE STUDIES:
## WHAT CAN WE LEARN?

It is our hope that this book affords teachers, administrators, policymakers, and others the opportunity to examine school structures and practices that contribute to educational inequity. As we continue to strive toward more equitable school experiences for all children, it is essential that we develop ways in which we can take action to ensure that students from diverse backgrounds are validated and appreciated within our schools. The studies presented in this book showcase the idea that:

> Teachers are not merely practitioners, professionals, facilitators, pedagogists, test preparers and administrators, or even competent content specialists . . . [M]ore than anything else, teachers are thinkers and decision makers who have a deep, thorough understanding of their content as well as a repertoire of teaching skills from which they choose and match these skills and content knowledge to classroom behaviors, situations, students, and curricula. (Irvine, 2003, p. 49)

The challenges ahead are complex and demanding, and efforts to implement equity pedagogy will most likely continue to be contradicted by policies and practices within and outside schools. We have assembled this general overview of the themes and ideas presented in this book so that readers can appreciate the challenges and can develop an agenda that addresses their particular needs. The following sections frame a possible agenda for equitable schooling by drawing on the themes developed throughout this volume. This agenda entails the following elements:

1. Attention to achievement gaps;

2. Empowerment of students from diverse backgrounds;

3. Engagement through culturally responsive practice; and

4. Activism.

## Attention to Achievement Gaps

The authors of the previous 10 chapters provide detailed descriptions of the work that needs to occur in order to address the ever-present—and growing—achievement gaps among students from different backgrounds. Lyman provided evidence that minority students' levels of reading comprehension are substantially lower than those of their White classmates. Hanson's discussion of standardized test scores across the district illuminated the problems associated with instruction that is geared to preparing students to successfully navigate these exams. From a national, comparative perspective, Williams noted Wisconsin's abysmal graduation rates, in comparison to other states, for African American students.[1] Nguyen examined district data to shed light on the responsibilities educators have to minority students. Shager discussed the dropout problem within the district. The list goes on and on. Everywhere there is evidence of a crisis.

What makes these studies remarkable is the willingness of these teachers to utilize classroom action research as a mechanism for change. The authors provide a plethora of strategies, activities, and ideas that might be adapted to and attempted in other settings. These include placing students in leadership roles, examining inequitable school policies, creating sacred time for struggling students, designing collaborative, community-building classroom activities, and developing personal connections with students who are located, or place themselves, outside the mainstream.

Several of the teachers whose research is included in this volume also recommend ways in which school, state, and federal policies might assist educators in their quest for equity. Nearly every study mentions the need for additional time and resources; several of the authors question the validity of the standardized tests used to measure intelligence and school success; and many studies point to the need for schools to attend to the realities of students' lives away from school. If educators and policymakers are to make a difference, attention must be paid to the inequities inside *and* *outside* of our educational institutions that lead to the marginalization of poor and minority students. If these ideas are ignored, the achievement gaps will continue to cloud the educational futures of our nation's children.

## Empowerment of Students From Diverse Backgrounds

Because current structures and practices within many schools exclude a wide variety of students, educators and policymakers must begin to develop programs and practices that empower and acknowledge students from diverse backgrounds instead of marginalizing them. Examples of this type of work have been documented throughout this book. Richards detailed the interviews she conducted in order to assist her English language learners as they attempted to understand and follow directions during class. By validating her students' feelings of frustration, she empowered her students to play a key role in evaluating and altering teacher practices. Hammatt Kavaloski's construction of a service-learning project created opportunities for students to capitalize on their abilities and expertise while working with younger students. Hanson's use of native Spanish speakers as teaching assistants is another example of creating leadership positions for traditionally silenced populations.

Again, many of these practices are adaptable to other settings. More important, these studies call for action on the part of educators and policymakers. This can be accomplished, as several of the authors have suggested, by differentiating learning experiences; by seeking, validating, and utilizing knowledge that students bring to school; by analyzing philosophies and practices that marginalize poor and minority students; and by encouraging and funding action research at the classroom and school level that focuses on issues of equity. González, Moll, & Amanti (2005) believe that:

> The border between knowledge and power can be crossed only when educational institutions no longer reify culture, when lived experiences become validated as a source of knowledge, and when the process of how knowledge is constructed and translated between groups located within nonsymmetrical relations of power is questioned. (p. 42)

## Engagement Through Culturally Responsive Practice

As we discussed previously in this chapter, teachers who use culturally responsive practices create learning opportunities and environments that engage all students. Lyman's classroom practices—focusing on issues of bullying, reproductive health, drugs, and AIDS—add to the list of ways in which teachers used the experiences of students to engage them academically. By addressing topics that other teachers readily label as inappropriate for elementary school students, Lyman created an honest, realistic forum for the exchange of ideas.

Teachers, administrators, policymakers, and others who engage in culturally responsive practices can try some of the following ideas: listen to stories about, and participate in, students' lives outside of school; use background knowledge about students' life experiences to drive curricular choices; hold high expectations for all students; work against traditional practices that marginalize, silence, or ignore students from diverse backgrounds; and insist that schools demonstrate the capacity to ensure that all students receive a fair and equitable school experience.

## Activism

By simply completing their studies, the authors of the Classroom Action Research projects have shown their willingness to make a difference in the lives of all children. However, their work did not end there. Many of the teachers continue to participate in action research groups in the Madison Metropolitan School District. Some have taken leadership roles in schools and utilize their power to promote change. Others work outside the schools to instigate social transformation. Most important, each teacher has taken action. Shager inspired his students to become researchers themselves by collecting information, analyzing data, and sharing their findings with a variety of audiences. His work provided opportunities to excel to students who had been unsuccessful in traditional models of schooling. Lyman's class decided to make a difference by selling ribbons to support AIDS charities. By incorporating health, mathematics, and other subject areas, Lyman taught her students that inquiry can lead to activism. Valaskey's study questioned and dismantled a department-wide tracking system that teachers had previously taken for granted. The model of service learning that Hammatt Kavaloski introduced is still being used at her alternative high school. This type of leadership from these classroom teachers is an example of the power of action research to stimulate activism by teachers.

Educators, policymakers, and members of the general public can further capitalize on the findings and actions of these teachers. By participating in discussions about inequities, by questioning unjust school practices, and by creating safe spaces in which this dialogue can occur, educators and concerned community members can begin to form networks that take action toward change. A shift in world views, leadership from inside and outside of schools, and resources such as time and money are needed for these goals to become a reality.

## TEACHERS PRODUCING EDUCATIONAL KNOWLEDGE

In addition to providing examples of practices that can be adapted to other settings to promote greater educational equity, the 10 teachers whose studies are published in this book have made important contributions to the knowledge base about equity pedagogy. In the previous section, we have shown some of the intersections among the 10 studies and the research of other university academics and teachers about similar issues. Traditionally, it has been assumed that research that contributes to the official knowledge base about teaching and learning is exclusively the job of university-based academics, who publish their work in peer-reviewed books and journals. Action research by elementary and secondary teachers primarily has been considered to be a form of teacher professional development that benefits the teachers doing it, and their pupils. Even when elementary and secondary teachers have published their research in journals and in books such as this, many policymakers and university academics have not taken their work seriously (Huberman, 1996).

We have attempted to demonstrate in this book the value of viewing the practice of equity pedagogy from the perspective of classroom teachers who are engaged in it. We agree with Cochran-Smith & Lytle (1993), who argued that examining classrooms from insiders' perspectives can provide questions, insights, and ideas that are not possible to achieve from richly contextualized classroom studies conducted by outsiders to these settings, even if these studies are richly contextualized. The kind of detailed, concrete, and specific information in these studies about various aspects of promoting greater educational equity potentially can help reduce the current disconnect between teachers and educational research (Hiebert, Gallimore, & Stigler, 2002). Our view of education research incorporates both practitioner-generated knowledge that arises out of and is integrated with practice and outsider-generated knowledge that helps us see across educational settings (Zeichner, 1995). Historically, there has been very little integration between the action research studies of K–12 teachers and the research of university academics around particular issues and topics. The studies presented in this book have illuminated particular aspects of the practices associated with equity pedagogy. The action research of K–12 teachers has the potential not only to provide concrete and specific examples of practices in different settings, but also to challenge, and help revise and elaborate our theoretical understandings of particular issues.

As Caro-Bruce and Klehr (this volume) note:

> Understanding that teacher action researchers are unique and important sources of pedagogical knowledge—and that their intellectual and leadership capacity remains largely unrecognized and untapped by the academic community—reflects a potential for new working relationships between teacher researchers and academics. (p. 22)

It is our hope that studies such as those presented in this volume will allow discussions between communities of researchers in order to act on the knowledge of those who strive to realize equitable schools for all children.

## CONCLUSION

As noted at the beginning of this chapter, there is much work to be done if we are to change the societal factors that influence our nation's educational institutions. While many may see this as an overwhelming, or perhaps even impossible task, some educators and some school districts are attempting to deal with issues of educational equity at a grassroots level. The authors of the previous 10 chapters and the Madison Metropolitan School District are examples of the beacons of hope that exist in many classrooms and districts across our country.

In the words of Villegas & Lucas (2002):

> We are not so unrealistic as to believe that our schools can single-handedly change the inequities that are imbedded throughout society far beyond the schoolhouse door. However, there is much that we can and must do, and the time to start is now. (p. 201)

## NOTE

1. Education Trust (2004) states, for example, that in 2001 the high school graduation rates in Wisconsin were 44 percent for African Americans, 55 percent for Latinos, 54 percent for Native Americans, and 87 percent for Whites.

## REFERENCES

Ballanger, C. (1998). *Teaching other people's children: Literacy and learning in a bilingual classroom.* New York: Teachers College Press.

Banks, J. A. (1993). Multicultural education: Historical development, dimensions, and practice. In L. Darling-Hammond (Ed.), *Review of research in education* (Vol. 19, pp. 3–49). Washington, DC: American Educational Research Association.

Banks, J. A., Cochran-Smith, M., Moll, L., Richert, A., Zeichner, K. M., LePage, P., Darling-Hammond, L., Duffy, H., & McDonald, M. (2005). Teaching diverse learners. In L. Darling-Hammond & J. Bransford (Eds.), *Preparing teachers for a changing world: What teachers should learn and be able to do* (pp. 232–274). San Francisco: Jossey-Bass Publishers.

Caro-Bruce, C., Flessner, R., Klehr, M., & Zeichner, K. (2007). *Creating equitable classrooms through action research.* Thousand Oaks, CA: Corwin Press.

Cochran-Smith, M., & Lytle, S. (1993). *Inside outside: Teacher research and knowledge.* New York: Teachers College Press.

Compton-Lilly, C. (2004). *Confronting racism, poverty, and power: Classroom strategies to change the world.* Portsmouth, NH: Heinemann.

Darling-Hammond, L. (1997). *The right to learn: A blueprint for creating schools that work.* San Francisco: Jossey-Bass Publishers.

Darling-Hammond, L., & Post, L. (2000). Inequality in teaching and schooling: Supporting high-quality teaching and leadership in low-income schools. In R. D. Kahlenberg (Ed.), *A notion at risk: Preserving public education as an engine for social mobility* (pp. 127–168). New York: New Century Fund.

Darling-Hammond, L., Wise, A. E., & Klein, S. P. (1995). *A license to teach: Building a profession for 21st-century schools.* Boulder, CO: Westview Press.

Education Trust. (2000). *Honor in the boxcar: Equalizing teacher quality.* Washington, DC: Author.

Education Trust. (2004). *Education watch Wisconsin: Key education facts and figures, achievement, attainment, and opportunity from elementary school through college.* Washington, DC: Author.

Fecho, R., & Allen, J. B. (2002). Teacher inquiry into literacy, social justice, and power. In J. Flood (Ed.), *Handbook of research in the English language arts* (pp. 232–246). Mahwah, NJ: Lawrence Erlbaum Associates.

Fisher, J. (1996). Open to ideas: Developing a framework for your research. In G. Burnaford, J. Fisher, & D. Hobson (Eds.), *Teachers doing research: Practical possibilities.* Mahwah, NJ: Lawrence Erlbaum Associates.

Florio-Ruane, S., & deTar, J. (1995). Conflict and consensus in teacher candidates' discussion of ethnic autobiography. *English Education, 27*(1), 11–39.

Gay, G. (2000). *Culturally responsive teaching: Theory, research, & practice.* New York: Teachers College Press.

Gittell, M. J. (Ed.). (1998). *Strategies for school equity: Creating productive schools in a just society.* New Haven, CT: Yale University Press.

Gittell, M. J., & McKenna, L. (1998). Introduction: The ends and the means in education policy. In M. J., Gittell (Ed.), *Strategies for school equity: Creating productive schools in a just society* (pp. 1–5). New Haven, CT: Yale University Press.

Glazier, J. A. (2003). Moving closer to speaking the unspeakable: White teachers talking about race. *Teacher Education Quarterly, 30*(1), 73–94.

González, N., Moll, L. C., & Amanti, C. (Eds.). (2005). *Funds of knowledge: Theorizing practices in households, communities, and classrooms.* Mahwah, NJ: Lawrence Erlbaum Associates.

Hiebert, J., Gallimore, R., & Stigler, J. (2002). A knowledge base for the teaching profession: What would it look like and how would we get one? *Educational Researcher, 31*(3), 3–15.

Huberman, M. (1996). Moving mainstream: Taking a closer look at teacher research. *Language Arts, 73*(2), 124–140.

Irvine, J. J. (2003). *Educating teachers for diversity: Seeing with a cultural eye.* New York: Teachers College Press.

King, J. E. (1991). Dysconscious racism: Ideology, identity, and the miseducation of teachers. *Journal of Negro Education, 60*(2), 133–146.

Kozol, J. (2005). *The shame of American education.* New York: Crown.

Ladson-Billings, G. (1994). *The dreamkeepers: Successful teachers of African American children.* San Francisco: Jossey-Bass Publishers.

Lortie, D. C. (1975). *Schoolteacher: A sociological study.* Chicago: University of Chicago Press.

Michie, G. (1999). *Holler if you hear me: The education of a teacher and his students.* New York: Teachers College Press.

Moll, L. C., Amanti, C., Neff, D., & González, N. (2005). Funds of knowledge for teaching: Using a qualitative approach to connect homes and classrooms. In N. González, L. C. Moll, & C. Amanti (Eds.), *Funds of knowledge: Theorizing practices in households, communities, and classrooms* (pp. 71–87). Mahwah, NJ: Lawrence Erlbaum Associates.

National Commission on Teaching & America's Future. (1996). *What matters most: Teaching for America's future.* New York: Author.

Nieto, S. (2002). *Language, culture, and teaching: Critical perspectives for a new century.* Mahwah, NJ: Lawrence Erlbaum Associates.

Noffke, S. (1997). Professional, personal, and political dimensions of action research. *Review of Research in Education, 22,* 305–343.

Oakes, J., & Lipton, M. (1999). *Teaching to change the world.* Boston: McGraw-Hill College.

Paley, V. (1979). *White teacher.* Cambridge, MA: Harvard University Press.

Phelan, P., Davidson, A. L., & Cao, H. T. (1991). Students' multiple worlds: Negotiating the boundaries of family, peer, and school cultures. *Anthropology & Education Quarterly, 22,* 224–250.

Rose, M. (1989). *Lives on the boundary: A moving account of the struggles and achievements of America's educational underclass.* New York: Free Press.

Troen, V., & Boles, K. C. (2003). *Who's teaching your children?: Why the teacher crisis is worse than you think and what can be done about it.* New Haven, CT: Yale University Press.

Villegas, A. M., & Lucas, T. (2002). *Educating culturally responsive teachers: A coherent approach.* Albany, NY: State University of New York Press.

Vitullo-Martin, T. (1998). Charter schools and tax reform in Michigan. In M. J. Gittell (Ed.), *Strategies for school equity: Creating productive schools in a just society* (pp. 115–129). New Haven, CT: Yale University Press.

Zeichner, K. (1995). Beyond the divide of teacher research and academic research. *Teachers and Teaching, 1*(2), 153–172.

Zeichner, K. M. (1996). Educating teachers for cultural diversity. In K. M. Zeichner, S. Melnick, & M. L. Gomez (Eds.), *Currents of reform in preservice teacher education* (pp. 133–175). New York: Teachers College Press.

# Index

**CORWIN**
**PRESS**

The Corwin Press logo—a raven striding across an open book—represents the union of courage and learning. Corwin Press is committed to improving education for all learners by publishing books and other professional development resources for those serving the field of K–12 education. By providing practical, hands-on materials, Corwin Press continues to carry out the promise of its motto: **"Helping Educators Do Their Work Better."**

NSDC's mission is to ensure success for all students by serving as the international network for those who improve schools and by advancing individual and organization development.